Soil Survey and
Land Evaluation

Soil Survey and Land Evaluation

DAVID DENT and ANTHONY YOUNG

School of Environmental Sciences,
University of East Anglia, Norwich

London
GEORGE ALLEN & UNWIN
Boston   Sydney

George Allen & Unwin (Publishers) Ltd,
40 Museum Street, London WC1A 1LU, UK

George Allen & Unwin (Publishers) Ltd,
Park Lane, Hemel Hempstead, Herts HP2 4TE, UK

Allen & Unwin Inc.,
9 Winchester Terrace, Winchester, Mass 01890, USA

George Allen & Unwin Australia Pty Ltd,
8 Napier Street, North Sydney, NSW 2060, Australia

First published in 1981

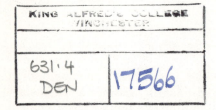
British Library Cataloguing in Publication Data

Dent, David
  Soil survey and land evaluation.
1. Soil-Surveys
I. Title   II. Young, Anthony
631.4'7   S591
ISBN 0–04–631013–4
ISBN 0–04–631014–2 Pbk

Library of Congress Cataloging in Publication Data

Dent, David
  Soil survey and land evaluation.
Bibliography: p.
Includes index.
1. Soil-surveys.   2. Land use — Planning. I. Young,
Anthony.   II. Title.
S592.14.D46   631.4'068   81-10834
ISBN 0–04–631013–4   AACR2
ISBN 0–04–631014–2 (pbk.)

Set in 10 on 12 point Palatino by Bedford Typesetters Ltd
and printed in Great Britain
by Mackays of Chatham

Preface

The objectives of this book are threefold: to give a compact summary of techniques and procedures for those actively engaged in soil survey and land evaluation; to provide a basic text for those studying for this profession; and to give an appreciation of the state of the art for land use planners, agronomists, economists and all who are likely to be involved in commissioning a soil survey or making use of its results.

We have not included step-by-step accounts of methods where technical details are readily available in published handbooks and survey manuals. A selected bibliography of these is provided. Where not yet available elsewhere, particularly in the case of land suitability evaluation, more detail on procedures has been included. For the most part we have attempted to outline and appraise the basic concepts and principles of these methods, so that they can be chosen and adapted to meet the varied requirements of different kinds of land planning, development and management.

There are three main sections, covering soil survey (Chs 1–7), land evaluation (Chs 8–11) and aspects common to both of these (Chs 12–15). There is, however, no hard-and-fast line between soil survey interpretation and land evaluation, only a difference in emphasis and approach. The *general reader*, that is a planner, an agronomist, a farmer, an engineer or the like who is considering commissioning or using a survey, could begin by reading Chapters 1, 8 and 15 which are directed towards the kinds of information that soil and land evaluation surveys can provide. He can then turn to such detailed material in the remainder of the text as may be relevant to his interests or needs. The *professional surveyor* will probably turn first to those aspects of which he has special knowledge or interests, to compare the views expressed, to disagree with some of them, and hopefully to pick up some new ideas. The *student* may work through the book from beginning to end, for it is written with this intention, being based on a course of the same title given by the authors at the University of East Anglia.

To avoid repeated qualification, the term 'surveyor' is used to cover a survey organisation, field survey team or individual surveyor. It does not imply that we are thinking in terms of one-man surveys. The rather awkward term 'user' is also employed for brevity, to comprise planners, agronomists, foresters, farmers, engineers, economists and all others who make use of the results of surveys.

Soil survey and land evaluation is a field in which the prime qualification is experience. We have gained ours by working with other surveyors in several national survey organisations and consultant companies. The ideas of many colleagues have been incorporated in this book and we warmly acknowledge our debt to the soil surveyors and other specialists with whom we have worked. Specific quotations have been acknowledged but, to avoid littering the text with references, acknowledgement of material already published is implicit in the further reading lists given at the end of each chapter.

Norwich 1980

DAVID DENT
ANTHONY YOUNG

Acknowledgements

The authors are grateful for helpful and constructive comments on the draft for this book from Dr J. A. Catt, Professor H. S. Gibbs and Dr G. W. Olson, and for comments on Chapter 3 from Dr J. A. Allan and Chapter 11 from Dr R. K. Turner.

The authors and publisher are grateful to the following for permission to reproduce photographs, figures and tables:

Plate I – Aerial Survey Unit, University of Cambridge; Plate II – Dr R. Price, Department of Geography, University of Glasgow; Plate III – Superintendent of Surveys, The Gambia; Plate IV – Commissioner for Surveys, Malaŵi; Fig. 3.1 and Table 3.2 – Cambridge University Press; Fig. 3.2 – Prof. R. U. Cooke, Dr J. C. Doornkamp and Oxford University Press; Fig. 4.2 and Table 4.2 – The Director, Soil Survey of England and Wales; Fig. 6.1 – Dr P. H. T. Beckett and ICI Ltd; Fig. 7.1 – Dr G. Murdoch; Fig. 10.1 – the Food and Agriculture Organisation of the United Nations; Figs 10.2 & 12.1 and Tables 11.3, 11.4 and 12.1 – The Royal Geographical Society; Fig. 10.3 – Dr K. J. Beek and the International Institute for Land Reclamation and Improvement, Wageningen; Table 9.3 – Mr T. F. Shaxson and the Malaŵi Ministry of Agriculture and Natural Resources; Table 10.8 – the FAO.

Contents

List of Tables

List of Plates

(between pages 48 and 49)

Plate

What Soil Surveys Can and Cannot Do

An assessment of the properties of soils and their response to management is required in agriculture and forestry, for informed decision making in rural and urban planning, for feasibility and design studies in land development projects, and for many engineering works. The practical purpose of soil survey is to enable more numerous, more accurate and more useful predictions to be made for specific purposes than could have been made otherwise.

To achieve this purpose, it is necessary to determine the pattern of the soil cover and to divide this pattern into relatively homogeneous units; to map the distribution of these units, so enabling the soil properties over any area to be predicted; and to characterise the mapped units in such a way that useful statements can be made about their land use potential and response to changes in management.

Soil survey is not a simple process of mapping discrete parcels of the landscape. Each soil property changes more or less gradually in both vertical and horizontal directions. Change in one property will not necessarily be in phase with change in another, so that identical combinations do not necessarily reappear in the landscape. However soil individuals are defined, their boundaries are transitional and intergrades are common. This is in contrast with the discrete individuals of the living world, in which species may be recognised, each with a limited range of characteristics, and where there are relatively few hybrids or other transitional forms.

The first step in making a soil map is to define the units to be mapped. If the purpose of the survey is narrowly specific and the soil properties relevant to that purpose are known, then these properties can be mapped directly. If the purposes are more wide-ranging, then the soils are usually classified and mapped according to their morphology, that is, the properties that can be observed in the field. Other properties are measured on representative samples of each morphological group.

The usefulness of a soil survey depends on two things: the accuracy with which soil properties are mapped, and the relevance of those properties to the purpose in hand. The usefulness for any particular purpose depends on the degree of correlation between soil properties relevant to that purpose and those on which the map is based. Soil characteristics which can be measured by hand and eye can be mapped very much more quickly and cheaply than those which require laboratory analysis. Therefore an essential part of soil survey is research to establish the relationships, if any, that exist between soil morphology and other properties of interest.

It is sometimes said that 'the purpose of a soil survey is to make a soil map'. As a statement of purpose, this is inadequate. What is misleading is the implication that the map is a desirable end in itself. Tacit acceptance of this notion can lead to an imbalance of effort, with unnecessary time and expense being devoted to mapping soil distributions and routine analyses to characterise the mapped units, with insufficient effort devoted to finding out what the map is likely to be used for and what soil properties have a bearing on possible courses of action. A soil survey is not an end in itself. Its utility should not be simply equated with the accuracy with which it predicts soil properties, without regard to whether these properties are significant in practical land management. A soil survey is usually a means of helping farmers, foresters, engineers, planners, development agencies and other users to make wise decisions about land use and management. Accordingly, in the initial stage of a soil survey, much attention needs to be given to who the potential users of the survey are likely to be and what kinds of soil information they are likely to require. Conversely, anyone commissioning a soil survey should give careful thought to what he needs to know, and should communicate this clearly to the survey team.

General-purpose and special-purpose soil surveys

It has become a tenet of soil survey that if the initial mapping is carried out in enough detail, with sufficient characterisation of each mapping unit, the basic soil map can be interpreted for many purposes without the need to resurvey for each new management problem that arises. However, if the requirements of users are to be met other than by chance, they must be embodied in the concept of the survey – the choice of mapping units, scale of mapping, intensity of survey and kind of report.

Soil survey may thus adopt one of two strategies, general-purpose or special-purpose. **General-purpose soil surveys** are expected to provide the basis of interpretations for many different purposes, some of which may not yet be known. In the absence of any practicable alternative, the mapping units must be based on soil morphology. The most suitable unit is a group of soils with the same sequence of horizons, developed on similar parent material, under similar external conditions; this is the definition of the soil series. Soils grouped in this manner have a lot in common, and the soil series has proved to be a useful unit both for general-purpose interpretation and as a basis for research on soil–plant relationships.

General-purpose soil survey involves the production of a pedological map, which shows the distribution of soil units defined primarily according to their morphology, and the acquisition of field and laboratory data on other physical, chemical and biological characteristics of these units. A general-purpose soil map may serve as the basis for a further stage of interpretation, namely land evaluation, which involves not only the characteristics of the soil units but also other relevant physical, economic and social factors.

Special-purpose soil surveys are carried out where the purpose is known and specific, for example irrigation, land reclamation or the cultivation of a particular crop such as tea or sugar cane. A special-purpose survey may be carried out providing that the purpose is clearly defined, the soil characteristics relevant to that purpose are known, and these soil characteristics may be mapped – either by inference from observable features or, if not, then by arduous grid sampling and analysis. This can be done, for example, in irrigation developments, since the relevant soil properties and their limiting values have been established and the economic investment justifies intensive field survey.

General-purpose surveys are most useful in less developed regions, where little is known about the physical environment and hence about potential land use. The range of possible uses is wide and likely to include both arable and non-arable; basic information on soils must be collected before decisions on land use are made. Such surveys are also necessarily adopted by those national soil survey organisations which attempt uniform coverage of a country. Special-purpose surveys are most useful where a good deal is already known about an area and its land use potential, a situation more likely to be the case in developed or densely settled regions.

The deficiency of general-purpose surveys is that they cannot serve all purposes equally well. The logic of this applies conversely to special-purpose classifications. The more closely tailored that a survey is to one specific purpose, the less likely it is to be of value for other purposes; a survey intended specifically as a basis for estate sugar cane production will be inadequate for planning mixed arable cropping by smallholders. If further information is required, another survey will most likely be necessary.

Planning environments

The kinds of decision on land use and management that are made, and hence the uses to which soil surveys are put, differ according to the social and economic context of the country or region. The two main distinctions are between developed and less developed countries, and between closely settled and sparsely settled or empty areas. For want of a better term, the divisions made on the basis of these distinctions may be called **planning environments.**

Developed and closely settled areas are illustrated by Western Europe and the north-eastern United States. There is competition and conflict of interest between agriculture, forestry, recreation and urban and industrial uses of the land. Decisions on land use changes are heavily constrained by legal and institutional factors, subject to the attentions of pressure groups and sometimes a public inquiry. In such circumstances the quality of the soil is but one consideration among many, although one of the more objective. Much land remains under the kind of use to which it has long been subject, bound by legal rights or private interests, so that one of the roles of soil survey is to improve management under that use. The existing users have a fund of experience and knowledge of soil properties, a heavy capital investment in the land and well developed scientific and advisory support.

In developing countries, soil survey operates largely within the context of land development planning, often financed by overseas aid. In sparsely settled or empty areas, development takes the form of land settlement schemes; in settled areas that of land reorganisation or development schemes. Sparsely settled areas with potential for settlement are most extensive in South America, less so in Africa, confined to restricted parts of Asia (e.g. Sumatra) – and in all continents are becoming ever less widespread. These provide the simplest context for soil survey: take empty land under government ownership and allocate each part to the most appropriate use. There is a corresponding disadvantage, that the absence of population means that there is no local farming experience on which to draw.

The planning environment of empty lands in developed countries does not differ greatly, as regards the kinds of land use decisions possible, from similar land in developing countries. Parts of interior Australia and northern Canada are of this type. The nature of possible land uses is influenced by the high cost of labour and greater availability of capital, and conservation interests may be stronger. The context for soil surveys is basically the same: there is land for which the initial decisions are whether to develop it at all and, if so, how to apportion it between various kinds of use.

In the closely settled parts of less developed countries, represented in extreme form by much of the Indian subcontinent, changes in kind of land use are not ruled out but must take place with the consent of the existing population. Standards of land management are constrained by the educational levels and capital resources of the people. There is a fund

4

of farming experience but it relates mainly to farming with low inputs and simple technology. There is frequently a planning requirement to incorporate sufficient areas under food crops to meet the needs of the rural population.

For some purposes a further important context is that of the centrally planned economies. These include developed and closely settled areas as in Eastern Europe, closely settled developing areas such as the farmlands of China, and empty areas as in Siberia and Mongolia. There are large national soil survey organisations, notably in the USSR, and soil surveys are certainly numerous, but it is difficult to obtain information on their role. So far as can be seen, there does not appear to be any fundamental difference between the uses of soil surveys in such economies compared with corresponding environments in the West.

Users of soil surveys

Actual and potential users of soil survey information include farmers, agricultural advisory staff, research workers, foresters, planning agencies, development organisations, engineers and private investors.

Farmers. Since arable farming is the kind of land use to which soil survey is most frequently directed, it might be expected that the main users would be farmers. In practice, most farmers make little or no use of soil surveys. They may already have a far better knowledge of their own soils than the surveyor is likely to acquire. Farmers' views on their own soils are strongly orientated towards significant management characteristics: texture (heavy and light land, when ploughed), drainability (wet land), nutrient retention (hungry soils) and the structural condition of the topsoil (tilth, heart). Not only are such characteristics known for every field (in Britain many have connotative names) but sometimes also variations within a single field. Paradoxically, so long as he is continuing with the same enterprises and on the same land as in the past, a farmer often does not need a soil survey.

It is different where innovation (for example, the introduction of supplementary sprinkler irrigation) or utilisation of new land are contemplated. Any new agricultural enterprise requires capital investment, in developed countries on a large scale. Bush clearance, drainage or land reclamation are also expensive. In either of these circumstances, mistakes can be costly, and avoiding them in advance by means of soil survey is cheaper by at least an order of magnitude than finding out from mistakes.

Agricultural advisory staff. The principal users of soil surveys in many countries are staff of the agricultural extension service, for example

ADAS (Agricultural Development and Advisory Service) in Britain. In some developed and densely settled countries the work of the national soil survey organisation is largely directed towards their needs. Advisory staff have the task of carrying experience from one farm to another and of introducing new techniques, derived from research. The soil series has been found to be the most convenient unit for this purpose, and the advisory service progressively builds up a body of management experience linked to series.

A further type of advisory service is the farm conservation plan. This was developed in the United States, and is now standard practice for more advanced farmers in developing countries. The two main components of such a plan are the allocation of each part of the farm to a major kind of land use (rotational arable, permanent pasture, forest lot, etc.) and the incorporation of soil conservation measures. The layout of farm tracks and siting of boreholes, farm buildings, etc., are also included. Land capability classification was designed for this purpose and serves it well.

Research workers. Agricultural research work should always be related to the climate and soils under which it is conducted. This applies both to the two most common forms of applied research, fertiliser response and crop variety trials, and to other kinds of field experimentation, e.g. into disease resistance. It is by no means yet the universal practice to preface reports on agronomic experiments with details of the climate, weather in the years covered, soil type (on both a local and international nomenclature) and main soil properties. As a consequence, there is a great deal of unnecessary duplication of work and, sometimes, attempts to extend results to environmental conditions to which they do not apply.

Foresters. Forestry is a major use of rural land, often under governmental rather than private management, in which case the advisory staff and operators may be one and the same. There are many analogies with the needs of arable farming: tree species, like crops, vary in their soil preferences and tolerances; input costs, for example the establishment and maintenance of forest roads, are as important as timber yields. A distinctive feature is the long-term nature of forestry, so that the initial matching of species to site is critical. Once a forest reserve has been acquired, it is desirable to have a soil survey as the basis for layout, planting and management. Whilst soil series can form a basis for planning and management, phases of series may be more useful, e.g. steepness, depth, drainage, erodibility, frequency of outcrops and boulders. As in the case of agriculture, interpretative groupings of basic mapped units can be made.

Planning agencies. Whereas farmers, agriculturalists and foresters operate within the context of a limited range of uses, planners are concerned with decisions over changes between major kinds of use, e.g. rough grazing to forestry, arable to urban. In developed countries, these agencies are the rural planning authorities of local government; in Britain, for example, they include the Planning Departments of County and District Councils together with quasi-governmental organisations such as the Countryside Commission and the National Park authorities. Given the heavy constraints under which land use changes are made in developed and settled countries, there is a need to assess suitability of land for specific purposes in some detail. For large changes in land use, some countries, led by the United States, require environmental impact assessments, which must include an appraisal of soils and their likely response to proposed changes.

Development organisations. In less developed countries, the primary call for soil surveys comes from the agencies responsible for rural land development. These include international organisations such as the World Bank and the Food and Agriculture Organisation (FAO), national overseas aid organisations, as well as national and sometimes regional government agencies of the countries concerned. The element of risk is greatest where a large investment is contemplated in an area about which little is known and where there is little experience of the kind of land use proposed.

Following upon several disasters, most notably the East African Groundnuts Scheme of 1947, soil surveys have become a standard part of land development projects.

Engineers. The use of soil surveys by engineers is relatively new but rapidly expanding. Their objectives include road alignment and foundations, building foundations and disposal of sewage and other wastes including toxic materials. There is now a large body of evidence to demonstrate that engineering parameters (e.g. shear and compressive strength, plasticity, shrink-swell characteristics, corrosivity to steel and concrete) are significantly related to soil types. Soil surveys can provide a basis for stratified sampling of the landscape, so greatly reducing the quantity and cost of engineering tests.

Private investors. Under this heading can be included also banks and other credit agencies. People with money at risk have been understandably cautious about the use of soil surveys, preferring where possible the judgement of the experienced man on the spot. Such intuitive judgement is most likely to be sound in regions with much previous experience of the type of enterprise concerned. But where new land is being taken into production, or a different enterprise is being considered, the investor is in the same position as a development agency (except that he can less afford to make mistakes). A soil survey provides information that can contribute to sound decisions.

Applications of soil surveys

Three broad categories of soil survey applications can be distinguished: the planning and management of farming, ranching and forestry; interpretations for engineering and a variety of specialist purposes such as waste disposal; and urban and regional planning which requires an evaluation of the suitability of land for a variety of alternative uses. In each situation the soil map serves basically the same purpose. It is a means of applying knowledge of soil properties and experience of their response to different treatments from areas that have been studied in detail to similar soils in other places.

Applications in developed areas

Management. In developed areas, with their high standards of management and fund of experience, soil survey forms a bridge between experimental science and practical agriculture and forestry. First, it enables the results of research and experience of soil use to be transferred to particular locations, to help decide on the optimum cropping system and management of soils. Secondly, it is an aid to the identification of soils that will respond to new crops and techniques.

Research. Soil survey is a basis for and a stimulus to research into relationships between soil and plant and between soil and technique, particularly for specific soils on which management problems have been encountered.

Planning. Rural and urban planning mechanisms come into operation in most developed countries where a change in major kind of land use is contemplated. The value of the land under alternative uses must be assessed, and the response of the soil to proposed changes in use predicted. The growing insistence upon environmental impact assessment for major developments has increased the need for soil surveys, although the soil is only one of many factors to be considered. Some countries use soil surveys as an objective basis for assessing the value of land for taxation purposes.

Engineering. Data from soil surveys are not normally available to depths below 1.5 m, but this is still of considerable value in the initial planning of engineering works. First, it enables hazards and problem areas, such as swelling clays and peat, to be located and avoided at an early stage. Secondly, it provides a sampling basis for essential but expensive detailed site investigations. Thirdly, it is a guide to the location of sand, gravel and other constructional materials. Direct use can be made of detailed soil survey for engineering works of relatively low capital cost such as forestry roads, low-density housing, sewerage and storm water disposal. In such cases the basic characteristics relevant to engineering are assessed during the survey.

Most applications of soil survey in developed, closely settled areas require detailed and very specific information, and predictions of relatively high precision are needed. Reconnaissance maps serve no direct useful purpose, except insofar as they provide a scientific framework for soil classification and a basis for teaching and learning. Detailed soil survey is necessary and a mass of fundamental data, or research information, must be acquired before the results of surveys can be applied. Coverage of all areas in the same degree of detail is not necessary, but as the proportion of the country or area surveyed increases, so also does the frequency with which it is put to use. Special-purpose surveys are often required and are economically justified by the high capital and social investment. Series and phases of series are the preferred mapping units for general-purpose survey, and these may subsequently be grouped and reinterpreted when the survey is applied to specific purposes. Many countries have national surveys producing general-purpose maps and broad interpretations, e.g. land capability classification. Special-purpose maps are commonly the province of the private consultant.

Applications in sparsely settled areas

Land development projects in sparsely settled or empty areas of less developed countries constitute one of the major and most clearly defined applications of soil surveys. There is, however, no fundamental difference between this situation and that of investment in sparsely settled regions of developed countries, the differences being in matters of detail such as the higher cost of labour but greater availability of capital. These two planning environments can therefore be treated together. The applications of soil survey are well established, and form a spectrum of increasing scale and intensity.

Resource inventory and project location. There is frequently a dearth of basic geographical information on the resources of large areas. Surveys at the reconnaissance scale provide a first approximation to such data, enabling an estimate to be made of the broad nature and extent of land development possibilities, together with the provisional identification of promising areas for specific projects. This need is served by general-purpose surveys, not confined to soils and frequently employing the land systems approach.

Project feasibility. A feasibility survey is one carried out before the decision to invest has been irretrievably taken. Its purpose is to investigate the ecological, technical and social consequences of a proposed development, together with its economic viability. The boundaries of the project are subject to modification, or there may also be a choice between alternative projects. Soil survey at the semi-detailed scale is normally appropriate.

It is particularly at this level of scale and intensity that two specific functions of soil survey are important: hazard avoidance, and guidance on suitability for major kinds of land use. **Hazard avoidance** refers to prevention of human distress, and loss of capital, caused by such environmental hazards as flooding, crop failure through drought or disease, or salinisation brought about by irrigation. Avoidance is achieved either by taking appropriate measures to counteract the hazard or by not using the most seriously affected land, whichever is the cheaper course of action. Guidance on **suitability for major kinds of land use** refers to the blocking-out of land into irrigated, rainfed arable, pasture, forestry, water catchment and other uses as appropriate. This is always a major component in land development planning in sparsely settled areas. Land suitability evaluation, giving the suitability of areas for each of several uses, is needed for this purpose.

Project planning. At this stage in development the decision to go ahead with a project has been taken, its boundaries are more or less fixed, and planning needs are concerned with the layout of physical infrastructure, e.g. roads, canals, farm or other management units, supply centres or soil conservation works. Further soil surveys at the detailed scale may be necessary for all or parts of the area.

Management. Here a project is already under way and a management problem has been encountered, such as salinisation, poor yields over part of the area, or drainage problems. Detailed or intensive special-purpose soil survey of selected areas will be necessary.

Applications in closely settled but less developed areas

This is the most difficult planning environment for the application of soil surveys, as indeed it is for land development in general. The value of soil maps in transferring experience depends on the quality of that experience. Its value in extending the results of research depends on the relevance of the research to the actual farming situation and also on the level of advisory services available. The existing population have established a *modus vivendi* which, if not always very productive when viewed from the standpoint of the national economy, is at least failsafe when it comes to provision of subsistence food supplies. In such a situation, changes are particularly risky, socially, economically and environmentally. Soils information is required for hazard avoidance, and as a means of ensuring that such changes that are implemented will be not only successful but sufficiently advantageous to be perceived as such.

In a few cases, the consent or desire of the local people may be obtained for a complete land reorganisation project, involving reallocation of property rights and changes in major kinds of land use. The most common, although not the only, situation for this is where an irrigation scheme is contemplated. The applications of soil survey are then similar to those of the development of empty areas, with the added constraints set by the present population.

Who carries out soil surveys?

Soil survey organisations of national governments. Most governments, other than those of some of the smaller developing countries, now have their own soil surveys. The Soil Survey of the US Soil Conservation Service and that of the USSR are the largest soil survey organisations in the world. That of the USA has 1800 professional soil scientists. In Australia, special-purpose soil surveys are made by staff of state conservation, forestry and agriculture departments. Two divisions of the Commonwealth Scientific and Industrial Research Organisation (CSIRO), are also involved: the Division of Land Use Research for reconnaissance surveys based on the land systems method, and the Pedology Division for pedological survey and research. Britain is unusual in that the Soil Surveys of England and Wales, on the one hand, and Scotland, on the other, whilst nominally combined, are in fact separate organisations using somewhat different methods. Most developing countries, formerly dependent on surveyors from colonial powers, now have their own soil surveys. In many cases soil surveys are responsible to ministries of agriculture, which may constrain their terms of reference to agriculture only; this is the case in Britain. General-purpose surveys for resource inventory are frequently carried out by national organisations, although their work is by no means confined to such activities.

Branches of other specialised government agencies. Land reclamation, irrigation and forestry organisations sometimes employ their own soil surveyors. Some have developed survey methods or soil classification systems different from their own national surveys and more suited to their particular needs; examples are the survey methods and site classifications of the US Bureau of Reclamation, the Ijsselmeerpolder Authority in the Netherlands and the British Forestry Commission.

Government agencies of developed countries specialising in overseas development. Some of these grew out of former colonial organisations: in Britain, LRDC (Land Resources Development Centre, formerly Land Resources Division); in France, ORSTOM *(Organisation scientifique et technique d'outre-mer)*; and in Belgium, INEAC *(Institut nationale pour l'étude agronomique du Congo)*. Their work is not necessarily confined to their former dependent territories; in particular, the LRDC operates also outside the British Commonwealth. Other such organisations were established for foreign aid purposes, e.g. the US Agency for International Development (AID). Surveys are often linked to specific aid-assisted development projects, but also include reconnaissance surveys for resource inventory.

International organisations. The Food and Agriculture Organisation of the United Nations (FAO) employs its own field survey staff, but, with no central laboratory or drawing office facilities for project work, it is dependent on those provided by governments or consultants. The World Bank (International Bank for Reconstruction and Development) has a few soils specialists for commissioning and evaluation work but employs consultants for field surveys.

Consultant companies. Firms specialising in technical consultancy for agriculture have grown greatly in number in recent years. In Britain, Hunting Technical Services, Booker Agriculture International and ULG Consultants are among the largest and longest-established. Other well known companies include ILACO (Netherlands) and SOGREAH (France). Engineering consultants requiring soil surveys for irrigation schemes usually work in association with agricultural consultants.

Some principles

Gathered under this heading are a number of general considerations related to soil surveys and their applications, directed partly at those who commission or make use of such surveys and partly at those who execute them.

A soil survey must have an object or aim. This may be wide-ranging, such as to provide a relatively stable data base that will last for many years and be usable for a variety of purposes, some not yet envisaged; or it may be narrow and specific, such as to delimit the land suitable for irrigation that lies within the command area of a particular dam site. In the former case it is not to be expected that the initial survey will collect all the data needed for each purpose; supplementary investigations, specific to the purpose, will frequently be needed, but the existence of the initial survey should avoid the need to repeat the time-consuming process of mapping soil distributions. In the latter case the basic research into soil–management relationships and the mapping of distributions are both integral parts of the soil survey, which should then provide direct guidance on the questions asked of it.

A soil map must show soils. The map produced by a survey is a soil map if the mapping units are based in substantial part on soil profiles. Many surveys rightly include features of landforms in the descriptions of mapping units. A map based on classes such as 'soil–landform association' is a soil map if it is directed towards showing the distribution of soils, the landforms being used as a means to that end. If, on the other hand, it is primarily a map of landform units, with soils being added to the legend as an ancillary feature, then it is a geomorphological map. Agro-ecological surveys in which the mapping units are based on vegetation, or vegetation with climate, are not soil maps even though the legend includes a description of the soils associated with each unit.

The distinction between what is and what is not a soil map is more than just a matter of terminology. Soils have characteristic distribution patterns, which differ from those of geology, landforms, vegetation or other environmental factors. Hence the nature of the units employed, the methods of survey and the range of interpretations differ.

The approach of land systems mapping (Ch. 7) is a special case. Land systems, and their subdivisions, land facets, are identified and mapped mainly on the basis of landforms, sometimes also vegetation, and are subsequently described in terms of the total physical environment. A land systems map is not of itself a soil map although land system surveys are closely related to soil surveys. A land systems map can be used as the basis from which, by subsequent more intensive and specialised field survey, a soil map can be obtained. Moreover, the mapping units obtained from the initial air photo-interpretation phase of a soil survey are indistinguishable from those obtained at the same phase of a land systems survey; in the former case the field observations are directed towards soils, in the latter they require equal attention to be given to landforms, climate, hydrology and vegetation.

Land resources do not consist of soils alone. Whilst obvious to the practical farmer, forester, engineer or planner, it is well to set this statement down as a principle, if only to draw it to the attention of the overenthusiastic soil specialist who momentarily loses sight of the broader picture. The potential of land to support crops depends on climate as much as on soils, and, wherever soil–water relationships can be advantageously modified, these merit particular attention; landforms and the characteristics of the deeper regolith are frequently more important to the engineer than the upper 1 or 2 m of soil studied by the soil surveyor; applied ecological surveys are more important than soils as a basis for livestock production and extractive forestry. When commissioning or considering a soil survey, one should bear in mind what other kinds of natural resource information will be necessary, and whether these can be incorporated into the soil survey or will require other specialist investigations. Conversely, soil surveyors need to have an appreciation of how their specialism interacts with other kinds of environmental information.

The soil map and report are complementary. The products of a soil survey include both a map and a report; neither is more important than the other for they are mutually indispensable. The amount of information that can be printed on the face of a map is limited and must be amplified by data given in the survey memoir or report. The report is, however, more than just an amplified legend. It contains in addition background material on other environmental factors, information on land potential and probable responses to various alternative forms of management, and sometimes also land use and management recommendations. One report may serve several map sheets.

A soil survey is not the sole basis for decisions on land use and management; it is only an aid. This principle applies also within the broader context of land evaluation surveys. Decisions on land management are invariably influenced by economic considerations, social and institutional factors, often by existing legal land rights and sometimes by political constraints. Even within the more limited sphere of the physical environment, the soil is only one factor; thus slope angle frequently has a dominant influence on the choice between arable and non-arable use, and climate is the main determinant in choice of crops. To view the soil, or the physical environment as a whole, as the controlling influence on land use is a one-eyed attitude. Rather, the findings of soil and land evaluation surveys are of a conditional nature: if such a course of action is taken, certain results will ensue, or certain measures will be needed to prevent adverse consequences.

What soil surveys cannot do

It is well to list certain attainments which are sometimes thought to be within the powers of soil surveys, but which they cannot achieve. These should be appreciated by all who commission soil surveys.

Map soils to a high accuracy with little effort. Soil survey is a slow business and the information obtained depends on the effort expended. The boundaries between soil mapping units are complex and not always visible by eye, whilst the mapped units themselves are by no means homogeneous. Modest levels of predictive accuracy are obtainable relatively cheaply, but there are thresholds of accuracy that can only be crossed by intensive and time-consuming survey and analysis. These levels of accuracy, and the scales and intensities of survey necessary to achieve them, are discussed in detail in Chapter 6.

Produce one soil classification that meets the needs of all users. The criteria employed in a classification should be those that are significant for the purpose for which it is intended. Even within the limits of arable use, different criteria are significant for different crops; thus, for example, sorghum is more sensitive to subsoil drainage impedance than is maize, whilst rubber has lower nutrient requirements than has oil palm. For other kinds of use, such as road foundations, the significant criteria are quite different; many good agricultural soils have poor foundation properties. No single soil classification can be devised that will meet all the varied needs of different kinds of land use.

Grade land uniquely from 'best' to 'poorest' quality. This situation arises from the previous aspect. Not only are soil and other land requirements specific to each use, but what is better for one use may be poorer for another. Some extreme examples are that level, poorly drained land is unsuitable for most crops but favourable for swamp rice, whilst vertisols that are excellent for growing cotton make appalling road foundations. Grain crops generally give better returns on soils of medium to heavy texture, root crops and groundnuts on lighter textures, whilst some crops have very specific requirements (e.g. tea requires available aluminium). The practice of grading land into a single ranking, such as is done in land capability classification, contains many tacit assumptions and is only valid for certain generalised purposes.

Produce, by soil survey alone, accurate estimates of crop yields. Broad estimates of ranges of crop yields, and other levels of production, can and should be obtained in the course of soil surveys for project feasibility studies, and in planning situations involving choice between alternative competing kinds of productive use. Nevertheless, a warning is necessary that all such estimates have a substantial range of error, of the order of ±33%; are highly dependent on levels of inputs and standards of management, which thus need to be described carefully; and can only be obtained if field survey activities are directed specifically towards this end.

Tell the user of the land what to do. Soil surveys and land evaluation studies can only provide information relevant to certain aspects of land management decisions. These frequently take the form that, if such a course of action is taken, certain consequences will follow. In land management decisions, these considerations will be taken into account, along with others derived from, for example, economics, social custom or political necessity. However, to suppose that soil surveys provide a full and infallible guide to the many and complex decisions involved in land use planning and management is to invite disappointment.

Further reading

Gibbons (1961), Mulcahy and Humphries (1967), Charter (1957), Avery (1962), Davidson (1980).
See also references for Chapter 15.

Planning a Soil Survey

Overall planning and the organisation of the various contributing activities are critical components of any soil survey. Mistakes made at the planning stage cannot easily be rectified, no matter how well the field survey and other individual activities are carried out. At the same time, this is the hardest stage at which to get things right, for you are trying to anticipate the contingencies and to some extent the findings of the survey.

Many details of planning are affected by the circumstances of the particular survey. Two extremes are represented by, on the one hand, a national soil survey organisation pursuing an on-going programme of systematic general-purpose survey and, on the other hand, a consultant company competing for contracts. A typical contract might be for soil survey and accompanying land evaluation as part of a land development project overseas. The same principles apply to the planning of all individual survey projects but here they will be outlined primarily in terms of a survey to be carried out within a fixed time for a specified purpose. A checklist of planning activities is given in Table 2.1.

Aims

The first decisions to be made are the location and the extent of the area to be surveyed and the objectives of the survey. The organisation requesting or commissioning the survey must specify in advance the information that it requires or the problems that the survey is intended to solve, how the findings are to be presented, and the time and finance available.

The surveyor carrying out the work or bidding for the contract must first make an appreciation of the aims and problems of the survey. This involves an appraisal of existing environmental data, in particular climate, geology and Quaternary history, topography, aerial photography and other remote-sensing data, and any previous soil or resource surveys. On the basis of this study the surveyor can formulate proposals for the methods to be employed and the staff, time and costs involved. He can also present a model of results, both showing what they will look like and indicating how they will solve the problems set. This can sometimes be assisted by showing the results of a previous survey of comparable type.

The more clearly the aims are defined, the more likely that ways will be found of achieving them. The location of the survey is broadly deter-

Table 2.1 Survey planning checklist.

Activity	Responsibility

(1) identification and definition of objectives:
    location, extent and boundaries of survey area
    problems to be solved
    time available
	user

(2) appraisal of physical and social environment	surveyor

(3) survey design:
    publication scale
    field mapping scale
    observation intensity, location and depth
    role of remote sensing
    additional field studies
    laboratory requirements
    role of automatic data handling
	surveyor initially, details agreed in consultation with user

(4) soil classification and map legend	

(5) interpretative/land evaluation activities:
    field studies
    interpretative legend	

(6) check availability and suitability of air photographs and topographic base: commission special photography as required	surveyor
(7) survey schedule	

(8) staffing:
    project leader
    professional staff
    support staff	

(9) mobilisation arrangements and logistics:
    survey field base
    accommodation
    travel
    transport for field parties and equipment
    equipment and materials
    laboratory facilities	

(10) publication of results:
    form of publication
    method of printing
    number of copies
	user

(11) costing	surveyor, firm agreement or contract with user

mined by the aims. What needs to be decided is whether the extent and boundaries are fixed or whether they are subject to modification in the light of the initial findings of the survey. Provision for the latter should be included in terms of reference wherever it is a possibility. A fundamental question is whether the survey is intended to be general-purpose or special-purpose. Partly linked to this is the question of the intended life span of the findings. By and large, soil surveys, in contrast with economic analyses, are expected to remain valid over a substantial number of years, but it may be that some immediate decision is to be taken – such as whether there is sufficient irrigable land to justify building a dam.

Survey design

Scale

The cost of the survey is directly related to the scale. The decision made on publication scale, viewed in the light of available knowledge of soil and terrain and of experience in comparable surveys, provides the basis for estimating staff, timing and budget requirements (see Ch. 6).

The greater the degree of detail required, or the smaller the minimum area to be shown, the larger must be the publication scale. This depends upon the intensity of land use to be served by the map, the stage of development planning and the intricacy of the soil pattern. In practice, pragmatic considerations may override technical requirements. When a survey is one of a series, the common scale may not take into account local variations in land use or soil pattern; the contrast between needs in the lowland arable parts of Britain and in the mountain and moorland areas is an example.

The scale of available aerial photographs or topographic field sheets may influence the scale of field survey, but it is best to conduct field surveys and compile the draft map at about twice the scale of intended publication. This allows space for soils information to be clearly drawn on the field sheets and allows a final reduction of scale to minimise the imperfections of the mapping. A field scale more than 2.5 times the publication scale is likely to lead to wasted effort in surveying boundaries to a degree of detail that cannot be represented on the final map.

In some circumstances it may be useful to employ two scales within one survey project. The whole area is covered at a reconnaissance or semi-detailed scale, from which a selection of the land best suited to a specified purpose, say irrigation or intensive arable use, is made. This land is resurveyed at a detailed scale for farm planning and advisory purposes.

The role of remote sensing

Following largely as a consequence of scale, but in part also from the nature of the country to be surveyed, come decisions on the extent and manner of use of air photographs and other imagery. The first is whether air photo cover of suitable scale, quality and date for the survey already exists and, if not, what additional photography should be commissioned (Ch. 3). The surveyor should also be clear in his own mind to what extent boundaries (as distinct from what lies within them) are to be inferred from photo-interpretation and to what extent they are to be traced in the field.

Density of observation

The intensity of field survey required to produce accurate maps at the required scale can only be determined on the ground, but where a commercial contract is involved it has to be agreed in some detail in advance. Value for money in soil survey is only achieved by a compromise between the quality of mapping and the effort required. The relationships between cost, time and the density of observations is straightforward; the relationship between the density of observations and the accuracy of mapping depends on the nature of the soil pattern, its external expression and the ability of the surveyor.

Obviously the density of observations must increase with the publication scale; if a map is to be at a large scale, it must be based on a high density of observations, and these must be of a degree of detail and to a soil depth adequate for the purposes of the survey. In intensive surveys for irrigation development, additional time-consuming infiltration measurements, deep borings to 3–5 m and basin permeability and leaching tests may be required, and a field laboratory may be set up for routine determinations of salinity and pH. Table 2.2 gives a general indication of the observation densities and consequent rates of progress associated with different intensities of survey.

Location of observations

A choice must be made between free survey, rigid grid survey or some compromise between these sampling designs (Ch. 4). The optimum method can only be decided when the nature of the soil pattern has been established, although the scale of mapping and the quality of the staff available exert some control. At the planning stage, it is best to specify an appropriate overall density of observations. The surveyor can then restrict superfluous fieldwork and concentrate effort in key areas: those of obvious importance to the objectives of the survey or, in the case of

Table 2.2 Observation density and time requirements* associated with different intensities of soil survey.

Examples of purposes	Scale	Average density of observations 0.5 per cm² of map	Rate of progress per 22 day month	Approximate time required for different activities (days per month)				Report preparation (weeks)
				Basic survey	Representative profile description and sampling	Field tests and field laboratory	Office	
implementation of land reclamation or irrigation projects; management problems; urban and industrial developments	1: 5000 1: 10 000	2 per ha 1 per 2 ha	250–500 ha 450–800 ha	8	2	8	4	6–12+
general- and special-purpose project planning, irrigation and urban fringe surveys	1: 20 000 1: 25 000	1 per 8 ha 1 per 12.5 ha	1000–15 000 ha	12	2	5	3	6–12
general-purpose: project feasibility and regional land use planning	1: 50 000	1 per 50 ha	30–100 km²	16	3	–	3	4–8
resource inventory, project location	1: 100 000 1: 250 000	1 per 2 km² 1 per 13.5 km²	150–500 km²	16	3	–	3	2–5

*In addition to the time requirements indicated here, 10 to 30% should be added for contingencies such as bad weather and difficult access.

general-purpose regional mapping, the areas of more complex soil pattern.

Soil classification and mapping legend

A decision on the soil classification system to be employed is usually made in advance of fieldwork. Most national soil surveys have evolved their own system of pedological classification for general-purpose surveys, each adapted to the range of soils found in the country. This often determines the system to be employed, because the existing store of research findings, agricultural extension advice, and farming, engineering or other experience is built upon it. A case in point is the vast store of interpretative data built upon the US *Soil taxonomy*. Where surveys of developing countries are financed in part by foreign aid, there may be pressure to employ the classification system favoured by the donor country. Whilst political/administrative considerations will often in practice dictate the classification system, the question that should really be asked is 'which system will both facilitate soil mapping at reasonable cost and best meet the needs of users?'. Whichever system is employed it is desirable, for purposes of international correlation and transfer of technical knowledge, to place the soil units distinguished in a recognised soil classification. The most widely known systems are the legend to the FAO *Soil map of the world* (FAO–Unesco 1974) and the US *Soil taxonomy* (Soil Survey Staff 1975). If the US taxonomy is used, you are committed to the considerable number of analyses necessary to establish the classification of each soil unit. These soil relationships are shown as a correlation table, stating whether this shows precisely determined equivalents or only approximate estimates.

For special-purpose surveys it will usually be most efficient to devise a classification system specifically for the purpose in hand, if necessary during the research phase of the survey (Ch. 4). In course of time, survey organisations may build up a set of classifications, each for a specific purpose, which can subsequently be applied to different parts of a country or within a climatic zone. For example, there is already a specialised body of knowledge on soil suitability for sugar cane.

The nature of the mapping legend will also be discussed between surveyor and client at the planning stage. The purpose of the survey, the anticipated nature of the country and, above all, the scale of the survey will indicate whether soil–landscape units, soils alone, or only selected soil properties are likely to form the better basis for map units. Decisions on the relative extent to which simple mapping units (e.g. soil series) and compound units (e.g. soil associations) are to be employed can be based on previous experience in a similar type of country; such decisions can only be provisional, since the nature and complexity of the soil pattern is not yet known.

Interpretation or land evaluation activities

The interpretative aspect of soil survey is not an office exercise but requires field activities directed specifically towards this end. These may include, for example, visits to experimental stations, field trial sites, forestry growth plots and to ordinary farmers, assembling information on crop yields, management problems, etc., and observing the soils to which those records and experience refer. In some special-purpose surveys these activities may come into the research phase, preceding routine soil mapping. A specific decision is whether soil engineering aspects are to be included in the survey. If so, this affects staffing, field equipment and laboratory support. It has frequently been found satisfactory for engineers to accept the mapping units and boundaries determined in the course of soil survey for agronomic purposes and to base their geotechnical investigations upon these.

The same planning procedures apply as for soil mapping. The commissioning organisation outlines the kinds of interpretative data that it requires. The surveyor assesses how these can be obtained and how much time will be required. Normally a specific and substantial amount of field survey time should be set aside for evaluation activities, additional to the time calculated as necessary for mapping.

Staff

The quality of the professional staff is the main guarantee of the quality of the survey. Inexperienced surveyors do not produce good maps. On the other hand, the salaries of professional staff are the major cost of soil survey and, as at every stage of the work, a balance must be struck between quality and cost. In the case of surveys with straightforward objectives, use can be made of competent junior staff under good direction. Free survey making extensive use of air photo-interpretation requires the greatest ability and experience, whereas grid survey requires the least. Surveys by outside organisations in developing countries commonly use counterpart staff, inexperienced graduates and technicians from the host country who learn the job in the field by accompanying expatriate surveyors. Counterpart staff are provided at no cost to the survey organisation; they can be invaluable as interpreters, although, as may be expected, their ability and usefulness in soil survey varies widely.

The key appointment is the project leader, who is normally responsible for the scientific quality of the survey and for its efficient progress. The team leader must be a strong and competent administrator and an able scientist. It is, however, vital to avoid the situation in which the team leader, with the experience necessary for soil correlation, interpretative activities and other scientific coordination, has to spend much of the time attending to the servicing of vehicles and recruiting camp cooks. For a soil survey forming part of a development project overseas, this problem is solved by making use of the project administrative staff. Otherwise it becomes worth while to appoint a full-time administrator when the professional survey staff exceeds 6 to 10 people. Additional scientific support may be provided by short-term visits by a specialist consultant or, in the case of systematic regional surveys, by a national soil correlator.

Equipment

Transport

In developed countries, planning transport to and within the survey area is a straightforward matter of estimating distance and multiplying by a unit cost. In developing countries, it is a major consideration and one that causes more problems than any other aspect of the survey. In overseas surveys, the client usually undertakes to provide vehicles, fuel and drivers; the surveyor must ensure that the vehicles supplied are suitable and properly equipped. Long periods of field survey time can be lost for want of fuel or while essential spare parts are air-freighted out, only to be held at customs. Measures that can ease these problems include the following.

(a) Obtain new or good used vehicles, with long wheelbase, four-wheel drive, winches for wet forested country, sand ladders for deserts and padlocks for fuel tank and bonnet.
(b) Make a servicing and repairs arrangement with the best agent in the district and carry essential spares in the vehicle. It is desirable that the surveyor should have some mechanical ability or that he recruit a driver who has.
(c) Request a letter signed at a high level of government giving the survey organisation customs clearance, travel authorisation and fuel priority as necessary.

Transport is required for the survey party, labour and any additional equipment, such as 50-gallon drums of water for infiltration tests. Horses or boats may sometimes be necessary. Needless to say, these arrangements are a considerable element in the costs of the survey, second only to staff salaries.

Field survey equipment

A checklist of field equipment is given in Table 4.3 (p. 68). Specialist items such as a mirror stereoscope, levels and Munsell colour charts are supplied by the surveyor. Many expendable items such as picks and shovels are available locally. Additional equipment may be required for some special-purpose surveys, for example equipment for permeability tests in surveys for irrigation. Where access is good, vehicle-mounted power augers or excavators can offer substantial savings of time and effort. Similarly, traces can be cut through bush more rapidly by bulldozer than by hand.

Base maps and field sheets

A base map is the topographic map onto which the survey data will be transferred and on which the data will ultimately be presented. Field sheets are the working documents used during the field survey; they may be maps or aerial photographs.

The base map should be sufficiently detailed to enable soil boundaries to be placed accurately in relation to streams, roads, buildings and any other relevant features. Soil boundaries that are difficult to trace owing to meagre base information lose much of their practical value and are a recurring source of annoyance to users of a soil map.

The availability of base maps should not determine the scale of publication. Scale can readily be reduced and the production of a controlled topographic base map is sometimes a prerequisite of regional development planning. Transparent base maps on a stable film base permit survey data to be transferred directly from the field sheets and allow prints to be made for preliminary distribution and colouring to show the soil pattern and interpretative groupings. The base data are checked and amended as necessary during field survey.

For most purposes vertical air photographs are the best field sheets because they show all the topographic detail that is needed for navigation and location of boundaries. They are also used for on-site revision of the preliminary photo-interpretation. The choice of scale for field mapping is important; a scale that is too large results in the inconvenience of handling large numbers of prints in the field and the temptation to map in greater detail than can be shown on the final map. If air photo cover is inadequate, new photography must be commissioned at the planning stage.

Supporting services

Laboratory support

The requirement for laboratory studies must be established at the planning stage because they are expensive and time-consuming relative to field observations. There is often unnecessary expenditure on so-called 'routine' analyses that are thought to be essential to the appearance of a soil survey report and yet are usually relegated to an appendix. An early decision may be guided by the following questions.

(a) Is there an identifiable problem that specific laboratory data will help to solve?
(b) Will the purpose best be served by determinations of a few properties for a relatively large number of samples, or by wide-ranging analyses on strictly selected samples?
(c) Can the purpose be more efficiently achieved by a greater number of much less expensive field measurements, for example, colorimetric pH determinations, salinity measurements using a portable conductivity meter, or hand shear vane measurements?
(d) Are the soils concerned of substantial extent or importance?
(e) Is there a definite plan for using the data?

Special-purpose and general-purpose soil surveys have different requirements for laboratory support. In general-purpose surveys, extensive analyses including physical, chemical and mineralogical studies are carried out on representative profiles. The purposes of the analyses include the placing of soil types within a classification, guidance on agronomic and forestry capability and management practices, and guidance on engineering works such as road layout. In the case of special-purpose surveys carried out under contract, the time and expense of laboratory analyses demand that they are strictly relevant to the objectives of the survey. Paradoxically, special-purpose surveys are often committed to a large number of routine analyses of individual properties to support interpretative assessments; for example, in surveys for irrigation projects, salinity and exchangeable sodium may have to be determined for many samples, perhaps collected on a strict grid basis.

However, results from laboratory analyses are often far from absolute. Standardisation of methods of analysis and laboratory procedure is essential if different profiles and classes are to be compared. For example, shall cation exchange capacity be measured at field pH or buffered at pH 7.0 or 8.1? Which method of analysis shall be used for phosphate or organic matter?

National survey organisations have their own laboratories and have developed standard laboratory methods for the characterisation of mapping units. Where the standard methods are inadequate or where special techniques are necessary, e.g. for waterlogged soils, the field pedologist should discuss these requirements with his laboratory counterpart in advance and make provision for any special transport and storage requirements of the samples.

Official laboratories typically have a backlog of between one and four years for routine analyses, so special arrangements must be made for priority samples. For commercial contracts, provision must be made for the required analyses to be carried out within the work schedule by a laboratory of proven reliability. When laboratory support is to be provided by a host country, the quality of this work must be checked, and training and supervision provided where necessary.

Data handling and presentation

Decisions are needed on how the survey data are to be stored, processed and presented. Computerised methods should not be used for prestige alone. The circumstances under which they are likely to be useful, and also where they will waste time, are discussed in Chapter 12. Like everything else, this service needs to be costed.

The findings of the survey must be presented in such a way that the information can easily be found and its significance readily appreciated by the user. Aspects to be decided include:

(a) what maps should be presented (e.g. soils, land capability or suitability, agricultural development potential, erosion hazards, salinity hazard;
(b) whether these maps should all be colour printed, or whether some (e.g. for use in farm layout) can usefully be photocopied;
(c) what form the report should take, how many volumes, how much of the supporting data are to be printed, and how many copies are to be printed?

Presentation of results is discussed in Chapter 13. The time and costs of cartography and publication must be considered at the planning stage.

Administration and logistics

This is a far more substantial element in surveys in developing countries. Apart from the provision and maintenance of equipment and essential services, aspects which need both to be planned and costed include:

(a) travel to and from the survey area and transport of equipment and samples;

27

(b) accommodation and base facilities;

(c) supplies: a regular supply system for water, food, fuel and money;

(d) local technical staff and labourers;

(e) interpreting: public relations, i.e. explaining what you are doing to local farmers and village authorities; possibly translation of documents and the project report;

(f) health care;

(g) communications between the survey team, cooperating agencies and headquarters.

Responsibility for the provision and maintenance of different items must be unequivocably established at the planning stage to avoid later misunderstandings which might lead to a breakdown of relations between the surveyor, the client and co-operating agencies.

Timing and costs

Work schedule

Once decisions have been made about the objectives and the design of the survey, supporting services and the relationship of soil survey activities to other integrated studies, a work schedule is drawn up for each phase of the project from mobilisation of staff to production of the final report. Depending on the nature of the project, the work schedule may vary from a statement of the number of man-hours required to a detailed breakdown of survey stage and activities.

In most work programmes the completion of various supporting activities is necessary before the next stage can begin. Thus field activities can only start when transport, maps, equipment and accommodation are supplied; a large team of surveyors cannot begin mapping before a preliminary mapping legend has been developed; and final interpretation of mapping units cannot be made before essential laboratory results are available.

In addition to the time requirements of the survey programme, the time scale may be constrained by the specifications of the terms of reference and, in integrated studies, by the needs of other components of the study to have information by a certain date. In our experience, the research stage of soil survey, with production of the provisional legend, needs to precede the fieldwork of other kinds of survey. Soil surveys usually take a longer time and, unless information is available to other parties, they are not properly integrated into the final evaluation. In many tropical countries the duration of the rainy season, in restricting travel, is a major constraint. The size of the survey team may have to be adjusted to meet specified deadlines.

Table 2.3 is an example of a work schedule appropriate for the planning stage of a soil survey. For large, complex operations, network analysis may be carried out to highlight the relationships between different activities and identify possible bottlenecks.

Cost estimates

There is a substantial difference between national soil survey organisations and consultant companies in the detailed costing of individual projects. In any soil survey the principal cost is that of staff salaries and related overheads, including accommodation and fieldwork allowances. These are related principally to the amount of fieldwork and hence to the scale of mapping, as are some other items including travel and vehicle running costs.

In addition, consultant companies must meet within the budget for each project any of the following not provided by the client: headquarters supporting staff; overseas allowances and family benefits; rent, furnishing and equipment for field stations; maps and air photographs; freight, postage and telecommunications; cost or depreciation of vehicles and field equipment; laboratory costs; publication costs. They must also provide for a proportion of the company's overheads, physical contingencies and a commercial profit.

Table 2.3 A simplified work schedule for a soil survey.

	Week										
	1	3	6	9	12	15	18	21	24	27	30
staff mobilisation	▬			▬							
field research	▬			▬▬							
preliminary air photo-interpretation			▬▬▬▬								
systematic mapping					▬▬▬▬▬						
field tests							▬▬▬				
laboratory analyses				▬▬▬▬▬▬▬▬▬							
interpretative activities						▬▬▬▬▬▬▬					
survey field checks							▬▬				
draft report					▬▬▬▬▬▬▬▬▬						

Survey specification

All the above decisions and plans are brought together in the specification for the survey. In the case of in-house work by an established survey organisation, the specification is a basis for policy decisions and the allocation of effort and resources.

The planning and preparation of commercial contracts is discussed in detail by Western (1978). The outline procedure is as follows. The commissioning organisation states outline requirements and invites tenders. Consultant companies make an appraisal of how these requirements can be fulfilled, and submit proposals. One firm is selected, and the proposals may then be considerably refined by discussions between client and consultant. The outcome of these deliberations is the agreed terms of reference, incorporated in a formal contract signed by both parties.

Further reading

Soil Survey Staff (1951) is the fundamental text, a revised edition of which is in preparation; Western (1978), Stobbs (1970), Young (1973a, 1976 Ch. 19).

Remote Sensing

Air photograph interpretation became an integral part of soil survey in the 1950s. Its value was first recognised for reconnaissance studies of large areas, both in developing countries and in empty areas of developed countries, such as northern Australia. In countries where there had been little previous soil survey, photo-interpretation was employed immediately for detailed work also, but its adoption was slower in some countries with established survey organisations. It is not so much true to say that photo-interpretation revolutionised methods of soil survey; rather, it made possible surveys of a scale, detail and extent that could never have been carried out had this technique not existed. Today, the air photograph is as much a part of soil survey as the auger.

From the late 1960s a number of other kinds of photographic and quasi-photographic imagery became available, first from sensors carried by aircraft and subsequently from sensors on satellites. The term **remote sensing** was coined to refer to these new kinds of imagery, although it covers conventional photography as well. It might have been supposed that these new and more sophisticated kinds of remote sensing would have an impact on soil survey equal to or greater than that of air photographs. This has proved not to be the case. A considerable volume of research into the potential of the newer kinds of remote sensing has been carried out. The outcome has been to find that each technique is well fitted to specific tasks, some of which have applications in soil survey; but the added information obtainable is relatively small when compared with that to be gained from standard air photography.

Air photographs and all other forms of remote sensing suffer the inherent limitation that they cannot sense subsurface colour, mottling, texture, kind of parent material and most other characteristics used to identify and differentiate soils.

Air photographs

Immeasurably the most useful product of remote sensing in soil survey is the air photograph, by which is meant the black-and-white or panchromatic, vertical photograph, 23 cm square and flown in parallel strips with stereoscopic overlap. The resolution now obtainable is very high, finer than 0.01 mm on the print, which is equivalent to less than 1 m on the ground even at small scales.

Air photographs have two principal uses in soil survey, and these are of equal status:

(a) *As base maps,* for planning routes, finding one's way about, and recording the location of field observations and soil boundaries. Photographs are valuable for this purpose not only in the obvious situation of unmapped country but also in empty or sparsely settled areas which lack roads, houses, field boundaries and other features shown on topographic maps.

(b) *For interpretation,* where they are a source of primary information of a different character from that gathered by field observations; field observations tell you more about conditions at a site, but photographs show spatial distributions much more effectively.

One of the first steps in a soil survey is to find out what photo cover exists and to commission more if necessary. Recent photography is preferable for route finding and location, especially where there have been recent changes in land use, although good use may still be made of older cover if costs so dictate. In recently afforested areas, photography flown previous to afforestation is invariably more useful for recognition of the soil pattern. For surveys of developing countries, photogrammetric production of topographic maps may form part of the project as a whole, in which case high-quality photography will be obtained. For reasons of security or bureaucracy, permission to purchase photographs must usually be obtained from the appropriate Department of Surveys or in some countries from higher levels.

Having obtained the photographs, the next substantial task (rarely mentioned in manuals of interpretation) is to locate them. Flight cover diagrams are often illegible, lacking in base detail, or missing. Make a complete print laydown. Draw up your own cover sketch, giving run numbers, print numbers at the ends of runs, orientation, and sketch in the principal roads, rivers and settlements. Write names of these features on the backs of the photographs and add north points. If a base map exists, it is worth while to mark the principal points of all photographs on it.

Put each run into a polythene envelope, labelled with run and print numbers. Make sure every photograph carries enough information to enable anybody to restore it to its correct envelope. Time spent in sorting, labelling and locating the photographs pays off in time saved and irritation avoided at later stages of the survey.

Other products obtainable are enlargements, mosaics and orthophotographs. Enlargements to 40 or 50 cm square are good for display purposes, and can be used in the field as a base map in very detailed surveys, but add little to interpretation; the stereoscopic effect is lost on enlargement, and fine detail is better obtained by binocular magnification.

Mosaics are of two kinds, uncontrolled and controlled. Uncontrolled mosaics can readily be made by trimming and joining overlapping prints. Controlled mosaics can be prepared commercially by rectifying individual prints for scale and tilt distortions to give a better geometric fit; a degree of ground control can be introduced to improve the planimetric accuracy of the mosaic. Controlled mosaics can be used as map substitutes both in the field and for the final soil maps. They can be rephotographed and reproduced relatively cheaply, although the initial production is a skilled and expensive job. Mosaics were formerly used to provide a broad overview of an area, but this purpose is now better and more cheaply fulfilled by satellite imagery.

A more recent development, the orthophotograph, achieves the planimetric accuracy of a detailed, large-scale map by separate rectification of small elements on the original negatives, so that the correction is consistent across each frame. Because of the sophisticated equipment required, orthophotographs are expensive.

Properties of air photographs

Knowledge of certain properties and limitations of the air photograph is necessary as a preliminary to interpretation and as a means of avoiding certain pitfalls. These properties, explained at greater length in introductory texts on photo-interpretation, are as follows.

(a) The photograph is an image of the land surface on which differences in surface reflectance of light appear as differences in tone, black–grey–white, on the photograph.

(b) The photograph is not planimetrically correct, that is, it is not constant in scale across the print. Variations in scale are caused first by the projection, scale being accurate only close to the centre of the photograph; secondly by relief, hill tops lying closer to the camera than valleys and so appearing at a larger scale; and thirdly by aircraft tilt. For interpretation and for use in the field, these scale variations are unimportant and the photograph can be treated as if it were a map. For transfer of boundaries from photograph to map, the variations are significant and hence simple tracing is inadequate.

(c) Through stereoscopic viewing of adjacent pairs, an enormous increase in the information content and utility of photographs is achieved.

Photo-interpretation depends on recognition of differences in the grey scale together with relief. Variations in the grey scale occur in different ways, termed tone, texture, pattern and shape.

Tone is the shade of grey, ranging from black to white. Rock and bare soil (unless black) show light tones; wet soil is darker than is dry soil. Coniferous trees appear darker than broad-leaved trees. Water absorbs visible light, so usually appears dark unless it is turbid (e.g. glacial meltwater streams) or very shallow.

Texture is the fine pattern of tone contrast, at a scale too small for the individual elements to be distinguished. Bare mudflats give a smooth texture, forest canopy a moderately rough one. Most crops have a characteristic texture; unfortunately, small grains (wheat, barley, etc.) have similar textures to grassland, but they can be distinguished by tone, varying with season or stage of growth.

Pattern is regular variation in tone at a scale at which the individual elements can be seen. Examples of features which produce clear and characteristic patterns are orchards, badlands, termite mounds and shifting cultivation. Features that show as pattern on large-scale photographs become texture at small scales.

Shape refers to individual features not repeated as a pattern.

These variations in the grey scale are combined with information on relief. **Relief** visible in photo-interpretation consists of relative height differences within the area covered by the overlap of a single stereoscopic pair. Where ground control is established, absolute heights and accurate contours can be mapped by photogrammetry. Such accuracy is unnecessary for general-purpose soil survey, but it is likely to be needed for irrigation planning and many engineering works.

Landscape features are usually identified by convergence of evidence, without giving conscious thought to the separate properties listed above. It is useful to refer to these properties, however, when describing to someone else (or even rationalising to yourself) how a particular landscape feature can be identified, for example, 'the lighter tone is some special kind of grass, possibly indicating shallow laterite', or 'the almost regular pattern of spots on flat ground indicates gilgai'.

Scale

Useful photograph scales in soil survey range from 1:50000 to 1:5000 (Table 3.1). It is obvious that large scales allow finer detail to be seen and smaller mapping units to be delineated. Set against this are four disadvantages of large scales:

(a) *Number and cost of prints.* The number of prints needed to cover a given area is four times greater for every doubling of scale. Flying

Table 3.1 Air photograph scales.

	Scale	Area covered by one whole print (km²)	Working area on one print* (km²)	Number of prints per 100 km²	Ground equivalent of 1 mm (m)	Ground equivalent of 1 cm² (ha)
very large	1:5000	1.3	0.8	240	5	0.25
large	1:10000	5.2	3.3	60	10	1
	1:20000	21	13	15	20	4
medium	1:25000	33	21	10	25	6.25
	1:30000	47	30	7	30	9
	1:40000	84	53	4	40	16
small	1:50000	131	84	2.4	50	25
Landsat image	1:1000000	34000	20000+	0.005	1000	10000

*The 'working area' is that covered by a single print after omitting overlap with adjacent runs and with next-but-one prints in a run, i.e. the area on which boundaries are drawn on alternate prints.

costs rise at somewhat less than this rate, since the cost of getting airborne is only met once.

(b) *Difficulty in seeing landscape patterns.* Since on large-scale photographs only a small land area can be viewed stereoscopically at one time, repeating patterns of landforms or other features are hard to identify – the geomorphological equivalent of being unable to see the wood for the trees.

(c) *Superfluous detail.* Experience shows that interpreters find it impossible to resist drawing boundaries wherever they can be seen. If the photo is on a much larger scale than the intended map, it will become covered with lines which cannot be verified in the field, represented on the map, or both.

(d) *Time taken over interpretation.* Through a combination of the above reasons, the time taken to interpret rises almost proportionally to the number of prints, i.e. three to four times as long if the scale is doubled. Useful information obtained, namely soil boundaries which prove significant, increases very much more slowly.

For these reasons, a good general rule is to choose the smallest scale compatible with the accuracy or fineness of detail required on the final map. Except in reconnaissance surveys, this will usually be 2 to 2.5 times the map scale.

For reconnaissance surveys of large areas, a photograph scale of about 1:40 000 is best. Landform units and other spatial patterns can be seen readily. It is reasonable to interpret 4–8 pairs of photographs, and thus 100–200 km², in a day. It is rather difficult but still possible to use 1:40 000 prints to find your way in the field. Even though the intended map may be at 1:250 000 or smaller, the boundaries on photos at scales smaller than 1:50 000 are packed too closely together.

Photograph scales of 1:20 000 or 1:25 000 are suited to a wide range of soil surveys in which photo-interpretation is balanced by a substantial element of field survey. Broad landform patterns can still be identified (though less easily than at smaller scales), whilst at the same time detailed land facets can be delineated. Where required, quite fine detail can be picked out under ×3 magnification. Tracks and individual trees can be seen, invaluable for planning routes and locating observation sites.

Scales of 1:10 000 or larger are suited to detailed special-purpose surveys, including surveys of peri-urban areas. Landform patterns are lost and interpretation must be based on slope facets or detailed vegetation characteristics. Often such photographs are primarily used as base maps for intensive field survey.

Equipment for photo-interpretation

All that is essential for interpretation is a good mirror stereoscope. A moving table and ×3 binoculars are desirable, whilst an interpretoscope, zoom stereoscope or similar instrument is a luxury (albeit a pleasant one) unless photo-interpretation is a major component of total survey effort. The essential design feature in a mirror stereoscope is that the whole of the stereoscopically common area shall be easily visible at once. A moving table allows different parts of the view to be brought under binocular view without disturbing stereoscopic alignment.

A zoom stereoscope gives a continuous change in magnification whilst remaining more or less in focus; a cheaper alternative is to add ×8 binoculars.

For field use, two kinds of pocket stereoscope are available. The conventional lens type produces a ×2.5 magnification but only 6 cm wide strips down either side can be viewed without bending the print. The pocket mirror stereoscope can be used to view the whole stereoscopic overlap by moving the instrument, but is more expensive and also less convenient to use.

Subsequent transfer of boundaries from photograph to map may be done in two ways: by plotter or by sketchmaster or similar instrument. The stereoplotter is an advanced photogrammetric instrument which rectifies scale errors on the photograph. Its principal use is in the production of orthographic base maps. A skilled technician is required to operate such an instrument, which can be economically justified only by full-time use. If your survey organisation does not possess a plotter, the cost of subcontracting should be written into the contract.

It will not always be the case that the precision of soil boundaries justifies photogrammetric accuracy; provided there exists a topographic map at a scale not too dissimilar from that of the photographs, a competent job can be done with sketchmaster or stereosketch, matching features on the base map, i.e. tracks, rivers, etc., to those on the photograph.

Use of air photographs in soil survey

The applications of air photographs may include any or all of the following.

(a) To make the base map, by photogrammetry.
(b) For the main photo-interpretation, the drawing of provisional boundaries prior to field survey.

(c) To plan field operations. This can include selection of routes, traverse lines, variation in sampling density, omission of certain areas altogether (e.g. mountains), and in some cases marking of individual observation sites in advance. Locating good catena transects is particularly valuable. The use of photographs to locate representative sites, though frowned on by the statistically minded, is widespread in practice.

(d) To find your way about in the field, and to locate observation sites. Take trouble to locate these carefully, e.g. by pacing from identifiable detail, mark immediately with crayon or a pinprick ringed in crayon, and add the observation number to the photograph.

(e) For revision, or post-field interpretation. A good many of the pre-field provisional boundaries may need to be erased, having not proved to be of significance for the purposes of the survey. Except in reconnaissance surveys, there will be new distinctions, not previously noted on the photographs but identified in the field. Once these are known, they can sometimes be extrapolated on the photographs, e.g. as a slightly darker tone or a small change in slope or vegetation, or, failing that, simply by drawing a line which follows the same position in a catena.

(f) For presentation. The final soil map is sometimes published on a photographic base in preference to a map; this is now standard practice for US 1:20 000 surveys. Publication in this form limits the map to symbols, preventing use of colours unless by transparent overlays. The product is less artistically pleasing but a photographic base of good definition is of more value to users, who can locate soil areas directly on the ground by features familiar to them.

Interpretation

One basic fact cannot be too strongly emphasised: the photograph is only an image of the land surface and you cannot see soils on it. Two consequences follow: that interpretation must be based on what can be seen, namely landforms, vegetation and possibly land use; and that the usefulness of the interpretation for soil survey depends on how clearly the relationships between these visible features and soil types can be established in the field.

In many cases the soil cannot be seen at all, being covered by forest, grass or crops. Where bare ground is present, either because of arable use or aridity, it is only the surface skin that is reflecting light into the camera. Differences in surface reflectance may be caused by topsoil colour, soil texture or moisture content, usually darker tones indicating heavier texture or moister sites. There are special circumstances where this can prove of value, such as on depositional landscapes under arable use, e.g. the English Fenlands (Plate 1) and some semi-arid regions. But to suppose that soils can be identified or even mapped directly by photo-interpretation is at least as absurd as to suggest that field survey can be accomplished without spade or auger.

The features of the landscape visible on air photographs are landforms (including surface water), vegetation, land use, the tone of bare soil, and man-made structures. Interpretation is sometimes based mainly or entirely on landforms, making a deliberate decision to exclude other features in the interest of having a uniform basis, or on landforms and vegetation combined. Circumstances calling for the use of vegetation alone are flat or swampy landscapes. Land use needs to be used with discretion, whilst soil reflectance is locally of importance. Generally, however, the interpreter makes use of whatever can be seen on the photograph, regardless of its origin; this may include features with a distinctive photographic appearance, the meaning of which is not known at the time of interpretation.

Landforms. Geomorphic units can be distinguished at a wide variety of scales, ranging from subcontinental to the parts of a single slope.

Major structural and relief units, such as shield areas, downwarped basins, dissected fold mountains or coastal plains, act as a setting; in surveys of large extent they provide a framework, or higher category of landscape classification, but many projects or other local surveys will lie wholly within one such unit.

Relief units are geomorphologically distinct areas such as an undulating plain, a range of hills, an escarpment, or an alluvial plain. They are identified on photographs as repeating patterns of smaller relief elements. The extent of a relief unit varies widely, from 1 km to over 100 km, and the degree of homogeneity permissible within a unit is a matter of subjective judgement. Relief units are the geomorphic basis of land systems.

Relief units may be described in terms of six characteristics: relative relief, drainage spacing, slope angle distribution, plan form (including degree of orientation), slope profile form (shape in cross section of interfluves, slopes and valley floors) and height distribution (Fig. 3.1 and Table 3.2). Examples are (a) gently undulating plain, relative relief 50–100 m, slopes 0–5°, widely spaced dendritic valley system with no preferred orientation, broadly convex interfluves and concave valley floors; (b) ridges 200–300 m high, slopes 15–35° with strong NE–SW orientation.

Slope facets are the smallest geomorphologically homogeneous areas that can be distinguished on air photos, typically 20–500 m in extent.

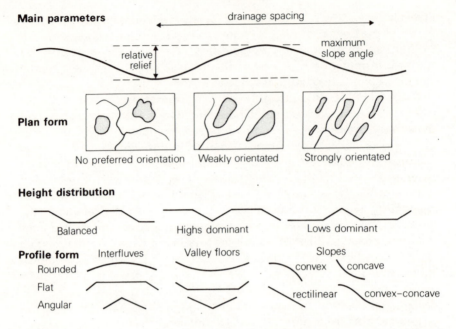

Figure 3.1 Parameters for the description of landforms (cf. Table 3.2). From Young (1976).

They may be rectilinear, defined by their angle; or convex or concave, defined by their curvature plus average steepness. A rectilinear facet at 0° is a flat. Slope facets are the geomorphic basis of land facets (p. 105). Although sample slope angles can be measured with a parallax bar or plotter if wished, it will usually be sufficient to record during interpretation in terms of 'steep', 'moderate', 'gentle', etc., since more accurate angles will be recorded in the field at all observation sites.

The technique of **morphological mapping** provides a useful method of recording detailed relief features, both in the field and from air photographs (Fig. 3.2). The land surface is regarded as being made up of morphological units, bounded by breaks of slope (abrupt changes in angle) or changes of slope (gradual). Units may be rectilinear slope facets, characterised by their angle, or continuously convex or concave units. Most major and some minor breaks of slope correspond to differences in soil type.

Geomorphological photo-interpretation is by no means limited to the description of ground surface forms in a static sense. The processes responsible for landforms also strongly influence parent materials and soils; hence recognition of landforms in dynamic terms, with respect to both past processes and those currently operative, is equally important. This aspect is particularly significant in landscapes of depositional origin, e.g. an alluvial plan, till plain, or glaciofluvial complex. Where the

Table 3.2 Classes for the description of landforms (cf. Figure 3.1). From Young (1976).

relative relief (valley depth) m

<10	very low	depositional relief
10–30	low (shallow)	plains of low relief
30–100	moderate	plains of moderate relief
100–300	high (deep)	hills
>300	very high (very deep)	mountains

drainage spacing (valley width) m

<100	very close (narrow)	badlands
100–400	close (narrow)	
400–1500	moderate	
1500–3000	wide	
>3000	very wide	

slope angle (degrees)

0–2	level to very gentle
2–5	gentle (gently undulating)
5–10	moderate (moderately undulating)
10–18	moderately steep
18–30	steep
30–45	very steep
>45	precipitous to vertical

plan form
no preferred orientation
weakly orientated (give direction)
strongly orientated (give direction)

height distribution

balanced (neither highs nor lows predominant)	normal valley relief
highs predominant (>66% of area)	dissected plateau
lows predominant (>66% of area)	plain with hills

profile form

interfluves	rounded, flat, or angular
valley floors	rounded, flat, or angular
slopes	predominantly convex, rectilinear, or concave; combinations of these forms (from crest to base), e.g. convex–concave, convex–rectilinear, convex–rectilinear–concave

processes responsible can be established, a range of soil properties and the broad soil pattern can be predicted by interpretation of surface features, in the first instance from air photographs. Table 3.3 summarises the topography and soil parent material properties of four model glacial landscapes, two of which are illustrated by Plate 2. The same approach can be applied to other land systems. The use of a model in no way substitutes for systematic field investigation, but by anticipating important soil characteristics the model serves as a guide to field investigations. Sampling sites may be chosen to characterise well defined areas efficiently and to establish the characteristics of doubtful areas, and many soil boundaries may be drawn on the basis of their surface expression.

Table 3.3 Soil characteristics of model glacial landscapes. Partly from Boulton and Paul (1976).

Landscape	Topographic features	Soil parent material features
I subglacial and proglacial	**Till surface** bears **drumlins** moulded in the direction of ice flow; superimposed on this are **flutes** and **push moraines** but on old till surfaces microtopography is rarely visible except on air photos. Disordered surface drainage pattern	**Lodgement till**, laid down beneath the glacier, is unsorted (particle size ranges from rock flour to boulders); it may include preweathered material, clasts are mostly subrounded; it is strongly overconsolidated (shear strength much greater than remoulded strength), exhibits sub-horizontal fissuring due to unloading; upper layer less than 1 m thick, dilated and may be depleted of fines, common angular frost-shattered clasts; natural drainage variable, according to local topography
II supraglacial	**Eskers** are steep-sided sinuous ridges formed as subglacial meltwater stream fillings	Crudely sorted coarse sand and gravel with interbedded lenses of contrasting textures; clasts subrounded and rounded; very permeable; natural drainage invariably free
	Proglacial outwash – a braided pattern of stream channels commonly picked out by vegetation responding to variations in texture and drainage; sometimes cut into sharply defined **terraces** and pockmarked by **kettle holes**	Braided pattern of sorted sands and gravels, occasional thin beds of silt, clasts rounded, lensed in section; very permeable; upper terraces freely drained
	Proglacial lake beds – smooth surface, depressional sites	Varved lacustrine silt and fine sand with deltas of coarser material; mostly slowly permeable and poorly drained; commonly become peat-covered
	Undulating **kame** landscape; common **kettle holes.** Disordered surface drainage	Complex association of outwash sands and gravels, sorted and lensed, faulted and folded. Kames are composed mainly of outwash, sometimes capped and flanked by **flow till** and **melt-out till** which are unsorted, not overconsolidated, and exhibit vertical jointing. Remoulded shear strength similar to *in situ* condition. This association overlies **lodgement till**
III glaciated valley	**Nunataks** and **steep valley sides,** may bear frost-shattered **tors** flanked by scree	Coarse, angular stony drift and scree; bare rock on ice-scraped surfaces
	Medial and **lateral moraines** – hummocky deposits along valley sides and bottom	Supraglacial **morainic till** – unsorted, including angular boulders of great size but little fine material; high angle of friction; very permeable; usually naturally well drained

Kame terraces along valley sides, often associated with lateral moraine, often with kettle holes	Outwash sands and gravels – lensed, commonly folded and jointed; very permeable; drainage depends on local topography
Moraine-dammed lake beds in valley bottoms, associated with terminal or push moraine across valley	Varved lacustrine sediments and deltas of coarser material; invariably slowly permeable and poorly drained; commonly peat-filled
IV periglacial	
Modification of glacial or preglacial topography. **Solifluction lobes** and **terraces** on smooth convex slopes. Blankets of cover sand and loess winnowed from outwash deposits and till surfaces	**Stony drift** – angular, frost-shattered debris with little fine material derived mainly from upper convex slopes, sometimes overlies lodgement till on lower slopes
	Coombe – unsorted, normally consolidated, may include preweathered material
	Cover sand – variable thickness of well sorted medium and fine sand, deposited over existing till and terrace surfaces. Deposition close to source
	Loess – variable thickness of well sorted fine material, mostly silt. In thick deposits, layers of different textures and buried soil horizons are typical. Deposition at long distances from source.
	Surface deposits mixed with underlying materials by frost leaving lag of angular stones and gravel on surface. Depletion of fines in surface layer. Commonly accumulation of downwashed material in a dense silty layer over permafrost, rock or compact till

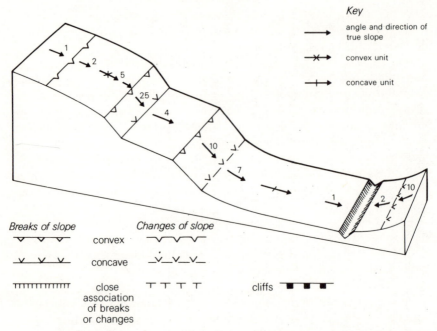

Figure 3.2 Symbols for morphological mapping. After Curtis *et al.* (1965).

Vegetation. Vegetation becomes a valuable guide to soils in two circumstances: where there are expanses of undisturbed natural vegetation, and on depositional landforms. If one can reasonably assume that the vegetation is unaltered by human impact, then it can prove to be a sensitive guide to soils, since vegetation sometimes responds to quite small differences in moisture, soil depth, reaction, salinity or other soil properties. This is particularly the case in the semi-arid zone. Where, however, there has been appreciable human impact, e.g. by cutting, burning or grazing, this can soon outweigh such natural responses, and produce prominent but spurious patterns.

It is often not possible to identify individual plant species on photographs, and hence interpretation must be of plant associations described in physiognomic terms. The main bases for description are the percentage cover of trees and shrubs, the proportion of trees to shrubs, their heights, and the density of cover by grassland or other herbaceous layer as indicated by the tone of this layer (Kuchler 1967, p. 191; Young 1976, p. 48). At the stage of initial photo-interpretation it is sufficient to describe the plant communities in *ad hoc* terms, whatever is recognisable. They can be related to a more definitive system of vegetation classification during fieldwork.

In depositional landscapes, for example, alluvial and intertidal plains, small variations in elevation are highly significant for soil morphology, soil chemistry, physical properties and land use potential. These height differences are too small to be measured directly by photo-interpretation, or even in the field without arduous levelling. In these circumstances it is often possible to make use of the response of vegetation to differences in hydrology, salinity, and active sedimentation processes, for example delineating different species or growth forms of mangroves and other plant communities (Plate 3). In effect, geomorphological units are mapped indirectly through their vegetation (Dent 1980). The kinds of units distinguished are cover floodplains, river and creek levées, back-swamps, abandoned channels, sand bars, silted lagoons and mudflats. The subsequent task of field research is to establish the relationships between these vegetation indicators, landform units and significant soil characteristics.

As in the case of geomorphology, and indeed all environmental features used to identify soil patterns, the better understanding that the surveyor has of the physiology and ecology of vegetation, the more skilled he will be in using it as an indicator of soils.

Land use. This can be readily seen on air photographs, including such aspects as the proportions of arable and maintained pasture, forest plantations, orchards, the pattern of fields and the extent of urban or village use of land. Maps showing the existing land use have many planning applications, both in developed and developing countries, and air photographs with a measure of ground control are eminently suited to this task. But land use is a fickle guide to soils. A line separating cultivated from unused land can sometimes indicate the margin of, say, shallow laterite, but it can also be caused by domestic water supply, settlement history or land tenure.

Ground surface. Differences in reflectance from bare ground can be useful in certain environments. Rock outcrops can readily be seen. In deserts, formations of sand dunes, playas and saline depressions can be mapped. On *prima facie* grounds it should be possible to distinguish the main classes of topsoil texture, although field checks of such attempts have sometimes shown low levels of prediction. Soil erosion, especially gully-ing, shows up clearly on photographs, provided the scale is large enough; sheet erosion shows as paler tones on arable land, and cattle trampling in valley floors as white patches. Patches of salinisation brought about by irrigation are also readily seen.

A further use of surface reflectance arises in depositional areas under arable use. Plate 1 shows an example of soil patterns in the English Fenland: light tones define former creek levées of silty clay texture, dark tones indicate hollows and old creek channels infilled by peat. The differences in relief are so slight that these features are difficult to pick out on the ground and the pattern is so complex that it can be delineated only on aerial photographs.

Interpretation procedures

The procedures of photo-interpretation, and the mapping units that can most usefully be distinguished, vary considerably with the type of landscape and the scale and purpose of the survey. The following outline procedure for the main pre-field, interpretation is conceived in terms of a general-purpose survey of an area of the order of 100 km^2, using prints of about 1: 25 000 scale, such as might be applicable in a multipurpose land development project.

(1) Make a print laydown of the whole area. From this (or in conjunction with satellite imagery), make a first identification of the main landscape units or visible patterns.

(2) Work quite rapidly through all the photographs, under stereoscopic viewing. Make descriptions of each of the mapping units identified, noting pairs of photos on which each is characteristically represented. In most circumstances, use landforms as a basis, supplemented by vegetation patterns where necessary.

(3) Now carry out the main interpretation, working more slowly through the prints and drawing in boundaries. There is a simple rule for this stage: start by delineating the most conspicuous features (e.g. hills, swamps, sand dunes), and only then proceed to more uncertain divisions such as those between plains of differing character. Often it will be found that a valley floor or ridge forms a convenient break between plainlands with gradually changing properties. Bolder individuals will interpret each run of photographs separately, reconciling joins which do not match subsequently; the more timid may transfer unclosed boundaries successively from run to run.

(4) Whichever procedure has been followed at run junctions, there are likely to be awkward joins remaining, areas which do not fit into the scheme devised, or places where one mapping unit seems to fade into another without an identifiable boundary. Landscapes often really are like this, and there is nothing to be done but accept the fact and include some rather arbitrary boundaries.

(5) Next, fill in slope units or other more detailed mapping units. Whether this is done for the whole survey area, for limited parts of it (e.g. potential arable land) or only for sample areas will depend on the requirements of the survey.

In some landscapes, the patterns and units visible on the photographs are so clear as to dictate what shall be mapped. In others, problems arise as to the degree of generalisation to adopt, known as the 'splitting or lumping' question. When in doubt, the general rule is to split during pre-field interpretation, always provided that the units so distinguished can be shown at the scale to be employed on the map. Differences which are later found not to be significant can be readily eliminated during post-field boundary revision, when the rule becomes the opposite: if you cannot be sure that a difference is both valid and significant, eliminate it.

The most convenient practice is to mark boundaries directly on one set of prints with wax-type crayons ('chinagraph', 'omnichrom', etc.); these do not damage the photographs and can be readily cleaned off with a solvent. The boundaries should then be traced off as a protection against loss, and the marked prints used in the field. Where it is thought undesirable to mark the prints, they can be overlain with 'drawfilm' or similar material, which is very transparent but takes both crayon and a fine ink line. For fieldwork, make yourself a stout clipboard.

The relationship between photo-interpretation units and soil units

At reconnaissance scales, the units distinguished by photo-interpretation are relief units such as floodplain, escarpment and pediment. These units invariably correspond to substantial differences in the types of soils present and their relative proportions.

At larger scales, photo-interpretation units are differentiated on the basis of convergence of evidence (Plate 4). In general, major breaks in slope (separating units of substantially different angles) nearly always indicate soil boundaries. Minor breaks in slope sometimes do and sometimes do not correspond to soil boundaries; the likelihood of soil change is greater if slope, vegetation and surface tone are all different.

A combination of landform and vegetation which proves to be a good indicator of a particular soil type in one area may be quite misleading in an adjacent area, so thorough field checking of such relationships is always essential.

Photo-interpretation for soil survey and land evaluation requires interpretation of the whole landscape, including the processes by which it has been formed, and in particular the relationships between landforms, parent materials and soils. For example a steep-sided, sinous ridge in a glaciated landscape may be interpreted as an esker; this identification suggests a probable range of soil properties, both for agriculture and engineering purposes (Fig. 3.3). Whilst the value of photo-interpretation compared with field mapping becomes progressively less as the scale becomes larger, there is no point where it ceases to be of value. Air photographs can still make a substantial contribution to

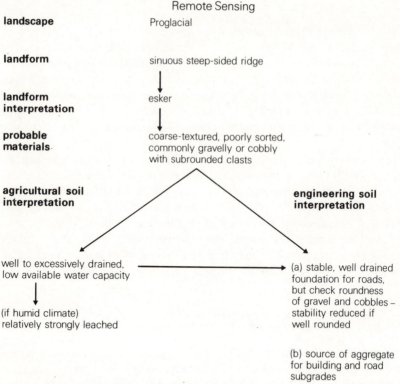

landscape   Proglacial

landform   sinuous steep-sided ridge

landform
interpretation   esker

probable
materials   coarse-textured, poorly sorted,
commonly gravelly or cobbly
with subrounded clasts

agricultural soil
interpretation

engineering soil
interpretation

well to excessively drained,
low available water capacity

(a) stable, well drained
foundation for roads,
but check roundness
of gravel and cobbles –
stability reduced if
well rounded

(if humid climate)
relatively strongly leached

(b) source of aggregate
for building and road
subgrades

Figure 3.3   Example of soil interpretations from air photo-interpretation of landforms.

survey, either by saving in time or improvement in accuracy, at scales of 1 : 5000 or larger.

Two environments present difficulties. In uncleared rain forest the tree canopy blankets the ground, softening relief to such an extent that first-order valleys cannot be distinguished, and only the main hills and swamps can be delineated, besides which the photographs are of little use for finding field locations. Secondly, in some lowland areas of developed countries, particularly Western Europe, the appearance of the photographs is dominated by field boundaries and crops, making any other pattern hard to distinguish.

From the fact that photo-interpretation for soil survey depends primarily on identifying significant landform–soil relationships, it follows that the most important qualifications for a good interpreter are an all-round knowledge of geomorphology coupled with field soil survey experience. The basic elements of photo-interpretation, such as the recognition of tone, texture and pattern and the different spectral reflectances of vegetation or water, will not alone take you far. Photo-interpretation calls for a knowledge not so much of photographs as of landscapes.

Plate 1 Depositional landscape, the English Fens. Estuarine creek channels and levées of stratified fine sandy to silty clay loam show as light tones; the intervening basins of peat overlying silty clay are indicated by dark tones. This soil pattern has been exhumed by wastage of the peat following deep drainage.

Plate 4 Savanna landscape, Dedza District, Malaŵi. A major soil and land system boundary commences at bottom centre and runs north-east close to the river. North-west of this, there is a soil catena from red ferruginous soils (FAO, ferric luvisols) on the interfluve crests through reddish yellow and brown soils down the valley slopes to valley floors consisting of a fringe of mottled sandy soils around poorly drained black heavy clays. The contrast between valley floor grassland and arable fields clearly separates the valley floors from the interfluves but the three upper members of the soil catena cannot be reliably distinguished by photo-interpretation. Patchy cultivation, more woodland and (in stereoscopic view) slightly steeper slopes in the south-eastern area correspond to less-fertile sandier soils. Note the importance of air photographs, as distinct from maps, to find your way amid such a network of tracks.

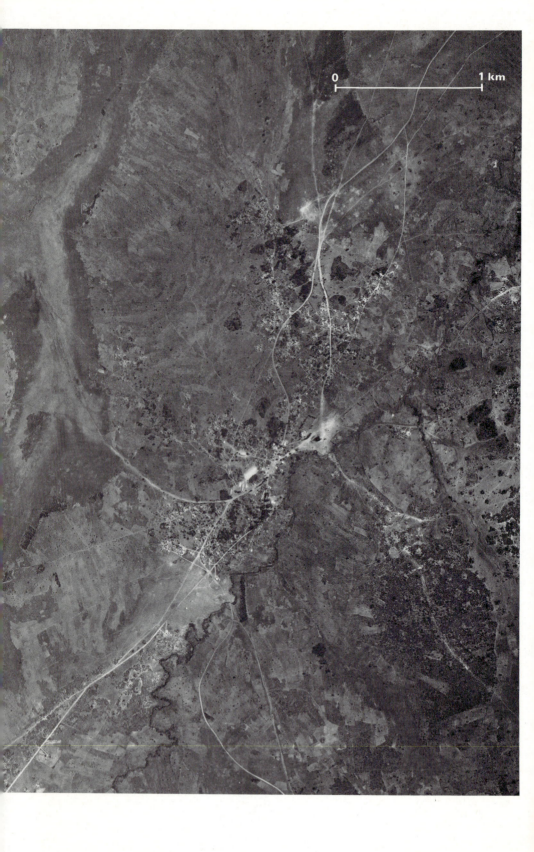

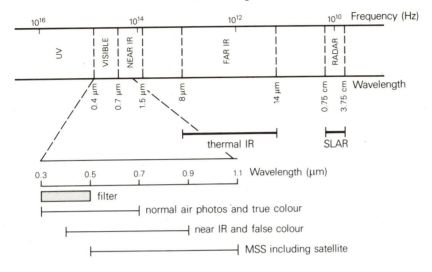

Figure 3.4 Wavelengths of remote-sensing systems.

Other kinds of remote sensing from aircraft

The wavelength ranges and other characteristics of the different imagery used in soil surveys and related land resource surveys are shown in Figure 3.4 and Table 3.4. Each kind of imagery has certain special attributes deriving from the nature of the image, and all have applications in some kinds of resource survey. The first four types listed in the table are forms of photography, namely imagery produced directly by light falling on a sensitised base, usually film; the last four types collect the initial data as other forms of signal, but for most purposes of interpretation these are subsequently converted into quasi-photographic images.

Near-infrared black-and-white photography

Standard panchromatic film is designed to be sensitive to the same range of wavelengths as the human eye, approximately 0.4–0.7 μm; in air photography it is used in conjunction with a filter to remove blue light which is subject to excessive scattering by haze. Infrared film extends the range of sensitivity into the near-infrared band, up to 0.9 μm. The special facility offered by this kind of film is to combine the character of a normal air photograph with added sensitivity to infrared radiation.

The image produced looks exactly like a normal air photograph but has certain added tonal contrasts. Water absorbs infrared radiation strongly, chlorophyll has a high reflectance in this band, and deciduous trees reflect much more infrared than do coniferous trees. Resolution is only

49

slightly lower than for panchromatic film and the cost difference is small. It is therefore worth considering using this kind of film if surface water or drainage impedance are known to be of particular significance in the area.

Colour photography

Colour air photographs cover the same spectral range as do black-and-white ones. They may be obtained either as colour prints, taken from colour-reversal negatives, or as colour-positive transparencies which must be viewed over a light. Colour photography requires more stringent atmospheric conditions than are necessary for black-and-white photography, and resolution is lower. Colour film is sensitive to small

Table 3.4 Some characteristics of remote-sensing systems in relation to soil survey.

Remote sensing system	Wavelengths	Resolution	Special facilities	Applications in soil or related surveys
normal air photography	0.4–0.7 μm	very high	–	numerous
near-infrared monochrome photography	0.7–0.9 μm) (plus visible, 0.4–0.7 μm)	high	chlorophyll reflects strongly, water absorbs	detection of drainage, impedance, surface water; differentiation of tree species
true-colour photography	0.3–0.7 μm	high	ground surface colour, vegetation colour	urban fringe surveys; display
false-colour photography	0.5–0.9 μm	high	emphasises variations in vegetation	vegetation and land use mapping; soil surveys in intertidal zone
thermal infrared	8–14 μm	low	records heat emitted by the ground surface	none
side-looking airborne radar (SLAR)	0.8–3.0 cm	very low	penetrates cloud	possibly reconnaisance in cloud-covered areas
multispectral scanning (MSS)	0.3–1.1 μm in bands	high	permits identification of spectral signatures	crop identification
satellite MSS imagery	0.5–1.1 μm in bands	high relative to small-scale image, low relative to ground	uniform coverage of large area	coverage of very large areas; initial overview in other surveys

differences in development, which, coupled with atmospheric variations, means that the colour match between adjacent runs is sometimes
poor. At worst, supposed colour prints come as a monochrome wash of
blue-green. Total costs are only 5–25% higher than for black-and-white
prints since the main cost is that of the aeroplane, but the cost of
additional prints is several times greater.

The human eye can differentiate about 100 times as many colour
combinations as it can tones on the grey scale. Moreover, really good-
quality colour photographs are a delight to the eye and interpreters like
using them. It is therefore disappointing that experience has shown that
the added information for soil survey is slight. The reason is that so much
of useful interpretation depends on surface form. The gain from seeing
topsoil colour is small since most topsoils are dark brown. For desert
landscapes, including identification of saline depressions, colour has
been found useful. In urban fringe surveys it can also be valuable,
though mostly for detecting land use, recreational pressure on grassland,
etc., rather than soils as such. In the general case, many soil surveyors
who have tried both would prefer to settle for really high-definition
monochrome prints in preference to colour.

False-colour photography

Originally devised as a means of camouflage detection in war, false-
colour film (commonly Kodak infrared Ektachrome 3443) produces a
striking and unfamiliar image. It operates over the same spectral range as
does monochrome infrared film, 0.5–0.9 μm, i.e. visible light plus near-
infrared. The problem of how to render the infrared band visible to the
human eye is solved by shifting all colour bands towards a longer
wavelength. Blue is filtered out, green (0.5–0.6 μm) is printed as blue,
red (0.6–0.7 μm) as green, and near-infrared (0.7–0.9 μm) as red.

Healthy vegetation and crops contain chlorophyll, which has a high
infrared reflectance, and thus they appear red. Diseased plants lose their
chlorophyll and appear yellow or blue-black, whilst crops suffering
moisture stress are darker. Ploughed land and other bare ground appear
blue-green, whilst poorly drained areas are darker due to the low infrared reflectance of water.

The strangeness of a false-colour image is an initial problem but soon
overcome. Vegetation communities, crops and other forms of land use
are more readily distinguished from each other in false colour than in
true colour. Hence the uses for which false colour has considerable
potential are vegetation and land use mapping, detection of disease in
crops or forests, and possibly identification of forest species. It follows
that its value in soil survey lies, if anywhere, in areas where vegetation is
an important indicator of soils. The intertidal and adjacent coastal zone,

where vegetation as an indicator is combined with presence of surface water, is one environment where it may be worth obtaining false-colour prints in addition to standard air photography.

Thermal infrared sensing

Thermal infrared detectors record the heat, or far-infrared radiation, emitted by the Earth's surface. As the atmosphere is a poor transmitter over most of the thermal range, it can only be recorded within atmospheric 'windows', usually 8–14 μm. Because of the longer wavelength, resolution is much lower than with light photography. For interpretation, the sensed heat signal is converted into a black-and-white image, which has the appearance of an air photograph on which something has 'gone wrong'.

Thermal infrared sensing has special uses, such as detecting poorly insulated buildings, places where tanks were parked a short time ago, or following the path of hot water emitted from power stations into an estuary. To attempt to detect soil types by their thermal emission characteristics might be a project for a research student but is certainly not practical soil survey.

Side-looking airborne radar

This form of imagery (known also as SLAR) depends on the reflectance from the ground of a radar signal (wavelength 0.8–3.0 cm) transmitted from an aircraft. The strength of the reflected signal is recorded electronically, and for interpretation it is subsequently converted into a black-and-white image. Beneath the path of the plane so much signal is reflected that it floods the receptor and the image lacks contrast; hence the imagery is obtained in bands on either side of the flight path, and because of perspective is not true to scale.

The strength of the reflected signal depends on the direction in which slopes face and the roughness of the ground surface. The image is palest where slopes face the flight path, whilst slopes with the opposite aspect produce black 'shadow' areas. Irregular or rough surfaces, including vegetation, contain elements which face the emitter, reflect the signal back, and so appear lighter than smooth surfaces. Smooth water reflects all the signal away from the receptor and appears black. The resulting image is something like a photograph of a relief model taken under hard lighting. Resolution is low and it is a clumsy form of imagery for soil survey. However, radar penetrates cloud and allows imagery to be obtained of rain forest areas which are rarely sufficiently cloud-free to permit aerial photography. The technique can be used for topographic mapping in such areas, and was the basis for a reconnaissance resource inventory of the Amazon basin.

Multispectral scanning

Multispectral scanning (MSS) records the reflection of sunlight by the Earth's surface separately in each of a number of spectral bands, within the visible and near-infrared range. The technique by which the imagery is recorded is very different from photography. It is based upon rapid scanning of the ground by rotating mirrors, the signal from which is reflected onto a detector, recorded electrically as a continuous signal, and stored on a tape. For most kinds of interpretation the signal is subsequently transformed into a quasi-photographic image of high resolution. The product is to all outward appearances a number of black-and-white photographs, but each is restricted to a single spectral band. The bands most often employed are the green and red parts of the visible spectrum plus one or two bands within the near-infrared range.

There are three ways of interpreting such data. The first is by automatic data processing. The recorded signal is fed directly into a computer, without conversion into a visible image. Programs are developed which 'recognise' the patterns of signal from particular features, e.g. crops. To develop such techniques is a major exercise, only to be undertaken by organisations with large reserves of time and money. The second possibility is to interpret the black-and-white prints visually, just as if they were photographs. This is a common method with satellite imagery, but from aircraft-borne scanners its only advantage over normal photography is the availability of images solely within the infrared band. The third method is to combine the signals from various bands into a single colour image, which can then be interpreted by eye; the combination can either be done by obtaining a false-colour composite, in which case there is little difference from false-colour imagery, or by viewing through a colour-additive viewer. The latter allows the colour combinations to be varied at will, so that once a feature of interest, say a particular kind of crop, has been identified it can be made to show up prominently. The particular combinations of waveband strengths and signal pattern belonging to a ground feature is known as the **spectral signature** of that feature. It should be noted, however, that spectral signatures cannot be extrapolated from region to region, and often not from one image to another.

Multispectral scanning from aircraft is little used in soil survey, since any advantages it may have over true- and false-colour photography are more than counteracted by the added time and expense, and very few soils produce a unique spectral signature. Its main potential in resource survey lies in situations in which there is a need to identify and to map all occurrences of a particular and uniform feature, say rice fields, over a large area.

Remote sensing from satellites

Imagery

Earlier satellite imagery has been largely superseded for resource survey purposes by the Landsat series: Landsat 1 (1972–8), Landsat 2 (1975–) and Landsat 3 (1978–). These carry a multispectral scanning system recording in four wavebands:

(a) band 4: 0.5–0.6 μm, green
(b) band 5: 0.6–0.7 μm, yellow to red
(c) band 6: 0.7–0.8 μm, near-infrared 1
(d) band 7: 0.8–1.1 μm, near-infrared 2.

Landsat 3 has in addition a low-resolution thermal infrared band.

Each image covers a ground area of 185 km×185 km, or 34000 km^2. The nominal ground resolution is 80 m, though this applies to features of high contrast, and in practice it is substantially poorer. Each satellite covers every point on the Earth's surface, land and sea, every 18 days, but repeat imagery is by no means available at this frequency as the transmitters are not often switched on. Cloud permitting, however, images at different seasons and in successive years are available.

The data are available in the following forms:

(a) as computer-compatible tapes
(b) as separate black-and-white quasi-photographs, separately for each spectral band (these can be obtained as negatives or prints at scales from 1:1000000 to 1:250000; the most widely used scale is 1:1000000)
(c) as false-colour composites.

Computerised image-enhancement services are available commercially and provide prints of improved resolution and sharper contrast. The most sophisticated product of remote sensing is an image-enhanced satellite colour composite.

On Landsat 3 there is a pair of return beam Vidicon (RBV, or television) cameras of longer focal length and higher resolution, nominally 50 m, recording in a single spectral band 0.5–0.75 μm. The cameras produce adjacent images each 99 km×99 km; two successive pairs of such images can be matched to a 185 km square MSS image.

For mapping at very small scales, e.g. about 1:5000000, one can use 70 mm 'chips' (positive transparencies); these are obtained in black-and-white, then combined as a coloured image by means of a diazo printer. For mapping at about 1:1000000 the best product is a Landsat colour composite at 1: 500000.

Anyone can obtain Landsat imagery, for any part of the world, by writing to the EROS Data Center, Sioux Falls, South Dakota 57198, USA, requesting a Geographic Computer Search Inquiry Form. Considering the technology involved, the product is available at a very modest and highly subsidised price.

Interpretation and applications

Compared with air photographs, the first major advantage of satellite imagery is its ready availability and cheapness. The second is that it provides coverage of very large areas on a small number of prints, and coverage of 34000 km^2 on a single print of uniform quality. A consequence of the large area covered is the obvious disadvantage of a much lower ground resolution. Even on the Landsat 3 RBV system resolution is about *100 times lower* than that of air photographs. A second disadvantage is the near-absence of a relief effect, owing to the altitude from which the images are obtained. These are not intended for stereoscopic viewing, although there is a limited stereoscopic facility in strips at the edges where images overlap.

Satellite imagery has the same limitation as air photography; all that is recorded is the light reflected from the surface of the ground. As in air photographs, the main features seen are landforms, vegetation and land use.

For reconnaissance surveys of very large areas, satellite imagery may be the sole form of remote sensing employed. It may also be used as a preliminary to conventional photo-interpretation (Ch. 7).

The use of satellite imagery alone has opened up a new possibility in soil survey, that of producing some sort of map of the whole of a large country in no more than a few months. Iran, for example, with an area of 1648000 km^2, is covered by 75 Landsat frames, and for the purpose of mapping soil degradation hazard was completely covered at a scale of 1: 5000000 in 1 man-month of interpretation. An area this size would need 40000 air photographs at 1: 50000 scale. Jordan, 98000 km^2, was mapped on a land systems basis at 1: 1000000 scale in 1.5 man-months of interpretation, 1 month in the field, 2 weeks' report and map preparation, plus printing and cartography (Mitchell & Howard 1978a, 1978b). On a commercial basis, interpretation of one Landsat image costs £250–£500 (1980), that is of the order of 100 km^2 for £1. Thus truly formidable tasks of interpretation have been reduced by satellite data to manageable ones. As a consequence, it is now a working proposition for the government of any country to set about producing some kind of uniform resource survey coverage within a period of the order of one to three years. Ethiopia, covered by 70 Landsat frames, has the production of a national master land use plan scheduled for 1979–1982, despite the very small amount of previous soil survey. Maps produced in this rapid way are not so accurate as those obtained by land system mapping at 1: 250 000 from air photographs, but they are uniform, and very few countries possess such coverage.

Employed as a preliminary to air photograph interpretation, satellite imagery can save time and temper. At a glance, the major landscape patterns are visible. A monochrome print, usually best in the $0.7-0.8 \, \mu m$ band, is sufficient for such an overview. Used in this way, the satellite image serves the same purpose as the initial print laydown of air photographs, and is better owing to its small scale, absence of print boundaries and uniformity of light conditions and processing. Additionally, a Landsat-based map can be used to plan the taking of new air photographs.

The interpretation of satellite images differs from that of air photographs in that no direct use can be made of height differences. Instead, relief must be inferred from its effects upon vegetation or other reflectance characteristics. It is possible to produce either a single interpretative map, showing something akin to land systems, or two maps, one of landforms and the other of ground cover. For landform mapping, a good example of the type of legend that can be devised is given by Mitchell and Howard (1978a). For mapping vegetation land use, a false-colour composite should be used. Natural vegetation can be classified by colour and, especially in arid regions, by percentage ground cover. Agricultural land use shows up clearly, either by regularity of pattern or by the redder image of crops.

Even more than with air photograph interpretation, the value of the map based on satellite imagery rapidly increases in proportion to the amount of field survey. No-one tries to employ photo-interpretation without field survey, yet the initial mystique of satellite data has led to a tendency to neglect so mundane an activity as walking about and seeing what is there. The large distances involved are an obstacle that must be overcome. Soil survey from satellite data rests on the same basic criterion as air photo-interpretation: it is valid to the extent that the units mapped from the imagery can be related to soil types on the ground.

Further reading

Carroll (1973), Carroll *et al.* (1977), White (1978), Soil Survey Staff (1966), Goosen (1967), American Society of Photogrammetry (1968, 1975), Speight (1977), Collins and van Genderen (1978), Townshend (1981).

Field Survey

There are three main phases of field soil survey: research, mapping and interpretation. The research phase is concerned with finding out which soil properties are important for the purposes of the survey, what are the field relationships of the soils with other factors, and how the soils can be mapped. In a national survey programme, or a project survey extending over a large area and a long period of time, this phase is not carried out as a single operation but is extended successively to different parts of the survey area.

The interpretation phase covers field survey activities related to evaluation and management of the soils. This is by no means a desk exercise carried out after completion of soil mapping, but requires specific field operations, which are not separated in time from the rest of the survey. Many, in some cases all, of the interpretation activities are carried out during the research phase, of which in some respects they form a part.

The research phase

The tasks of the research phase are to establish:

(1) which soil properties are important for the purposes of the survey;
(2) the field relationships between soil properties and surface features;
(3) the soil classes to be mapped and the mapping legend;
(4) how potential land productivity and recommended management practices are related to practicable mapping units.

The first of these tasks, to determine the soil properties which are significant to the purposes of the survey and thus need to be mapped, will already have been considered during the preliminary discussions preceding field survey. It may require further investigation in the field, following which the terms of reference of the survey may need to be modified in detail. For example, it may not be known in advance whether soil salinity is a significant hazard within the survey area. In the research

57

phase, a statistically designed set of sample transects will establish whether this hazard is sufficiently severe and widespread to necessitate routine sampling throughout the area as an essential prerequisite to land development or, on the contrary, whether such an operation will be a waste of money.

The research phase has sometimes been called the 'reconnaissance' or 'preliminary' phase. These are not merely misnomers but serious misconceptions, since they suggest that the research phase is only a minor element of field survey. Typically, the research phase should occupy about a third of the total field survey time in a general-purpose survey and up to half or more in a special-purpose survey. Indeed, one possible outcome of the research phase could be that the mapping phase as such is not necessary.

Research is the most difficult phase of survey, calling for both methodical investigation and skilled judgement. Its success relies heavily on the ability and experience of the surveyor, for which energy in the field is a poor substitute. The ultimate success of the survey also depends on the extent to which the soil properties of interest can be assessed in the field, and can therefore be mapped directly, or can be related to the mapping criteria.

Establishment of field relationships

The surveyor maps the soil continuum as a pattern of soil areas. Each mapping unit is characterised by selected properties of its soil profile and site and an estimate of the variability of these properties.

It is possible to examine the soil profile at any point in the landscape but there is an obvious practical limit to the number and detail of such observations. The only features of the landscape that can be mapped with speed and accuracy are surface features. Once the relationships between soil profile characteristics and surface features are established, the soil can be mapped according to its surface expression, with as much direct observation of profiles as is required by the scale of mapping and the complexity of the soil pattern. However, the particular relationships between any selected soil properties and mappable features have to be established in the field for each separate locality.

There is only one principle of universal value in soil mapping: Dokuchaiev's hypothesis that the soil profile is the integrated expression of parent material, climate, topography, living organisms and the age of the landscape. Where all these factors are the same, the soil will be the same; when any one of these factors is changed, the soil will change. Information about some of these factors may be gathered from previous studies; for example, climatic and geological data are often available. If not, it must be gathered in the course of the survey.

Preliminary photo-interpretation is principally a topographic or geomorphological interpretation of the landscape but, with adequate ground control, elements of vegetation and land use can also be mapped quickly and accurately from air photographs. Slope and surface form are also of importance in their own right as criteria for soil mapping.

Soil parent materials and their pattern of variation nearly always have a strong influence on soil properties. Existing geological maps may be of very limited value as indicators of soil parent materials, notably in glaciated regions and areas which experience deposition of volcanic ash or loess. The nature of the parent material can only be established by profile examination, but patterns of variation can often be predicted in a general way from geomorphology. For example, in recently glaciated areas, specific landforms can be identified on the ground and by stereoscopic study of aerial photographs. Each landform is associated with characteristic soil parent materials and the landform itself exerts a dominant influence on hydrology and related soil properties. Some field relationships in a young proglacial landscape are illustrated by Figure 3.3 and Table 3.3. In older glacial landscapes, relationships between landform and soil are modified by a long period of soil development and over wide areas preweathered material has been reworked; the relationships between landform and soil remain, but they are less obvious.

A contrasting example of more subtle relationships between landform and soil properties is provided by the intertidal zone where depositional and erosional landforms and their associated microrelief control stratigraphy, natural drainage, degree of soil ripening and the depth in the profile at which potentially acid (sulphidic) material occurs. In this case the landforms cannot be detected directly on aerial photographs and can barely be seen in the field since relief differences may be less than 1 m over distances of several kilometres. However, differences in microrelief and drainage are reflected by the natural vegetation, which can be used as a guide to soil mapping. Figure 4.1 and Plate 3 illustrate some relationships between landform, vegetation and soil properties in tropical and subtropical estuaries.

Superimposed on the pattern of parent material variation are the effects of soil-forming processes. These are dependent on climate, local differences in hydrology, natural vegetation, Quaternary history and the more recent but often far-reaching influence of man.

On the basis of his pedological analysis of the landscape, the surveyor divides it into areas within which the factors of soil formation are more or less uniform and, by implication, the soils should be uniform. Soil profiles are examined at a range of sites within each landscape unit and the surveyor builds up a conceptual model of the relationships between the soil and other observable elements of the environment. Each soil observation is a process of:

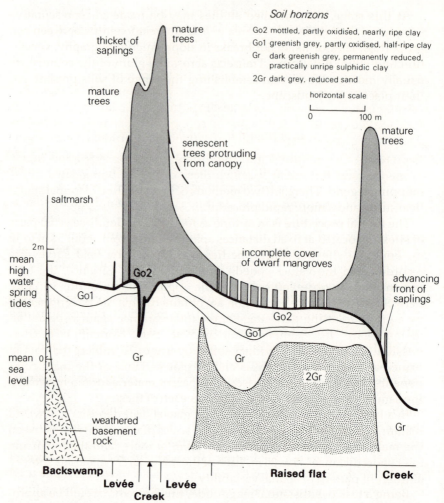

Soil horizons

Go2 mottled, partly oxidised, nearly ripe clay
Go1 greenish grey, partly oxidised, half-ripe clay
Gr dark greenish grey, permanently reduced, practically unripe sulphidic clay
2Gr dark grey, reduced sand

Figure 4.1 Transect across the intertidal zone, Kaipara Harbour, New Zealand, showing relationships between microtopography, vegetation and soil morphology. Adapted from Dent (1980). Only one species of mangrove, *Avicennia marina*, is present here, which responds dramatically to slight differences in elevation and surface drainage. Within the Tropics different topographic niches are typically occupied by different mangrove species, as shown in Plate 3.

(1) identification of a site – by its landform, microtopography, vegetation or other surface expression

(2) prediction of the soil properties on the basis of the conceptual model

(3) examination of the soil and recording its properties

(4) modification of the model in the light of the observations.

At this stage, very detailed studies may be made in representative samples of the whole survey area to find the relationships between soil properties, landforms, major breaks in slope, microtopography, vegetation and cultural patterns. Transects across the grain of the country are usually most productive in establishing the range of soils present and their place in the landscape.

Investigation of soil variability

Research is also required into the different scales of variation in soil properties and the extent to which these can be accommodated in the mapping legend. There are two methods of investigation, a formal statistical study and a more rapid procedure.

The formal procedure is in outline as follows. Randomly selected pairs of sites are located at fixed distances apart, ranging from about 5 km to 10 m. For each site the soil properties investigated by field survey are recorded and the values coded. Using analysis of variance, the total variance of the observed soils and the apportionment of this variance between each distance separation are obtained. This can be represented by a graph, plotting percentage of the total variance against separation distance (see, for example, Chorley *et al.* 1966, Nortcliff 1978). It is possible to use each individual soil property or to subject the data to principal components analysis and to plot variance of the main components. Where obvious landscape or parent material differences exist, the sampling should be stratified within each of these.

In a local study of soils developed on glacial drift deposits in lowland Britain, Nortcliff (1978) found two main scales of variation: that between the main types of drift, separated by 2 km or more, and that occurring over short distances, 5 to 25 m. Each of the main parent materials showed a different pattern of spatial variability.

Being a task of substantial magnitude, this procedure could be appropriately undertaken or sponsored by national survey organisations. For one-off surveys, such as for land development projects, this technique is far too time-consuming, but the principle of studying variability before embarking on mapping should still be applied. The pattern of variation can be investigated by short linear traverses within each major landform or parent material unit, and the amount of short-range variation within apparently uniform areas can be established by examining clusters of profiles within a 10 m radius.

Development of a provisional mapping legend

The soil classification to be used has already been decided. The provisional legend defines:

(a) the range of soils present and the taxonomic units to which they belong

(b) the nature and scale of variability of the soil pattern

(c) the mapping units to be employed, including decisions on which areas can be mapped as simple units (soil series, etc.) and which will be mapped as compound units (soil associations, soil landscapes, etc.)

(d) the relationships between the mapping units so defined and the landscape as a whole (landforms, vegetation, etc.).

For example, in an old glaciated landscape it may prove practicable to separate the soils of glaciofluvial terraces from the soils developed on lodgement till on the basis of consistent, gross differences in particle size distribution, consolidation and drainage, and associated profile morphology. Within the lodgement till unit there may be important point-to-point variations, for example in the depth to indurated subsoil or impeded drainage, which cannot be mapped, either because of absence of surface expression or because the pattern cannot be shown at the scale of the survey. In this case a significant variability within the mapping unit must be accepted and reported.

A further problem that arises in field survey is that the soil units which are practicable, or easiest, to map are not necessarily equivalent to the taxonomic classes of a standard system of soil classification. In most cases it is preferable to map the natural soil units that occur in the field; that is, to map what is there and to consider classification equivalents afterwards. The positions of many boundaries are dictated by the landscape, leaving the surveyor to describe as best he can what lies within them.

The provisional mapping legend should not be treated as a rough draft, but should be regarded at the time as the final map legend, lacking only minor details. The decisions on mapping units and permitted variability within them should avoid devoting unnecessary effort in the systematic mapping phase trying to map what cannot be mapped. This is particularly important when the mapping phase is to be performed by a large team of surveyors working to the provisional legend.

The detailed relationships established between surface features and soils will show, first, which boundaries can be reliably transferred from the previous photo-interpretation and which must be established by field traversing; and, secondly, which visible features to look for in field survey and in which landscape positions to site field observations. The more time and care that is devoted to research, the quicker, more accurate and thus more efficient will be the subsequent mapping phase.

At this stage it may be useful to collect samples from key sites for laboratory determination of properties that cannot be assessed in the field but which are important for the purposes of the survey and are required for the characterisation of mapping units.

The mapping phase

Mapping to the provisional legend at a specified level of intensity occupies the greater part of survey time in the field. Profile observations may be made on a strict grid basis, by free survey or according to some compromise between these two approaches.

Selection of observation sites

Grid survey. In a strict grid survey, observations are regularly spaced to produce a rectangular grid over the survey area. This is appropriate for large-scale intensive surveys, in which the usefulness of air photo-interpretation and the surface expression of soil classes is limited and where the high density of observations demands precise plotting of sites. There is no alternative to grid survey where there is no adequate aerial photography or topographic map for navigation. It is employed in dense forest and swamp where photo-interpretation is often of limited usefulness and there is no way of finding your position except by measurement; in these conditions a herringbone pattern of cut lines is useful, with a central baseline between regularly spaced straight traverses.

Grid survey is also necessary in areas of complex soil pattern where the detailed pattern could be mapped only at an impracticably large scale. Compound mapping units are then required and grid survey provides a statistical estimate of the proportions of different soil classes within these mapping units.

An advantage of grid survey is that it requires less experienced staff than subjective selection of observation sites. For the same reason, experienced surveyors dislike this approach, though it is worth pointing out that the use of a strict grid for locating profile observations does not preclude using ground evidence or photo-interpretation for drawing boundaries.

A major disadvantage is that it is inherently wasteful; a significant proportion of sites are unrepresentative, including for example settlements, or are near to landscape boundaries when the soil class is indeterminate. Inflexibility of site selection can also be a severe disadvantage where access is frequently interrupted by creeks, dykes and so on, so that time is wasted reaching the specified sites. Exact site location can be difficult; the statistical validity of the sample is lost if the man on the ground does not know precisely where he is and ends up by choosing the site within a 100 m radius. Some basic topographic survey, such as setting out lines of posts, may be required.

Free survey. In free survey the surveyor uses his judgement of the objectives of the survey and all the available air photo and ground evidence to locate profile observations at the most useful and representative sites. Each observation thus produces the maximum useful information; the density of observations is adjusted according to the requirements of the survey and the complexity of the soil pattern. Free survey requires good field sheets, either aerial photographs or detailed topographic maps, and adequate navigational features on the ground. To an expert surveyor it is technically more satisfying than grid survey and it is more efficient at small and medium scales.

However, map users and commissioning authorities may have more confidence in a grid survey because of its apparent objectivity and uniform coverage. Some compromise between the two approaches may be agreed where, for example, at least one observation must be made within each grid square, or within 100 m of each grid intersection. This maintains uniform coverage but enables the surveyor to avoid unrepresentative sites or crossings of an unbridged river or canal. Alternatively, a more widely spaced rigid grid may be employed, retaining statistical rigour but allowing the surveyor a proportion of additional observations at his own discretion.

Field observations

Soil profile observations are made at three levels of detail: representative profiles, intermediate descriptions and brief descriptions or soil type identifications. Each description comprises site information and profile morphology, in addition to which there may be field tests and sampling at the more detailed levels. The kinds of data typically recorded at each level are given in Table 4.1.

Site descriptions record two overlapping sets of data: the factors of soil formation, some of which, e.g. angle of slope, can be key features in the soil classification; and the observable landscape features by means of which the extent of the soil type observed at the site can be provisionally extrapolated. For each environmental factor other than climate, two aspects are recorded: the conditions of the site itself and those of the surrounding area. Thus the record of parent material includes the lithology and state of weathering of rocks in the profile and any nearby outcrops and also the geological formation, as shown by a geological map if one exists. In recording relief it is particularly important to note the position of the site (on the slope crest, upper slope, mid-slope, lower slope, bench, terrace, valley floor), since this is the basis for establishing

Table 4.1 Data recorded in field observations. *Key:* √ always recorded; (√) optional, according to the requirement of the survey.

Kind of information	Representative profile	Intermediate level	Soil type identification
(1) Identification and location:			
profile no., surveyor (initials), date	√	√	√
location, grid reference, map sheet/air photo no.	√	√	√
(2) Site information:			
landform of surrounding area, e.g. undulating plain, 2–5°	√		
of site: slope angle and shape (convex, concave, etc.)	√	√	(√)
position on slope (upper, middle, etc.)	√	√	
microtopography	√	(√)	
elevation	√	(√)	
surface stones and rock outcrops	√	(√)	(√)
evidence of erosion	√	√	(√)
hydrology of area, e.g. percentage poorly drained	√		
of site: natural drainage	√	√	√
depth to groundwater table	√	(√)	(√)
vegetation of area: physiognomic type, dominant spp	√		
of site: plant association, indicator spp	√	(√)	
land use of area, including percentage cultivated	√		
of site, including history if ascertained	√		
climate: added subsequently by analysis of records	√		
(3) Soil profile information:			
parent material: rock/drift type as on geological map	√	(√)	
lithology and degree of weathering	√	√	
horizon depths	√	√	√
colour, mottling	√	√	√
texture	√	√	√
structure	√	(√)	
consistence	√	(√)	
pedological features, e.g. cutans, nodules, cementation, pans	√	√	
pores, roots and features of biological origin, e.g. crotovinas	√	(√)	
content of rock and mineral fragments	√	(√)	(√)
nature of boundary	√	(√)	
(4) Field tests:			
pH	√	√	
salinity (EC)	(√)	(√)	
infiltration capacity	(√)		
saturated hydraulic conductivity	(√)		
sampling for laboratory characterisation	√	(√)	

catenary relationships which frequently dominate the local pattern of soils.

When working in uncultivated or partly cultivated country, the record of vegetation may include indicator species or plant associations which seem likely to be associated with particular soil types or properties and which can be used to extrapolate the distribution of these at later stages of mapping. There is no better way to build up your ability to identify plants than to make a collection of plant pressings, coupled with field notes, which at some convenient time can be identified by a herbarium or local ecologist.

Representative profile descriptions to characterise each taxonomic unit are taken from pits 1.0–1.8 m deep, greater depths being necessary for highly weathered soils. In surveys for irrigation, a proportion of pits extend to more than the standard depth. It is not necessary to leave representative profile descriptions until the end of the mapping phase as a separate operation; they can be made whenever a particularly appropriate site presents itself and provide a welcome break from routine mapping. Site data may be amplified, for example by sampling rocks for identification or by recording vegetation physiognomy and the species present in a quantitative or semi-quantitative manner. The soil profile morphology is recorded in the full standard form and samples are collected for laboratory characterisation. Management and crop yield data for the site are assembled if available and, for some special-purpose surveys, field tests may be carried out; for example in surveys for irrigation, infiltration and hydraulic conductivity measurements may be made. There is an element of ritual about the representative profile description, since by no means all the data recorded are ever used, and the laboratory determinations from one pit are of very limited value. The representative profile descriptions are most useful to the surveyor himself and to other pedologists who consult the survey record.

Descriptions at intermediate level may be taken from pits or chance exposures such as roadside cuttings, ditches or stream sections. Chance exposures should never be neglected since large sections cut back to present a fresh face can give information on parent material, stratigraphy and soil variability not obtainable from auger borings. Usually intermediate-level descriptions record the profile morphology in less than full detail, the selection being in accordance with the purposes of the survey. Thus for a general-purpose survey, the major properties used to characterise and map the soil units are recorded, e.g. horizon depths, colour, texture, structure and consistence. Sufficient detail is recorded to permit reallocation in the event of changes in mapping units.

The least detailed descriptions are **soil type identifications,** taken from auger borings or small inspection pits. Only the depth, colour, texture and structure of the various horizons and an assessment of natural drainage are recorded. Many brief descriptions are made to check the mapping unit and to locate boundaries. Where the soil type is obvious, they can be mere soil type identification with a record of some characteristic feature, e.g. 'Mulama Series, nodular laterite at 45 cm'. The soil type identifications cannot be subsequently revised – they are a once-and-for-all identification. It is therefore pointless making observations of this kind until the soil types and mapping units to be used are definitive.

The format and terminology for describing soil profiles are fairly well standardised, for the most part being derived from the US *Soil survey manual* (Soil Survey Staff 1951). The FAO *Guidelines for soil profile description* (2nd ed, FAO 1977) provides a convenient format for site and profile description and examples of descriptions both of individual profiles and of a series as a whole. Several national survey organisations have their own field handbooks.

A number of valuable chemical tests can be performed quickly in the field. The **presence of free carbonates** can be detected by applying 10% hydrochloric acid to a small sample and noting any effervescence. The amount of carbonates may be crudely assessed according to the scale in Table 4.2. Soil pH can be measured directly on a wet profile face or on a wetted sample using pH indicator papers. The Merck Company manufacture narrow-range indicators in the ranges 2.5–4.5, 4.0–7.0 and 6.0–10.0 which are affixed to plastic tabs. The indicator is held against the wet soil for 20 s and the colour compared with a standard chart. **Reactive hydroxy-aluminium** (allophane in volcanic ash soils and amorphous aluminium hydroxides in podzolic B horizons) can be detected by placing about 10 mg soil (the amount easily seen on the tip of a pocket knife) on a strip of phenolphthalein-impregnated filter paper or pH 8–10 indicator paper, and adding a drop of saturated sodium fluoride solution. After 2 min the pH or red coloration on the phenolphthalein paper is estimated. Non-calcareous mineral soils with significant amounts of

Table 4.2 Field estimation of carbonates. From Hodgson (1974).

Field description and limits of groups	$CaCO_3$ (%)	Audible effects (hold close to ear)	Visible effects
non-calcareous (less than 0·5%)	0·1	none	none
very slightly calcareous (0·5–1%)	0·5	faintly increasing to slightly audible	none
slightly calcareous (1–5%)	1·0	faintly increasing to moderately audible	slight effervescence confined to individual grains, just visible
	2·0	moderately to distinctly audible; heard away from ear	slightly more general effervescence visible on close inspection
calcareous (5–10%)	5·0	easily audible	moderate effervescence; obvious bubbles up to 3 mm diameter
very calcareous (more than 10%)	10·0	easily audible	general strong effervescence; ubiquitous bubbles to 7 mm diameter; easily seen

reactive hydroxy-aluminium give pH values of 10 or more. A weak reaction can also be produced by organic matter. Field tests for irrigation surveys are discussed in Chapter 14.

Location

The most detailed and perceptive soil description is of little use unless you know where you are. This needs to be determined to within about 2 mm on the field sheet (and thus 1 mm or equivalent on the final map), e.g. to within 50 m when using field sheets at 1:25000. In settled arable country, this can usually be done by pacing from a field boundary. In savanna and semi-arid country, position can frequently be determined by reference to individual trees or vegetation clumps. In featureless desert country, open grass range and rain forest, you have to survey your way to each site and the basic principle of topographic survey applies – establish the coarse framework with accuracy, the infilling less precisely. Those training for soil survey should not neglect this mundane but basic aspect.

Equipment

A checklist of field equipment is given in Table 4.3. Choice of equipment is dictated both by the task in hand and by personal preference. In general, and especially in the research phase, pits are preferable to auger

Table 4.3 Checklist of field equipment for soil survey.

Standard field kit	Additional items (for special purposes)
heavy, pointed spade	field stereoscope
auger – Jarret, Dutch, screw	pH/mV meter, electrodes, buffers, distilled water supply
broad-bladed knife or trowel	
notebook, pencils (B and photo-marker), pencil sharpener, rubber	EC meter
	NaF solution and phenolphthalein papers
clipboard or map case	30 m tape
2 m tape	gouge auger/peat sampler
soil colour charts	pick axe, shovel, machete, geological hammer
water bottle	Kubiena cans
acid bottle	core sampler and cylinders for water retention characteristics
field pH kit	
hand lens	infiltration equipment
compass	hydraulic conductivity equipment
Abney or Suunto level	water pump/bailer
sample bags, ties, labels	plastic balls/steel cylinders (for bulk density measurements)
description pro forma cards	
personal comfort and survival kit	camera
	dictaphone

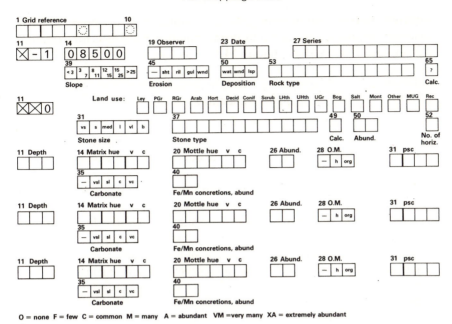

Figure 4.2 Example of a soil description pro forma of the fixed format type, for an auger hole description. (Soil Survey of England and Wales.)

borings. Do not use a screw auger too early or too much. All that can be ascertained using a screw auger is colour, texture and a guess about stones and gravel. Its sole purpose is to identify the soil type and it can only be used once you know exactly what you are looking for. The Dutch auger is preferable in moist or wet cohesive soils. In hard soils, a strong operator can make good use of the robust 'Jarret' auger which is essentially a large bucket auger. Both of these implements bring to the surface a large sample on which colour and mottling, texture and consistence can be assessed. A gouge auger is valuable in unripe cohesive soils and peat from which undisturbed samples up to 1 m long can be extracted in a few seconds.

Recording field observations

Each profile description, even the briefest, should be given a number and this should be marked on the field sheet with the site location. Where aerial photographs are used as field sheets, site locations may be marked with a pinhole. Where a topographic base map is used, coded information may be written in ink on the field sheet. If the field sheets are to be interpreted by others, a key must be provided and adhered to.

Traditionally field descriptions and other observations have been recorded in hard-backed notebooks. During the research phase, it is

Field Survey

(a) Site description   SITE NO. _____

Observer	Date	Type	Sampled?

LOCATION Country   District   Latitude   Longitude
Description
Grid reference   Air photo no.
Altitude

CLIMATE Type   Köppen class
Annual temperature   Annual rainfall   No. of dry months
Notes   (< 60 mm)

PARENT MATERIAL Geological formation
Lithology
Modification (weathering, colluvial, etc.)
Notes

RELIEF Area
Site: Angle   Position   Shape
Microrelief
Notes

VEGETATION Area
Site
LAND USE Area   Percent arable
Site: Present   Past
Notes

GROUND SURFACE Outcrops   Stones
Soil appearance
Human influence

MOISTURE Surface   Depth to water table
In soil

EROSION Description   Severity class
Other degradation

GENERAL Other site features
Site classification
Notes on site

LAND USE POTENTIAL
Land capability class: Field   Final

NOTES

Figure 4.3 Example of a soil description pro forma of the free format type, for a pit description (tropical soils).

(b) Profile description

SITE NO. _____

Horizon no	Depth	Symbol	Colour	Mottle	Texture	Stones, gravel	Structure Grade Size Type			Consistence	Clay skins

Horizon no	Concretions	Pores	Minerals	Roots	Fauna	(Other 1)	(Other 2)	Boundary	Samples Depth Sample no

Special features

GENERAL DESCRIPTION

CLASSIFICATION Drainage class

Soil type: Field

Soil series: Field

Notes

Cause (site, profile impedance)

Revised

Revised

useful to have all the information in one place, but for routine survey involving several team members and many descriptions specially prepared cards are preferred; examples are given in Figures 4.2 and 4.3. Cards may be held in loose-leaf binders and when completed they can be filed according to taxonomic unit, mapping unit or district and can be readily retrieved and compared.

Where it has been decided in advance that computerised data storage is to be used, time is saved and errors reduced if the information is directly recorded in coded form. This requires that the field record cards should have the codes together with mnemonic indications, e.g. abundance of roots (few, common, many, abundant) as fe 1, co 2, ma 3, ab 4. The revised edition of the UK *Soil survey handbook* (Hodgson 1974) has the codes overprinted in red throughout. Recording in digitised form and subsequently transferring to punched cards, with computerised retrieval, has displaced the earlier system of edge-punched cards.

Where the profile is recorded on standard cards or in coded form, do not leave it at that. Add a brief general description of the profile, noting prominent or distinctive characteristics, and how it compares with other soils in the same class. This aids the surveyor both at the time and in any subsequent reappraisal.

The benefits of careful, legible and consistent recording of data in the field cannot be overemphasised. Cryptic field notes, done to get back home quickly on a foul day, add to the time required later in the office and cannot be interpreted reliably by others, or even by the author.

Field survey is very productive of data and regular office sessions are necessary for air photo-interpretation, permanent recording and incorporation of new material into the survey data base, and interpretative assessment. They also provide a welcome break from otherwise continuous fieldwork. This is an important aspect in a long project where you must pace yourself over the whole period or the quality of the work will decline.

Mapping boundaries

In reconnaissance survey, almost all boundaries may be drawn during photo-interpretation; field survey consists of identifying what lies within them and deleting those that prove not to be significant. In semi-detailed survey most boundaries are inferred from surface evidence, profile observations being used to establish the soil classes within the mapping units. In intensive surveys most boundaries are checked in the field by traverses across them at regular intervals.

Boundaries are sketched directly onto the field sheets, using whatever evidence is available, for example a break in slope or vegetation change.

Boundaries drawn in the field will nearly always be better than those drawn afterwards by interpolating between observations, and can never be worse. Resist the temptation to resort to site recording alone in the hope that something will emerge from subsequent examination. What is not apparent in the field rarely becomes so in the office. The only exception is in grid survey for parametric mapping, e.g. of salinity, where you must interpolate either because there are no useful surface features or because the property being mapped requires laboratory analysis.

It is only prudent to check boundaries especially carefully where they cross roads or other places of easy access: this is where your work may be checked.

Glass-marker pencils are best for use on air photographs since the lines can be altered; but since they are also easily removed unintentionally by rubbing against the protective envelope, a permanent record should be made each day. A semi-matt finish on the prints retains markings better than a glossy finish.

Sampling

Laboratory determinations can only be made on a small proportion of the profiles observed in the field, which are in turn a tiny sample of the total soil cover. The requirements for laboratory data for special-purpose and general-purpose surveys have been discussed above (p. 26). For special-purpose field sampling, it will usually be desirable to decide upon a standard sampling practice and stick to it, e.g. samples at 10 and 50 cm depths. For characterisation of soil units in a general-purpose survey, a sampling site must be typical of the taxonomic class that it represents. Samples from a representative profile are normally taken from each horizon. In this case, resist the temptation to take a large number of samples from one profile. Take a maximum of four plus a topsoil composite sample; it will nearly always be more informative to have four samples from each of two profiles than eight from one.

Before taking a sample, decide upon the horizon boundaries very carefully; 'draw' them on the pit face with a knife or mark with pegs. Decide whether, for your survey, you are sampling over nearly the whole horizon or just its centre, i.e. whether a horizon extending from 50 cm to 100 cm depth is to be sampled in the 60–90 cm or 70–80 cm range.

Sample from the bottom of the pit first. Take about 1 kg soil. Polythene sample bags which can be sealed by two elastic bands or knotted at the neck are very convenient. Put the sample in two bags, one inside the other, with the label between; this both protects against splitting and keeps the label clean and dry. Samples from waterlogged soils should be kept in their reduced condition by squeezing entrapped air from the bag before knotting. If the presence of pyrite is suspected, the samples should be kept frozen until analysed, otherwise an acid sulphate soil develops in the bag.

Samples for determination of water retention characteristics are collected undisturbed in cylindrical metal canisters using a special sampling tool. Undisturbed samples for micromorphological study are collected in a rectangular metal frame, sometimes called a 'Kubiena can', although sardine tins may be used once their original contents have been eaten. Careful sampling is especially important for analyses such as water retention characteristics which are very expensive and therefore performed on only a few samples.

Record the site number and sampling depths accurately and legibly.

If samples have to be despatched by air freight, drying, grinding and separation of the coarse fraction by a 2 mm sieve may be performed at the field base to reduce weight and bulk; the weight and characteristics (lithology, rock or nodules; angularity) of the coarse fraction are recorded. Suitable packing must be provided and customs or other administrative arrangements attended to. A register of samples and analytical requirements should accompany the material despatched to the laboratory.

Correlation and quality control

Even the most intensive survey cannot produce a mere factual catalogue of soil properties and distribution. Soil surveys are interpretations of the landscape and no two surveyors will make identical interpretations; their conceptual models and consequently their final maps will be somewhat different. In the case of a team survey, the provisional mapping legend drawn up by the project leader sets the standards against which the soils are compared during the subsequent mapping phase and thus imposes a measure of uniformity. The role of the project leader during the mapping stage is in correlation. He must work regularly with each member of the team, ensuring that each interprets the legend in the same way and maintains a consistent standard and detail of mapping; he must maintain on-going revision of the legend and will be involved in integrated land evaluation activities.

Consistent quality of work throughout the survey is best maintained by regular team meetings in the field where an individual's assessment of basic soil properties such as texture, colour, structure and consistence can be checked with the leader/correlator and other team members. Where fine differentiation of textural groups of soils is important to the survey, field assessment of texture should be compared with laboratory determinations on samples from the area.

The purity of mapping can be checked during the course of the survey by inspection of random sites within each unit. If the purity is below an acceptable level, the standard of mapping or the legend must be in question. The location of boundaries can likewise be subject to spot checks, but detailed checking along their length is unrealistic.

In a systematic national survey the soil correlator has a further role in assisting individual surveyors with soil classification, ensuring that soils mapped as a named series in one district conform to the series at its type location, preventing series definitions from being unacceptably stretched to fit new soils, yet at the same time avoiding unnecessary proliferation of series. To this end, definitive series names should not be allocated too early in the survey. The careful compilation of soil unit sheets (see below) is particularly useful for correlation. In the United States there is a formal administrative and scientific procedure for the proposal, review and acceptance of new soil series.

Characterisation of mapping units

As the survey proceeds, **soil unit sheets** are prepared for each mapping unit. These contain the following information:

(a) the type locality: grid reference, map sheet, air photo pair;
(b) the environmental factors (landforms, vegetation, etc.) associated with the unit, together with those indicator features by which it can sometimes be recognised (e.g. colour/texture/tone in topsoil, plant indicator species, distinctive appearance on air photos);
(c) a detailed description of the profile at the type locality;
(d) the range of properties within the taxonomic unit to which the representative profile belongs;
(e) where the mapping unit differs from the taxonomic unit, the range of properties and associated soils within the mapping units, the relative (percentage) extent of these soils and their geomorphological or other genetic relationships within the landscape;
(f) records of present land use, management practices and problems, available data on performance (crop yield, tree growth, etc.);
(g) relevant laboratory data, added as they become available;
(h) the surveyor's estimate of land use potential, desirable land improvements and management practices, and other information related to the purposes of the survey.

These sheets are compiled in draft at the end of the research phase, progressively added to during the mapping phase, and form the principal basis for the final legend.

The interpretation phase

Just as soil survey consists of a lot more than mere soil mapping, so the field observations in survey are by no means directed exclusively towards mapping soil distributions. A soil survey produces a range of information required for its interpretation and application, including land use potential, management practices and avoidance of hazards, plus soil data needed as a basis for economic or other evaluation. The assembling of this information is not an office exercise but requires specific field activities, related to the various soil types present. These activities can either be carried out simultaneously with the research and mapping phases, collecting data wherever they are found, or they can be treated as a separate third phase, the interpretation phase. Time requirements vary with the purposes of the survey but it is by no means unreasonable to allocate up to 25% of total field survey time to activities directed towards interpretation.

In carrying out such investigations, the soil surveyor is not attempting to usurp the functions of the agronomist, forester, roads engineer or other specialists. The aim of the soil surveyor is to relate land potential and management recommendations, such as may be made by these specialists, to the different soil units mapped. Where it becomes apparent that there are no such differences, for example that several soil units are equally suitable for a particular crop rotation and fertiliser regime, this will be stated. It is likely, however, that some of these 'standard' recommendations for the area will require modification for certain soil types; the surveyor should draw the attention of other staff to this, and work out modifications jointly with them. In particular, the soil surveyor is often in the best position to identify and direct attention to environmental hazards, and in some cases to advise against using certain land for particular purposes.

Some interpretation activities, for example those directed towards engineering properties, are a matter of a sampling programme for laboratory determinations. The specific field tests and sampling needs in irrigation surveys are noted in Chapter 14. The variety of possible activities is large, particularly when surveys for urban-fringe planning, recreation planning, etc., are included. Two kinds of activity may be noted, those directed at crop yield estimates and soil response to specified management.

Crop yield estimates

A specific need commonly encountered is for estimates of crop yields on the different soil units present. These are required as a basis for cost – benefit analysis of land development projects, and may also serve to assess, for example, the potential benefit from increased agricultural advisory and/or marketing facilities.

Crop yields vary with management practices, weather in the year concerned and soil type; in developing countries the variation attributable to management may be fivefold or more, compared with only 50 to 100% with soil type. It is therefore essential to collect data, and present results, in terms of inputs and management. These can include specific details of crop varieties, fertiliser treatments, planting dates, etc., but in developing countries it is convenient to assemble the data in terms of three **levels of inputs,** low, intermediate and high, as defined in Chapter 10 (p. 156).

Crop yield estimates can be obtained in the following ways.

(a) by comparison with data from experimental sites on identified soil types, both within the survey area and on similar soils and climates outside it;

(b) by field experiments conducted within the survey area specifically for this purpose;

(c) from farm records, marketing board records, farm system studies, demonstration plots or such other data as may be found;

(d) by comparison of the known or supposed requirements of the crop with the physical and chemical properties of the soils.

The first of these will often be the most useful. This requires visits to sites where records of past experimental work exist, and identification of the soil type on which these results have been obtained. This need not be confined to the survey area but can be extended, with suitable reservations on climatic comparability, to sites on similar soils outside it. Agronomic trials established specifically for purposes of the survey suffer from the inevitable time delay, but for annual crops results from even one year, conducted during the survey, are better than nothing. In the long term, however, a set of such trials, deliberately established on representative sites on agriculturally important soils, can be of great value in augmenting the utility of the survey. These are now known as **benchmark sites.**

Estimates of the rate of tree growth can be collected in a similar way if forest yield sites exist in, or on comparable sites to, the survey area, or by direct measurement of tree height and girth increment using a coring device.

Soil response

Soil surveys are frequently carried out where changes in land use or management practices are contemplated. In these circumstances, an important function of soil survey is to predict how the various soils will respond to the proposed changes. Irrigation is a special and extreme case. Other examples of such changes are land reclamation, land drainage, clearance of natural vegetation and conversion to some form of arable use, and intensification of arable use. The soil properties likely to undergo substantial change usually include organic matter content and in differing circumstances also reaction, redox potential, salinity, etc.

There are as yet no standard procedures for making such estimates of soil response, but two approaches may be followed. The first is reasoning based on the observed soil properties, knowledge of the proposed changes, and physical and chemical deduction in terms of processes. The second is comparison with soils already under the proposed use. For example, sampling of fields under arable use of some years standing compared with adjacent sites under vegetation will give an indication of the order of magnitude of likely changes in organic matter content.

Assessment of **hazards** forms part of this study of soil response. It may be desirable, where necessary by cooperation between the surveyor and local land husbandry staff, to draw up an erosion hazard rating of the various potential arable soils.

Land evaluation or classification

Land evaluation in its own right is discussed in later chapters. However, in any soil survey, evaluation or classification of some type forms a part, and should be made provisionally in the field, at least for full and intermediate profile sites. This may consist of assignment to a capability class or estimates of suitability for arable, forestry or other specified uses. Such estimates will afterwards be revised for the soil mapping unit as a whole.

An active and on-going programme directed towards survey interpretation does more than relieve the monotony of soil mapping. It directs the attention of the surveyor to the objects of the survey, and thereby enables the research and mapping activities to be more profitably directed.

Further reading

Soil Survey Staff (1951), Taylor and Pohlen (1970), Hodgson (1978), Curtis *et al*. (1965). Soil profile description handbooks, e.g. FAO (1977), Hodgson (1974), Dumanski (1978).

Mapping **5** Units

A soil survey attempts to delineate areas that behave differently or will respond differently to some specified management. The mapping units serve as a basis for predicting soil behaviour. In general-purpose surveys, soils are mapped according to their morphology on the hypothesis that soils which look and feel alike will behave similarly and those that appear different will respond differently in many circumstances.

Mapping involves classification; the two processes cannot be separated. A soil map is itself only an interpretation of the landscape. It presents one pattern of mapping units out of an infinite number of patterns that could be distinguished. The value of the survey depends upon the way that the soils are grouped and upon how this classification serves the purposes of the survey, just as much as upon the accuracy of the mapping.

Taxonomic units and mapping units

In the field, the surveyor examines soil profiles, which are point samples of the soil cover. These sample descriptions are then sorted into conceptual groups, or **taxonomic units,** each of which is defined by a medial profile form, that is the central concept or middle of the range, and an allowed range of variation around it. Taxonomic units serve as a medium for the transfer of information and the prediction of soil response to alternative management practices, by enabling experience at one place to be applied to similar soils elsewhere. They can be further grouped and regrouped for particular purposes. Because of the intrinsic variability of soil, the central concept of any particular taxonomic unit exists in the field only, if at all, at the type location where it is initially described, but it serves as a standard for subsequent mapping. Thus a surveyor may refer to an individual profile as 'good Macmerry', meaning that it is close to the central concept of Macmerry Series, or may use some less complimentary term to indicate that the individual profile is not close to the central concept of a particular series but that there is no more appropriate classification.

Mapping units are not the same as taxonomic units. The taxonomic unit is conceptual and the limiting values of each property can be precisely defined. Mapping units are real soil areas. The surveyor inserts boundaries on the soil map which depict as faithfully as possible the perceived situation and which delineate units that are as homogeneous as possible; but real soils do not fit neatly into conceptual units. The properties of real soils always merge more or less gradually from the central concept of one unit towards that of one or more other units, and change in one property is not necessarily in phase with change in another. Inevitably mapping units will contain impurities, that is, soils which do not conform to the definition of the taxonomic unit by which they are represented; this happens either because a gradual boundary must be represented on the map by a line, or because the soil pattern is complex with inclusions of unlike soils too small to map. An allowable proportion of 15% impurities within a mapping unit is often quoted, without guidance as to how this optimistic value is to be achieved or checked.

Whenever possible **simple mapping units,** those containing soils of only one taxonomic unit, are used. This produces a map with the greatest predictive value. Where the soil pattern is too complex to be depicted faithfully by simple mapping units, **compound mapping units,** which contain soils of two or more taxonomic groups, must be used.

Criteria for the establishment of mapping units

If the purpose of the survey is precisely defined, then the soil characteristics that are relevant to the purpose are, to a degree, known. This is the case with surveys for irrigation projects, where limiting values, for example of topography, drainage, texture, reaction, exchangeable sodium percentage and maximum tolerances of salinity for different crops, have been established experimentally. The soils can then be grouped on an *ad hoc* basis according to similarities and differences in the key characteristics, and a map can be produced that is of high predictive value for the specified purpose.

Multipurpose soil maps present greater difficulties. Although the ultimate justification for soil surveys is a practical one, the multipurpose survey is avowedly not subordinated to any particular need of the moment. The rationale behind them is that it is possible to delineate 'natural' soil units at a taxonomic level comparable to the biological species; and that these natural units can be combined, analysed or otherwise interpreted for a variety of practical purposes without the need to resurvey. However, soil does not always occur in convenient natural units. The soil individual, whether a taxonomic unit or a mapping unit, is a matter of personal judgement. The judgement is guided by the following principles and constraints.

(a) The mapping units should be as homogeneous as possible. This is not necessarily the same as distinguishing soils with uniform characteristics, but the variation within a mapping unit is kept within defined limits and the kind of variation should be consistent within all mapping units given the same name.
(b) The grouping should be of practical value.
(c) It must be possible to map the units consistently.
(d) The mapping must be accomplished in reasonable time and with only such equipment as can be used in the field. This means that the soil characteristics used in mapping must be, in the main, visible and tactile properties such as colour and texture. Many properties of practical interest, for example, plant nutrients, cannot be directly observed and mapped in the field. The relationships between the mappable features and other critical soil characteristics must be established during the research stage of the survey.
(e) Relatively stable soil properties, such as texture and lithology, should be used to define taxonomic units, rather than properties which may change rapidly according to management, such as structure or topsoil organic matter.

This last principle is open to question, since one of the most important properties of soil from the point of view of management is its propensity for physical and chemical change under alternative treatments. The multipurpose soil survey should not only record the present characteristics of the soil cover but also gather information necessary to predict likely changes in these characteristics under alternative management practices.

Given these principles, two broad approaches to multipurpose soil survey can be adopted.

(1) *Soil survey based on soil morphology,* which is expressed in visible and tactile soil properties. Many useful predictions about soil behaviour and response to management may be made on the basis of morphological characteristics and related, accessory properties. Morphology is related to the soil-forming factors of climate, parent material, topography, drainage, vegetation and the age of the land-form. Some of these factors are readily mapped from their surface expression and, where they remain constant, so too does the morphology of the soil. Soils are therefore mapped *as if they were* discrete three-dimensional individuals by inserting boundaries where the rate of change of their morphology with distance is greatest. In

81

practice this has to be done largely according to their surface expression, inserting boundaries at changes in slope, vegetation or surface soil characteristics.

(2) *The land systems approach*: that of attempting a general-purpose land classification, integrating all the environmental variables likely to influence use of the land – climate, geology, landforms, vegetation and soils. Pedological soil classification is not central to the land systems approach. The map produced is not a soil map, and typically it is strongly biased towards landforms since these are relatively easy to map from air photographs. Some general predictions of soil properties and their response to management may be made, depending upon the intensity of supporting field soil observations.

Mapping units in detailed soil survey

Simple units

Soil series. The fundamental unit of a morphological classification which is to be the basis for practical interpretations should ideally be a simple one. This unit is most commonly known as the soil series. It is conceived as a grouping of soils which are alike in their characteristics and behaviour in the landscape. Soils within a series are developed on the same parent material in the same environment and have profiles that are almost alike, with horizons that are similar in their vertical sequence, thickness and morphological properties.

The concept is variously interpreted but the soil series is defined in terms of site characteristics and a medial profile with a restricted range of variability with respect to the horizons present, their thickness, colour, texture, structure, presence of carbonates or soluble salts, mineralogy and sometimes other properties. Each series is intended to have a unique combination of site features and morphological characteristics which can be assessed, for the most part, in the field (p. 223; cf. FAO 1977, p. 50).

Once a series has been defined and mapped according to its differentiating characteristics, many accessory properties of practical importance can be predicted. This should ideally be done by establishing mean values and variability upon a statistically valid sample of profiles from the series, although actual practice falls far short of this ideal.

The soil series serves as the primary taxonomic unit and also as a mapping unit. As a taxonomic unit it can be strictly defined, but it is less easily mapped, and series as mapped inevitably include soils of varying properties, all changing more or less gradually from the central concept of one series towards those of others.

Each established series is given a name, usually taken from the locality where the series is first recognised, for example Riponui Series. This is a useful reference term for local users of the survey such as extension workers and farmers.

Soil type. The US survey organisation and several others originally sub-divided the series into soil types on the basis of the texture of the topsoil. The type is designated by its series name followed by its texture, for example Riponui sandy clay, Riponui sandy loam. This practice has now been abandoned by most survey organisations, including that in the USA. In some kinds of landscapes, for example on glaciofluvial and alluvial deposits, textural variations are impossible to map consistently. Moreover, differences in texture are commonly associated with other significant profile differences, and differences between types within a series were often found to be of greater agronomic significance than differences between series. As the differentiating criteria of series have steadily become more tightly defined, the monotype series has become the norm and the soil type eliminated.

Soil phase. Series should be defined in the same way everywhere, regard-less of the immediate purpose of the survey. Where detailed interpreta-tions are required, the series can be subdivided into phases according to any characteristic significant to land use, for example depth, surface form, stoniness, texture, past erosion or salinity. Phases may be used to indicate transient or artificially induced changes in morphology. For example, drained phases are recognised where drainage has been improved artificially without significant changes in other differentiating characteristics; waterlogged phases are required where the series has become poorly drained as a result of waters being diverted from other areas in ill-managed irrigation schemes.

The phase is not a unit of taxonomic classification. It can be used at any categoric level to draw attention to differences of practical significance. It is usually used as subdivision of the series, for example Sourhope Series, steeply sloping phase, but is occasionally used when mapping broad units. For example, the FAO *Soil map of the world* at 1:5000000 scale recognises 12 phases, including stony, lithic, saline, sodic, petroferric (hard ironstone), petrocalcic and fragipan.

Soil variant. A soil that is closely related to an established series but which differs in some essential characteristic is called a variant when, for some reason or other, a new series cannot conveniently be established. The use of the variant enables the surveyor to avoid establishing separate series for soils of minor extent without jeopardising the narrow defini-tions of the series. A soil may be designated a variant in one survey and later raised to the rank of a separate series when it is subsequently found to be more extensive. As in the case of the phase, the variant may be applied to other categories of classification.

Compound mapping units

Soil association. The association is a group of geographically associated soils, each of which is confined to a particular facet of the landscape and which occur in a predictable pattern. Each component series is named and described, and the proportions of each lie within defined limits. An association is named after one or more of its principal members, for example, Foxton–Himatangi Association. The members of the geographical association are not necessarily related pedologically or lithologically.

Another concept of the association used in Canada and by the Soil Survey of Scotland is the hydrologic sequence: a group of series developed on the same parent material, differentiated according to drainage and associated characteristics. This has proved a useful unit for mapping at reconnaissance and semi-detailed scales in young landscapes where many soil properties are closely related to the parent material. The concept of the hill soil and steepland soil mapping units used in New Zealand is similar. In all cases, the association is used either where the scale of the map does not permit the depiction of series, or where the purpose of the survey does not justify more detailed mapping.

The value of a soil association is much increased if the relative proportions of the component series are specified, and still more by description of their relative positions in the landscape or other means whereby the user can find which series he is on. Thus a map merely showing the X–Y association has instantly lowered its predictive value by half. Analysis of some published maps, multiplying area of associations with numbers of series within them, has revealed average potential predictions of soil series as low as 30%. Specifying the X association as series X 40–60%, with Y and Z each 5–20%, is a little better. If it is stated, however, that X occupies most interfluve crests, Y the valley sides and Z is recognisable by the presence of acacia trees, the user is in a position to refine the map as and where he needs.

Soil complex. An association can be resolved into simple mapping units on ordinary detailed maps. If the soil pattern cannot be resolved because of its complexity, it is mapped as a complex. The complex is of limited predictive value and is therefore used only as a last resort. It may be given a local name or a composite name derived from the names of its components.

The distinction between an association and a complex has for long been a source of confusion. By definition, the difference is supposed to be that the separate units of an association could be mapped separately but the surveyor chooses not to do so, whereas in a complex the units are so intimately mixed that individual delineation would be impossible. This distinction is illogical, since by increasing the scale of the map and the effort expended, any pattern of identifiable taxonomic units could eventually be mapped separately. A useful working rule, based on current US practice, is to employ an association where the component series or other units could be mapped separately at 1: 20 000 scale but not at the smaller scale of the survey in hand, reserving a complex for cases where the units cannot be separated at 1: 20 000. The units of an association often, but by no means always, bear some clear relationship to relief or other visible feature.

Discussion

With the exception of the series, all the mapping units used in detailed soil survey are pragmatic groupings lying outside the taxonomic classification. The series is both a mapping unit and also the lowest category of any hierarchical taxonomic classification, such as the US *Soil taxonomy* (Soil Survey Staff 1975). The compound mapping units, associations and complexes may contain soils from several different taxonomic groups. Phases and variants can apply at any categoric level of the classification (Table 5.1). In practice there is variation in the definition and interpretation of each of these mapping units between different survey organisations.

Mapping units in special-purpose soil survey

The problem here is much more straightforward, the guiding principle being to make your mapping units relevant to the purpose. If the survey is to assess erosion hazard, and for that purpose only, the final map should contain units such as very severe, severe, moderate, low, etc., erosion hazard. This map is the primary guide to planning and management; it will be backed up by supplementary maps, not necessarily printed, showing slope angle, soil permeability and other contributory factors, but the integration of these is the job of the soil surveyor, accomplished during the research phase of the survey. Similarly a survey commissioned to assess salinity hazard should present mapping units defined in terms of salt levels. Ideally, confidence limits should be specified, although time may not allow collection of sufficient data for this.

Phases of soil series are sometimes appropriate mapping units for special-purpose survey. If a grid survey has been necessary and only a single property is to be considered, isolines may be drawn, for example between points of equal salinity or depth to a limiting horizon.

Table 5.1 Soil mapping units.

soil series	simple mapping unit; also a taxonomic unit
soil type	obsolescent; simple mapping unit, subdivision of the series
soil variant	simple mapping and taxonomic unit, usually employed at a level equivalent to the series
phase	mapping unit, usually employed as a refinement of the series in detailed mapping, but can be used as a subdivision of any kind of mapping unit
soil association	compound mapping unit
soil complex	compound mapping unit
soil landscape	compound mapping unit, based on landscape but defined in terms of soils
land system and facet	not defined in terms of soils; see Chapter 7
special-purpose unit	defined to meet user requirements

Mapping units in soil survey at small scales

If you are asked to map at a scale smaller than 1:50000, there is no possibility of mapping units that consist of one kind of soil only. Three courses of action are possible.

(a) Not to map soils at all, but to employ the land systems approach (Ch. 7). Provided the prospective users agree, this is probably the best course for resource inventory surveys at scales of 1:250000 or smaller, since maps purporting to show soils at such scales are unrealistic documents.
(b) To employ a compound mapping unit called the **soil landscape.** This is an association of soils delineated by landscapes. It represents a halfway stage between the soil and land system map; its object is to show soils, not the total environment, but landforms are employed as a means of identifying mappable areas of soils.
(c) To attempt to use taxonomic units higher than the series as a basis for soil mapping, for example the suborders or Great Soil Groups of the US *Soil taxonomy*. This does not usually work well, since topographically related, adjacent components of the soil pattern frequently belong to different higher taxonomic classes.

Compilations are soil maps not constructed by field survey but by assembling available information, supplemented by inference and not infrequently imagination. Most soil maps of countries are of this kind, as is the FAO–Unesco *Soil map of the world*. In compilations it is usual to employ soil orders or other high-category classes as a map legend, it being understood that these refer to the predominant upper-catena soils, excluding valley floor gleys and, unless predominant, lithosols. Sometimes the mapping units may be numbered with a legend indicating which associated soils and inclusions are likely to be found in each. This is of dubious value and nearly all users employ such maps solely as a guide to the dominant soil. In compilations, the element of fantasy present in all soil maps can on occasion attain substantial proportions.

Guidelines for the choice of mapping units

- In special-purpose surveys, use units directly relevant to the purpose.
- Ask the user in what form he wants the data presented.
- To whatever degree possible, employ simple mapping units in preference to compound ones. For obvious reasons, maps of associations and, worse, complexes have a low predictive value.
- Units that can be identified subsequently in the field are to be preferred to those dependent on refinements of the soil surveyor's art. (Units defined on false-colour air photos or other remote-sensing imagery might fall into the latter category.) If you have got it wrong, this can be redeemed if the man on the spot can correctly identify the soil by surface colour, texture or stoniness.
- Wherever appropriate and possible, use the soil series. 'Appropriate' means meeting the requirements of the user; 'possible' means a soil pattern that permits the mapping of units of reasonable purity. The series has stood the test of time. A warning is necessary that, if working in an area where most series have not already been established, one cannot set up a dozen or so in a few weeks' work. Series should be rigorously defined and some national survey organisations have not only scientific but also formal administrative procedures for seeking approval of a new series.

Further reading

Soil Survey Staff (1951) is the fundamental text, although national survey organisations have interpreted the definitions of units in different ways; Taylor and Pohlen (1970), Bie and Beckett (1971).

Scale, Accuracy, Costs and Returns

There is a chain of relationships between the effort put into a soil survey and the usefulness of the end-product. The manner in which soil properties are distributed over the landscape, their pattern and variability, determines what it is possible to map and how much survey effort will be required to achieve a given level of accuracy. The scale of the published map sets limits on the amount of detail that can be shown, whilst the scale at which field survey is conducted largely determines the time taken and therefore the major cost element of the survey. Thus for any given soil pattern, the information content of the soil map is related to the time and cost of the survey.

This chapter is concerned with these relationships, that is, with the question of how accurately you can predict soil properties for a given survey effort. As we have repeatedly emphasised, however, accuracy of soil prediction is by no means the whole function of soil survey. The economic benefits or other usefulness of a survey are determined to an equal or greater degree by the extent to which information based on the survey provides useful guidelines for land use planning and management.

Scale and level of intensity

The scale of a soil map should be decided by the purposes for which it is required. Survey cost rises sharply with increase in scale, so a decision on the degree of detail needed, and hence the scale, is one of the most important to be taken in discussions preceding the survey.

It is usual, and simplest, to describe surveys in terms of the scale of the published map. What matters more, however, is the level of intensity of soil observations that has gone into the making of the map. A survey with widely spaced observations could be published at a large scale, although it would be very misleading to do so. Levels of intensity can be described in terms of the number of soil observations per unit area and of boundaries checked in the field. The soil survey of Canada defines five survey **intensity levels,** corresponding to what are termed **orders** of surveys in the USA, level 1 being the most intensive.

Five ranges of scale, or levels of intensity, are recognised for soil surveys and maps: exploratory, reconnaissance, semi-detailed, detailed and intensive. These correspond to intensity levels 5 to 1 respectively (Table 6.1). In addition, there are maps produced by compilation at scales similar to the exploratory.

Exploratory surveys (intensity level 5). These are conducted to provide a modicum of soil information about otherwise unknown regions. They are carried out by road and track or helicopter traverses without attempting uniform coverage, with maps produced at scales between 1: 500000 and 1: 5000000. Milne's *Provisional soil map of East Africa* at 1: 2000000 (Milne 1935–36) was a classic of this type. This method of survey was used to fill some empty areas for the FAO *Soil map of the world*. Surveys based on satellite imagery with low-intensity ground checking also fall into this type.

Compilations are syntheses based on pre-existing soil maps at various scales, filled in by inference where there are gaps in coverage. The legend should include a diagram showing coverage by scale and reliability. The FAO–Unesco *Soil map of the world* (1970–80) is of this type, as are the national soil maps of most countries. Scales are usually 1: 1000000 or smaller, and mapping units are the higher categories of an international or national soil classification. Owing to the low and variable reliability, such maps cannot be used for practical planning. Their purposes include display, national atlases, teaching, answering enquiries from international organisations, and as a general orientation or background for soil surveyors.

Reconnaissance surveys (level 4). Such surveys achieve a uniform coverage of the survey area at a small scale, most commonly at 1: 250000. Mapping units are mostly based on landform–soil units or land systems and much use is made of air photo-interpretation and/or satellite imagery. Geographic soil associations or sets of similar profiles have been adopted where there has been a substantial field mapping effort, but in some landscapes it is not meaningful to map soils as such at this scale. A few countries now possess complete coverage at reconnaissance scale.

The considerable effort devoted to reconnaissance surveys since about 1940 has been an act of faith – that generalised information on natural resources and their distribution is a necessary first step in planning future land development. The limited direct practical use subsequently made of such surveys leaves this hypothesis unproven to date. However, their results are expressed in purely physical (i.e. non-economic) terms with a relatively long life. Countries such as New Zealand and the Netherlands which completed reconnaissance mapping at an early stage have had the advantage of a uniform and coherent basis for national soil

Table 6.1 Scales of soil survey. For rates of survey, see Table 2.1.

Kind of survey or map and level of intensity	Scales Range	Typical	Area represented by 1 cm² on map	Mean distance between field observations at 1 per cm²	Mapping units	Examples of purposes
exploratory surveys and compilations; level 5	1 : 1 000 000 and smaller		100 km² and less	–	taxonomic soil classes of high categories, e.g. brown earth, luvisols, mollisols, sols ferrugineux	display, national atlases, teaching; background for survey preparation
reconnaissance; level 4	1 : 500 000 to 1 : 120 000	1 : 250 000	6.25 km²	2.5 km	land systems or other landform – soil units, combining great soil groups	resource inventory at national or regional levels; national land use planning, tentative project location
semi-detailed; level 3	1 : 100 000 to 1 : 30 000	1 : 50 000	25 ha	500 m	associations, series; landform – soil units combining associations and series	project feasibility studies; regional land use planning
detailed; level 2	1 : 25 000 to 1 : 10 000	1 : 25 000 1 : 20 000 1 : 10 000	6.25 ha 5 ha 1 ha	250 m 200 m 100 m	series, phases of series, some associations and complexes	agricultural advisory work, project planning, irrigation surveys, some management and peri-urban surveys
intensive; level 1	larger than 1 : 10 000	1 : 5000	0.25 ha	50 m	series, phases of series, individual soil properties	management, peri-urban and urban soil surveys, invariably special-purpose

classification and soil survey interpretations. In developing countries, one more specific application is to aid in identifying provisional locations for development projects, which are then surveyed in greater detail.

Semi-detailed surveys (level 3). Semi-detailed surveys, typically at 1:50000, are the smallest scale at which soil series can be mapped, although some associations will nearly always be necessary. Air photo-interpretation and field survey both contribute significantly, but with substantially more time spent on fieldwork.

In developing countries, this is a good scale for feasibility surveys of arable or multipurpose land development projects. It provides the information necessary to allocate land to its major uses (arable, tree crops, pasture, forestry, etc.), and the areas under these uses give the basis for economic analysis. Whilst suited to feasibility studies, 1:50000 is not an adequate working scale for project design and management. For agricultural advisory purposes, the problem of this scale is that field boundaries cannot be shown. For many years the British soil surveys employed a system of published maps at 1:63360, but with manuscript maps available for inspection at the field survey scales – 1:10560 in England and Wales and 1:25000 in Scotland.

Detailed surveys (level 2). These cover both the 1:25000 and 1:10000 scales. Air photographs are still of substantial value but the bulk of survey effort is in the field. The usual mapping units are soil series, phases and other closely defined units. As 1:20000 is the standard scale for US county soil maps, more published surveys have appeared at this scale than at any other.

This is the ideal scale for agricultural advisory work. The farmer and the adviser can see the farm, field by field, at a manageable size, and the soil units mapped are for the most part of a size and kind that are practicable to use in management. It is also a good scale for detailed planning of development projects, it is indispensable for irrigation projects, and it is useful in some management and peri-urban surveys. Why, then, with all these advantages, is this scale range not universally employed? The answer is the rather slow rate of progress and hence considerable cost. There is no way around this cost; to do a proper job of mapping requires that amount of field effort. It is notable that the need for this scale was recognised in the USA despite the size of that country, and it may be that others will have to accept it if soil surveys are to realise their full potential.

Intensive surveys (level 1). Intensive surveys are at scales larger than 1:10000. Besides soil series and phases, maps of individual soil properties can usefully be produced. Owing to the very high cost per unit area, surveys at this scale should never be undertaken without knowing who is going to use them and for what purposes. The high value of land in the urban and urban fringe zone, coupled with the varied and specialised uses to which it is put, may justify intensive surveys. Agricultural experiment stations should be surveyed on this scale, and some enterprising farmers have commissioned intensive surveys when new crops or management practices, e.g. supplementary irrigation, are projected. It is appropriate wherever there is to be a large capital investment in high-value crops or new techniques, whether by government agencies or on privately owned farms.

Choice of scale

A decision on the publication scale is usually made at the planning stage of a survey. Scale is determined by the purpose of the map, mainly according to the degree of detail required. On grounds of cost, the scale selected will be the smallest that adequately meets the needs of the user. The most appropriate scale for any purpose is influenced by the intricacy of the soil pattern and the contrast between the properties of adjacent soils, but this is not always known until the survey is well under way.

Users by no means necessarily seek as much detail as possible. There is frequently a **minimum management unit,** the smallest area which it is practicable to treat differently. In mechanised arable farming, this may be a field of 5 ha or larger; even if within-field variations are known (as they often are to farmers), the whole field must be managed in the same way.

There are cartographic controls to the size and shape of areas that can be depicted. A map is difficult to use if it shows areas less than 1 cm across, unless they form a well defined pattern such as narrow strips along valley floors. For example, if the minimum management unit were considered to be approximately 10 ha or 300 m square, a scale of not smaller than 1:30000 is indicated. This accords well with the proven utility of 1:20000 or 1:25000 scales for farm planning and advisory work in the USA and UK respectively.

As noted above, field survey should be conducted on base maps 2 to 2.5 times the scale of intended publication.

Limitations to the accuracy of soil maps

Spatial patterns of soils

The spatial pattern of soil distribution is far from being random or arbitrary. It is determined by the factors of soil formation, in the first instance by climate, parent material and relief, each of which possesses a characteristic spatial distribution. These factors affect soil at a number of distinct scales.

Climate changes relatively gradually, creating what is broadly termed a zonal soil distribution,* a progressive change in the properties of freely drained soils on 'normal' parent materials. Examples are well known: the decrease in the thickness and organic content of the topsoil and concurrent rise of a calcareous horizon towards the surface from north to south across the Russian steppe and from east to west across the American prairies; in New Zealand within the group of yellow brown earths, the increase in weathering from south to north.

Climatically induced changes in soil properties usually occur gradually over long distances, apart from a few exceptions such as abrupt rain-shadow effects. Hence they give rise to soil boundaries on small-scale compilations but hardly ever in the field. Occasionally, a single parent material extends continuously across a range of climate, and the placing of a soil boundary must be arbitrary.

Relief, with its associated influence on hydrology, produces the detailed distribution patterns which dominate soil maps at medium to large scales: the catenary pattern in erosional relief and the pattern of depositional landforms on alluvial plains. Topographically induced soil boundaries can vary from quite sharp, occurring over 10 m or less, to transitional changes extending over 100 m. Except at very large scales, even the latter can be represented on maps as precise boundaries. In areas where there are large blocks of relatively uniform parent material, much of the field effort in soil survey is devoted to working out the relations between relief and soils. Even so, there are limits to the accuracy obtainable in this way; in some areas, a wide range of soil types can occur within the most detailed mapping units that can be distinguished on the basis of relief (e.g. Bleeker & Speight 1978).

Parent material affects soil distribution at two levels of scale, smaller than and larger than that of relief. The first is that of broad types of parent material, the main lithologies in areas of solid geology or the main types of drift material. Broad bands of soil types related to these materials sweep across the soil map, to some extent independent of relief. In some countries (e.g. Malaysia, Zimbabwe, England), the soil map looks somewhat like the geological map coloured differently. This is not entirely the result of substituting inference for soil survey; in Malaysia, the climate is so uniform that each parent rock corresponds to distinct soil series.

The second effect is that variations in the composition of parent material are probably the main cause of local variability in soil properties, over distances of 10–100 m or less. Such variations can sometimes be

---

*A zonal soil is commonly regarded as one in which the properties are primarily determined by climate. Experience suggests a revised definition: a zonal soil is the soil type that was thought to be present before anyone went to have a look.

regular and predictable, as in patterns resulting from patterned ground of periglacial origin, but are often for practical purposes random.

Soil variability over short distances

Studies of the variability of soil properties within small or apparently uniform areas have yielded results of much significance to soil survey, since they set limits to the attainable accuracy of soil maps.

The variability of a single soil property may be expressed as its coefficient of variation (*CV*), the standard deviation (σ) expressed as a percentage of the mean ($\bar{x}$) or

$$CV(\%) = \frac{\sigma}{\bar{x}} \times 100$$

Thus if five randomly chosen samples of topsoil from the same mapping unit give clay percentages of 22, 18, 28, 11 and 21, the mean $\bar{x}=20$, $\sigma=6.2$ and the coefficient of variation *CV* of the clay percentage is $CV=(6.2/20)\times100=31\%$.

Typical values for coefficients of variation within single fields, mapped soil series and great soil groups are shown in Table 6.2. Texture shows the lowest variability, which is to be expected for the case of soil series since it is used as a criterion in field mapping. Properties related to the organic fraction show greater variability and chemical properties greater still. Whilst part of this latter may be caused by management, e.g. irregular mixing-in of fertilisers, much is inherent; samples taken from uncultivated brown earths on a 1 m radius have shown *CV*s for exchangeable bases and phosphorus of 25–50% (Ball & Williams 1968).

It is clear that the analytical precision with which the results of chemical analysis for a single 'typical' profile are quoted is meaningless. Where it is really considered desirable to have a reliable estimate of the range of chemical properties within a mapped soil unit, a substantial programme of sampling and analysis is necessary. Thus for forestry plots of 0.01 ha in Scotland, the number of samples necessary to obtain mean values to within ±10% at 95% confidence was found to be six samples for N, nine

Table 6.2 Typical values for coefficients of variation of soil properties. Based mainly on Beckett and Webster (1971).

Soil property	Coefficient of variation, CV (%)		
	within a field	within a soil series	within a great soil group
sand, clay	15	20	30
carbon, nitrogen	25	35	36
Ca, Mg, K, P	30–70	60	60

for total P and 29 for acetic-acid extractable P and bases (Blyth & Macleod 1978). Taking composite samples, i.e. soil from several sites mixed in one bag, improves the estimate of the mean but masks variability.

Unpredictable or unmappable variability over a short distance is not confined to chemical parameters. In some complex alluvial landscapes and reworked glacial drifts, variations in sedimentation may have no surface expression but may produce short-range variations in physical characteristics that affect soil response to management and which should ideally be used to differentiate series or phases of series.

Choice and definition of mapping legend

Once the extent of soil variation has been established, the surveyor must choose between defining the mapping units tightly or loosely. If tightly defined, with as many simple mapping units as possible, then more precise and more useful predictions can be made about the behaviour of the soils of each mapping unit, but a greater survey effort will be required to achieve a given purity or mapping success. If the units are loosely defined, fewer and less useful predictions can be made for each unit but the mapping success for a given effort will be high.

It was formerly held that the purity of mapping units should be 85% (Kellogg 1937, Soil Survey Staff 1951, p. 277). This was an article of faith, or laudable aim for surveyors, and might have been attainable when soil series were more broadly defined than at present. On the definitions of soil series now in use, retrospective analyses of soil maps have repeatedly shown that the purity attained is usually only 50–65% (e.g. Ragg & Henderson 1980). This is not only because it is impossible to delineate all the details of the soil pattern but also because of imperfect understanding of its nature. This finding is not as disastrous as it might appear, for many of the profiles which fall outside the limits of depth, texture, etc., specified for the series do so by amounts which are small or are not significant for management (e.g. Courtney 1973).

Predictive accuracy of soil maps in relation to scale

The purpose of the boundaries on a soil map is to enable the user to predict the soil properties of the individual mapping units more precisely than those of the area as a whole, and to be in a position to manage each unit differently. A map is only worth making if each of the units shown both (i) differ significantly from each of the other units in respect of soil properties, and (ii) respond differently to at least some kinds of management. That is, the difference between mapping units must be both statistically significant and relevant to land use or management.

Table 6.3 Illustration of the calculation of relative variance for a soil map. The map contains two mapping units, A and B, occupying equal areas. Five randomly sited topsoil samples are taken from each of A and B, and their clay content is determined.

Clay (%)			Analysis of variance	
Unit A	*Unit B*	*Units A + B*	*variance within A*	154
22	31		variance within B	58
18	36		variance within mapping units	$\overline{212}$
28	41		total variance	852
11	34		variance within mapping units	212
21	38		variance between mapping units	$\overline{640}$
$\bar{x} = 20$	$\bar{x} = 36$	$\bar{x} = 28$	relative variance $= \dfrac{212}{852} = 0.33$	
$\sigma = 6.2$	$\sigma = 3.8$	$\sigma = 9.8$		
$CV = 31\%$	$CV = 14\%$	$CV = 41\%$	$1 - RV = 0.67$	

The method for measuring the degree of difference between mapping units is based on the relative variance (*RV*) defined as

$$RV = \frac{\text{variance within mapping units}}{\text{total variance over mapped area}}$$

An example showing how to calculate this statistic is given as Table 6.3.

The predictive accuracy of a map is given by $1 - RV$. A 'perfect' map, one in which the mapping units are all completely homogeneous internally but differ from each other, gives a value for $1 - RV$ of 1. A useless map, in which variance within mapping units is just as large as over the area as a whole, gives $1 - RV$ as 0.

The use of soil associations in a map legend greatly reduces the accuracy with which the soil at a given site can be predicted. A mapping unit given as 'Gruntling Association: Able and Baker Series' reduces the chance of correctly predicting the series at a chosen site to 50% or, given impurities, to 35–40%. By combining the number of soil series contained within each mapping unit with the area covered by that unit, a 'score' of attainable series prediction accuracy for a map can be obtained. Many maps have scores as low as 50% or even 25% on the basis of legend alone, leaving aside impurities (Bie & Beckett 1971).

As would be expected, predictive accuracy is low on small-scale maps and rises with increase in scale. The values differ for different soil properties and the change with scale is often irregular (Beckett & Webster 1971). What is significant is that for general-purpose soil survey, based on series or similar units, a maximum value for $1 - RV$ is reached, beyond which there is little or no further improvement in predictive accuracy with increase in scale. This is a consequence of the microscale variability. Research into the scale at which this levelling-off is reached is scanty, but it seems possible that for general-purpose soil maps it occurs at a map scale of about 1 : 25000, at which point $1-RV$ is about 0.5 for physical properties and 0.3 for chemical properties.

This situation sets a limit to the accuracy attainable by general-purpose soil surveys. The only way in which this ceiling can be penetrated is by special-purpose surveys in which the properties of interest are directly observed. Hence if it is known that one soil property, say salinity, is highly important to proposed uses whereas all other properties are of little significance, do not attempt to map soil series and then determine the salinity of range of each; instead, set up a grid sampling programme supported by mass laboratory analysis of salinity.

Costs and returns of soil survey

Costs: general considerations

The main components in the cost of a soil survey have been noted in Chapter 2: salaries, transport to and within the survey area, subsistence, air photograph acquisition, laboratory analysis, cartography, printing and overheads. Typically some two-thirds of the total consists of salaries, the greater part for time spent in the field. This being the case, one very approximate way to judge the order of magnitude of total costs is to estimate man-days needed in the field, multiply by a unit cost, and add 50%.

The main determinant of survey cost per unit area is the scale of mapping. In addition survey cost is affected by the following:

(a) Whether the survey is local or distant, i.e. whether near established survey offices, an air journey away, or overseas.
(b) Whether it is part of an on-going programme or started afresh. National survey programmes achieve economies through keeping a constant flow of work.
(c) The proportion of photo-interpretation to field survey.
(d) The difficulty of the terrain, and hence time taken to travel between observations.
(e) Whether general- or special-purpose and, if the latter, what kind of information is required.
(f) The extent of ancillary field investigations, such as hydraulic conductivity tests, and the sophistication of laboratory support.
(g) Who does it. Consultant firms have to charge true costs, including cover for slack spells between jobs. Government organisations, besides having continuity of work, may as a matter of policy choose to include an element of subsidy. Consultancy by university staff is relatively cheap, partly because they have no inter-project overheads and partly because they are accustomed to working to a small budget and finding ways to achieve desired results within it.

Costs in relation to scale

The above circumstances could lead to the cost of a survey at a given scale varying frequently by a factor of 2 to 5 times and occasionally more. But even a fivefold variation in unit cost is small compared with the effect of scale. The reasons are that the length of boundary shown on soil maps increases with increase in scale; the effort need to map a given length of boundary is more or less constant; and total survey costs are primarily determined by time spent in the field.

The first of these reasons calls for explanation. Experience shows that the spacing or density of boundaries tends to be constant *on the map*, regardless of scale; that is, a map at twice the scale of another will have almost the same map length of boundary and therefore about four times the ground length. One view, not without an element of truth, is that surveyors have an irresistible desire to map whatever is mappable. Less cynically, it may be supposed that those who commission surveys require boundaries of a given degree of detail and, correctly, select the smallest scale on which this detail can be shown.

It follows that man-days in the field, and hence total survey costs, rise rapidly with increase in scale. Were the above relationships wholly constant, cost should rise as the square of the scale, since doubling the (linear) scale increases the map area by four. Comparisons of published surveys show that the increase is at somewhat less than this theoretical rate. Bie and Beckett (1970, 1971) found the following relationships:

$$\log E = 7.41 + 1.57 \log S$$
$$\log C = 8.16 + 1.4 \log S$$

where E is the effort, in man-days per km^2 in the field, C is cost, in 1960 US dollars, and S is map scale, expressed as a fraction (e.g. $\log (1:25\,000) = -4.0$). Since these are approximate empirical relationships, the exponent in the first equation may be rounded off to 1.6. The constant 8.16 in the second equation changes with economic inflation, but the exponent 1.4 does not.

The meaning of these results is that if map *scale* is increased by a factor of n, field *effort* rises by about $n^{1.6}$ and total survey *costs* by $n^{1.4}$. Thus doubling the scale of a survey raises the field survey effort by 3.0 times and the cost by a factor of 2.6.

The effort and cost of mapping 1 km^2 at four scales are shown in Table 6.4, based on the above equations and with some other estimates added. Given the variation in survey circumstances, together with inflation, these values are best regarded as relative rather than absolute.

Despite qualifications, the essential message of this table is clear. Reconnaissance surveys can be accomplished rapidly and relatively

Table 6.4 Time and cost of soil survey, in relation to field mapping scale. Based partly on Bie and Beckett (1970, 1971).

	Detailed		Semi-detailed	Reconnais-sance
	1: 10 000	1: 25 000	1: 50 000	1: 250 000
survey effort (man-days/km²)	13·5	3·2	1·1	0·1
survey cost (1980 £/km²)				
cost of above at £25 000 per man-year	920	220	75	7
cost based on log $C=8·16+1·4$ log S, adjusted for inflation*	720	200	75	8
approximate costs given by Western (1978) for surveys by consultants	–	500	50–100	25–50
US Soil Survey estimate, adjusted for inflation	–	140 (1: 20 000)	–	–

*At 1960 US $1=1980 £2.

cheaply, of the order of 10 man-days and £1000 for 100 km². Surveys at least half as useful based on satellite imagery and mapped at 1: 1000000 might be achieved 5 to 10 times more cheaply.

At semi-detailed scales the unit cost is more than 10 times that of reconnaissance but still remains of modest absolute amounts, of the order of £50–£100 per km². It is thus well worth keeping to this scale wherever it will fulfil the survey purposes, as in some project feasibility studies.

Once into detailed scales, costs rise rapidly, by some 2.5–3 times on passing from 1: 50000 to 1: 25000 and a further 3–4 times from the latter to 1: 10000. The absolute cost reaches about £500–£1000 per km² at 1: 10000. Detailed soil survey can only be justified if benefits of the same order both can and will be achieved from the results.

Relation of scale, cost and predictive accuracy

It has been noted that the predictive accuracy of a soil survey rises rapidly with increase from small to medium scales, then more slowly, finally reaching a ceiling set by the microvariability of the soil continuum. Costs, on the other hand, rise exponentially with increase in scale. There is therefore a scale at which, for every landscape and type of survey, the ratio of predictive accuracy to survey cost reaches a maximum.

This point is reached at different scales for different types of survey (Fig. 6.1). Air photo-interpretation surveys (API), by which is meant those in which boundary delineation is entirely from air photographs and field mapping by selective traverses, reach their predictive ceiling at relatively small scales. It was formerly thought that they were most useful at about 1: 250000, although it may be that the combination of only partly

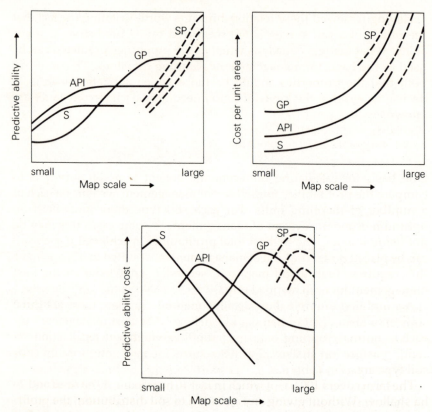

Figure 6.1 Relations between scale, survey method, cost and predictive ability of soil maps. S, surveys based on interpretation of satellite imagery; API, surveys greatly dependent on air photo-interpretation; GP, general-purpose soil surveys; SP, special-purpose soil surveys. Based partly on Beckett (1971).

reduced prediction with greatly reduced cost means that the best value for money for this type of survey lies somewhere between this and 1:1000000 (p. 107). General-purpose field surveys (GP), those based on a combination of photo-interpretation with substantial and systematic field coverage, probably give the highest prediction per unit cost somewhere in the scale range 1:50000 to 1:10000; we do not yet know more closely where this maximum lies. The cost of special-purpose grid surveys (SP) varies widely with the information collected, and is therefore shown on Figure 6.1 as a group of curves. They exceed free survey (S) in predictive accuracy only at very large scales.

It does not necessarily follow that surveys should be conducted at the scale where the accuracy–cost ratio reaches a maximum. Some circumstances require greater detail despite its cost, e.g. irrigation projects, or surveys of an agricultural experiment station.

Having reviewed these relationships it is worth restating the fact that the utility of a soil survey is not measured by its predictive accuracy alone. What matters equally is whether the properties predicted can be used as the basis for management or planning decisions. This requires both that the properties should be those which are relevant to such decisions and that the kinds of action needed in each circumstance are known.

The economic benefits of soil survey

One basis for calculating the economic benefit of a soil survey is to compare the profitability from different management systems on each of a number of mapping units. For each soil type there must exist an optimum economic system of management; in some cases this may be not using it at all. The highest total profitability is achieved if each soil can be placed under the kind of management most suited to it. To achieve this requires, first, a soil map and, secondly, knowledge of the best management for each mapped unit.

A simplified example illustrates the method. Suppose there are three soils on a farm, 'loam', 'sand' and 'shallow'. The best management for each is 'normal cropping' on loam, 'cropping with heavy fertilisation' on sand, 'pasture' on shallow. The net returns for each enterprise on each soil type are as in Table 6.5.

The farm covers 100 ha, of which in fact 40 ha is loam, 40 ha sand and 20 ha shallow. Without giving any attention to soil distribution, the profitability under each management system will be as shown in columns 2–4 of Table 6.5b, the best of which is £2400 under normal cropping. The profit is shown in the last column, £3200, a gain of £800 or 33% over placing the whole under normal cropping; this is on the unrealistic assumptions of perfect soil survey, the practicability of applying the right management to each soil, and that in the absence of a soil survey, no notice would be taken of differences in soil properties. In reality, the combination of limitations to both survey and management would reduce this potential advantage by at least half.

This concept can be extended to any number of soil units and management systems. The information needed to calculate theoretically the optimum intensity of soil survey is (i) the purity of soil mapping units achievable at any given intensity, and (ii) the net profit from a number of alternative kinds of management applied to each soil type. A computer program is available for such a calculation (Bie *et al*. 1973). This has rarely been done, for although estimates can be made of survey accuracy in relation to scale, people have very rarely attempted to assess inputs, crop yields or other benefits, and thus profitability in relation to defined soil types.

Table 6.5 Schematic calculation of the economic benefit obtainable by matching farm management systems to mapped soil types.

(a) Gross margin (£/ha yr).

	Management system		
Soil type	Normal cropping	Cropping with heavy fertilisation	Pasture
loam	50	40	15
sand	20	25	10
shallow	−20	−40	10

(b) Gross margin (£), farm of 100 ha.

	Management system			
Soil type	Normal cropping	Cropping with heavy fertilisation	Pasture	Optimum
loam, 40 ha	2000	1600	600	2000
sand, 40 ha	800	1000	400	1000
shallow, 20 ha	−400	−800	200	200
Total	2400	1800	1200	3200

Even if rarely applicable as a formal calculation, the principle embodied in this procedure, i.e. that of matching the best kind of land use management system to each soil type, is widely applicable. Besides the obvious case of choice of crops or farming practices, other examples are the selection of tree species in a forestry plantation or the amount and timing of irrigation water. In surveys of empty areas, the choice may lie between major kinds of land use. One 'management system' for which soil survey can often give guidance is when not to use certain land at all.

Does soil survey pay?

It is sometimes suggested that the costs of soil survey are not justified by the returns. Certainly this is true wherever no use at all is made of the results, a not-unknown circumstance. It could also apply on a land development project if those responsible for planning take the view that 'the soil survey tells us where the hills and the swamps are'. Officials in developing countries have been known to regard a soil survey as a costly formality that must be gone through as a matter of form if external aid is to be secured (Hills 1979).

Given, however, that the results are put to use, then the value of soil survey can be illustrated by consideration of the orders of magnitude involved. A survey at 1:25000 can be accomplished for about £2 per hectare. One hectare of an arable crop yields some 5 t of a grain crop or 30 t of root crop, valued at around £500. It is reasonable to assume that the benefits of all kinds from soil survey, including selection of planting areas, variation of treatments and avoidance of hazards, will have the effect of raising net gains by at least 5%, whether from increasing production or reducing costs. A 5% increase on £500 is £25, or over 10 times the cost of the soil survey in a single year.

The absolute cost of soil survey may seem high when taken out of context, but it is low in relation to the total costs of farming, establishing a forestry plantation or a land development project, and very low indeed in comparison with major engineering works such as a dam. Thus even if one assumes quite small relative improvements in productivity, or more likely savings in investment costs, the benefit–cost ratio of surveys is very high. Studies in both the USA and Australia have demonstrated benefit–cost ratios of the order of 40 : 1 or 50 : 1. Where a land development project involving major engineering works does not go ahead, or is substantially modified, as a result of a soil survey, the savings can be many hundreds of times the costs of the survey.

These estimates may be tempered by a note of caution. Soil survey can assist in making decisions but it does not make them. The right decisions might be made without the survey, or the wrong ones made despite the information it provides. Hence you cannot attribute the whole value of good decisions to guidance provided by soil survey, nor subtract the value of decisions which turned out badly despite being based in part on survey information.

Further reading

Beckett and Webster (1971), Beckett (1971), Burrough et al. (1971), Bie et al. (1973).

The Land Systems Approach

Purposes of reconnaissance surveys

Reconnaissance surveys are intended to provide a broad view of the land resources of an area, to serve as a guide for planning and development and a framework for more detailed surveys. They are by no means confined to soils but cover the whole of the physical environment to the extent that it affects land use potential. They are mainly of use in developing countries and in empty or sparsely settled areas. For development planners such surveys show the types of resources present and their location and extent; the nature of the resources will probably be known already (to inhabitants of the country if not to expatriate 'experts') but their extent is not. That is, agriculturalists, planners and even politicians will know perfectly well that there is opportunity in the 'Eastern Region' for a mechanised food farm, dairying scheme or fuelwood plantation; a reconnaissance survey shows whether there are 50, 100 or 200 km^2 of land suited to these purposes, and where this lies. This information can be used for project location, to identify and delimit one or more promising areas, to seek financial support on the basis of such information, and subsequently to proceed to feasibility surveys of those areas.

These purposes are adequately served only if as much effort is devoted to evaluation of the resources as to their mapping and description. Experience has shown that where reconnaissance surveys omit or only superficially cover the stage of interpreting the mapped resources in terms of land development, they are not used.

The scale most commonly employed is 1: 250000, reduced from boundary delineation on air photographs at 1: 40000 to 1: 50000. A considerably more rapid coverage can be achieved if satellite imagery is used, mapping at 1: 1000000. Even at 1: 250000, the smallest area that can be mapped is 5 km^2; it goes without saying that such maps cannot be used for planning (as distinct from identifying) development projects.

The mapping units employed are based on the total physical environment, or at least on some combination of landforms, climate, soils and vegetation, rather than upon soils alone. There are two reasons for

104

this, practicability of mapping and purposes of the map. On the one hand, all boundaries on a reconnaissance map are derived from photo-interpretation, and hence necessarily are based on landforms or vegetation, whilst areas several kilometres across so often contain such widely differing soil types that a map legend based on soils alone would be an uninformative list of associations. On the other hand, the purpose of reconnaissance surveys would not be served by maps showing soils alone; information is also required on landforms, climate, hydrology and vegetation.

The land systems approach

Origin and definitions

One method of conducting and presenting the results of reconnaissance surveys has been used far more widely than others and is superior for most purposes. This is the land systems approach, also known as integrated survey, meaning that all factors of the physical environment are mapped simultaneously. The origins of this approach lay in the application of air photo-interpretation to rapid reconnaissance mapping. Three organisations discovered independently that boundaries drawn from air photographs could serve a variety of purposes. The Division of Land Use Research, Australia, had the aim of rapid appraisal of the resources of large empty areas in the north and interior; the National Institute of Road Research, South Africa, was concerned with soil engineering properties for the design of road systems; and MEXE, an experimental unit of the British Army, wanted to know whether their tanks would sink into the mud and to know the answers to other military questions. On discovering this common experience, the approach was systematised and a nomenclature established (Brink *et al.* 1966).

Two principal mapping units are employed, the land system and the land facet. The **land system** is an area with a recurring pattern of topography, soils and vegetation, and with a relatively uniform climate. The **land facet** is an area within which, for most practical purposes, environmental conditions are uniform. Both definitions are rationalisations of units that arise naturally in the course of photo-interpretation; land systems are distinctive patterns extending across one or several photographs, whilst facets are the smallest areas that can be recognised and delineated (Plate 4). The facets within a system are not a random collection of contiguous areas but are often causally linked, by geomorphological processes, origin or groundwater flow. Hence an alternative definition of a land system is an area with a recurring pattern of genetically linked land facets.

Each land system is known by a local name, e.g. the Gwebu System, and is unique. There have been attempts at grouping them into higher categories but there is no generally agreed classification. The land facets within each system are numbered and given connotative titles, e.g. 1: gently sloping valley sides; 2: floodplains.

More detailed subdivisions, **land elements,** are sometimes initially distinguished then amalgamated into land facets under the qualification 'for most practical purposes'. One further term, **land units,** does not have a standard definition. As employed in Australian surveys it is in some cases equivalent to the land facet, in others it is more generalised. Landscapes are by no means invariably divided into two hierarchical levels, and land unit can usefully be reserved for cases where it seems necessary to distinguish a category between the system and the facet.

Procedures

The survey activities follow the same three phases as in soil survey – photo-interpretation, field survey and collation of results – but with a different emphasis. Photo-interpretation occupies a higher proportion of time and fieldwork a lower proportion; the relative percentages of time spent on the three phases might appropriately be 30:50:20.

The phase of photo-interpretation is similar to that for soil survey except that landforms and vegetation are mapped in their own right. The **defining features** of each land system should be systematically noted. A high proportion of both defining features and boundaries are based on landforms. This is not only for practical reasons. It is desirable in principle to identify, and as far as possible to define, land systems in terms of landforms, in the interests of having a uniform basis to the mapping. In flat areas, coastal and alluvial plains, vegetation must be used.

The identification and delineation of landform-based mapping units is nearly always done by judgement, and their description based at the photo-interpretation stage on qualitative terms, e.g. 'moderately sloping with closely spaced, narrow valley floors'. A parametric method is also possible. Individual elements of landforms are first measured and mapped: altitude, slope angle, profile curvature, plan curvature, aspect, basin size, etc. These are then combined to identify **landform elements** which are combined into **landform patterns.** These can form the basis of land facets and land systems respectively. Details of the method are described by Speight (1974, 1977). The parametric method gives a more objective and uniform basis to land system identification, but it is much slower.

Fieldwork differs substantially from that in soil survey. It is carried out by vehicle traverses, planned in advance to visit all or most of the provisional land systems identified by photo-interpretation. A convoy of landrovers sets off carrying, besides tents and supplies, a team of one or more geomorphologists, soil surveyors, ecologists, and possibly hydrologists and land use/farm systems experts. At each stop, survey is based on catenary traverses, by means of which the facets are described, their soils identified and their relative extent estimated. Mountains and other areas of low potential receive cursory visits.

Some land system surveys include derived maps of soils or vegetation. Where it has been decided that this is desirable, more extended and separate field survey of these factors is necessary. Owing to the reconnaissance scale this is necessarily obtained by stratified sampling, based on the photo-interpretation mapping units.

Reconnaissance surveys based on satellite imagery

The cost of the standard type of land system survey, based on air photos and mapping at 1: 250 000, is small per unit area covered, but for large regions it is by no means a negligible call upon survey resources. The utility of the results is limited by their highly generalised nature. This conjunction of substantial cost with limited utility has led some to express the view that extensive resource inventories are not good value for money.

Whilst not necessarily conceding this proposition, an alternative now exists. Land system surveys based on satellite imagery, in conjunction with field traverses, are not as good as those based on photo-interpretation but are not demonstrably very much worse. A tabular legend showing landforms, vegetation, etc., is again produced, and comparisons between soil boundaries initially based on satellite imagery with those subsequently derived from photo-interpretation show an acceptable measure of agreement. The smaller land facets cannot be delineated.

Set against this modest reduction in information, there is a considerable saving in survey effort. For example, air photo-interpretation at 1: 250 000 of part of Sudan took 8 man-months per 1000 km^2, compared with 1.5 man-months per 1000 km^2 for survey of a similar area using Landsat imagery in conjunction with partial photo-interpretation (Wilson 1979). The whole of Ethiopia has recently been covered by Landsat interpretation at 1: 1000 000 by a small team in one year, a task unthinkable using air photographs.

Thus the value of the results of satellite-based survey is lower, but not by a large margin, say something like 'half as good'; but the cost of completing such a survey is lower by a factor of ten or more. Hence the results obtained per unit cost are certainly greater; in addition, they are obtained much more quickly. Given that the usefulness of reconnaissance surveys in development planning is limited, it may prove to be that the

(a) Kildonan Land System, Swaziland

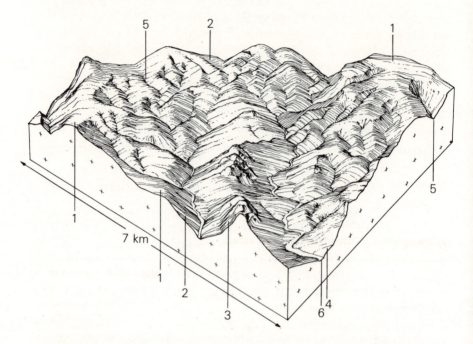

Figure 7.1 Example of a description of a land system. From Murdoch *et al.* (1971).

functions which they do serve can be achieved satisfactorily by satellite-based survey.

The initial stage, that of drawing provisional boundaries based on the satellite imagery, does not differ in principle from air photo-interpretation. Patterns of inferred landforms and land cover (vegetation/land use) are identified and delineated. Their provisional description is more inferential and tentative than from stereoscopic viewing of air photos, leaving more detail to be added or modified at the stage of field traversing. A nested procedure, combining complete coverage by satellite imagery with conventional photo-interpretation for sample areas, is now often the best way of conducting reconnaissance surveys.

Results

Since part of the essence of this kind of survey lies in the rapid communication of information, excessive proliferation of data should be avoided in the report. The vast amount of interesting information that will have been garnered in the course of fieldwork must be pruned down to its essentials. The results are presented as:

(b) Description of the land system as a whole

Climate	Mean annual rainfall 850–1400 mm, locally up to 2250 mm
Rock	Mostly granite and gneiss
Landscape	A high landscape of steep-sided ridges and hills
Hydrology	Perennial streams; groundwater influence marked in bottomlands, slight elsewhere
Soil	Yellow ferrallitic soils and raw mineral soils
Vegetation	Highland and mountain sourveld
Agriculture	Pine, gum and wattle plantations; extensive sheep grazing; rain-fed cropping (maize, potatoes)
Relative relief	Variable, 200–500 m
Altitude	600–1700 m

(c) Description of the individual land facets

Land facet	Form	Soils, materials and hydrology	Land cover
1	*Ridge crests* Convex in cross section or with straight sides, with slopes up to 10%; crests gently undulating, occasionally irregular; width usually about 150 m but occasionally up to 400 m; locally dotted with small rocky outcrops	Very acid deep yellow on red loam (NH set), grey on orange gravelly loam (QH set) and pale brown sandy loam on rotten rock (TH set); ferrallitic soils; freely drained	Mountain sourveld *Themeda triandra* *Rendlia altera* *Loudetia simplex*
2	*Hill slopes* Steep and mainly straight with convex upper margins; extensive along contour below facet 1; commonly 500–1000 m wide	Rock outcrops and stony ground; or very acid deep yellow on red loam (ferrallitic soil) U and NH sets	Highland sourveld *Themeda triandra* *Monocymbium ceresiiforme*
3	*Crags and rocky slopes* Irregular or rugged with steep to precipitous sides; up to 100 m high	Rock outcrops and stony ground	Mountain sourveld (as 1 above)
4	*Footslope terraces* Very gently sloping (about 2%); even; up to 200 m wide; occur adjacent to larger tributary streams	Grey sandy loam on hard iron pan (G set); or acid mottled sand to clay; periodic high groundwater	Highland sourveld (as 2 above)
5	*Tributary valleys* Narrow (up to 50 m across), gently sloping with occasional steeper portions in longitudinal section; . with (a) channel (up to 20 m wide) and adjacent flats (b) steep or very steep sides up to 5 m high	 (a) Acid mottled sand to clay often with shallow black peat (b) Deep yellow over red loam or shallow grey loam	Sedges and marsh grasses; highland sourveld (as 2 above)
6	*Main river* Winding with small and discontinuous terraces, river channel rock strewn and with an undulating floor (a) channel (b) terrace	 (a) Perennial river (b) Deep brown sand	Highland sourveld

(a) a map of land systems, with extended legend
(b) descriptions of each system, together with their component facets
(c) accounts of each of the factors of the environment
(d) a section on evaluation.

The main map shows land systems but not facets, together with an extended legend in the form of a table. For each system, landforms, soils and vegetation are invariably shown, and sometimes also altitude range, geology/soil parent materials, climatic indicators (e.g. January and July temperature, mean annual rainfall, number of dry months), hydrology, present land use (including percentage cultivated) and land potential.

The land system descriptions in the text are in two parts, the system as a whole and its component facets (Fig. 7.1). The first comprises a block diagram showing the system and its facets in schematic form, together with a table in which the information in the legend on the map is repeated and amplified. The second part gives information on each facet, omitting climate but including, for example, relief (especially slopes), drainage, soils, vegetation (trees and grass) and land use and/or potential. The relative extent of the facets should be indicated, and this can usefully be combined with a typical cross section. Maps showing the distribution of facets for small sample areas are occasionally included but are not essential.

The survey memoir includes chapters containing systematic accounts of geomorphology, climate, hydrology, soils and vegetation. All include text maps on a small scale, whilst features of principal interest, soils in arable regions and vegetation in regions dependent on livestock production, can be shown on separate maps at a scale equal to or half that of the land systems map. Evaluation, or interpretation in terms of development potential, is presented as a chapter together with at least one separate map.

Alternative approaches

A number of other approaches to reconnaissance resource survey have been attempted, some differing from land systems more in name than in practice. These include the following.

Ecological surveys. The *Vegetation–soil map of Northern Rhodesia* (Trapnell *et al.* 1948) was a classic reconnaissance survey, based on extensive field studies of vegetation and associated soils and landforms. It was valid because the country at that time possessed large expanses of vegetation little changed by the low intensity of cultivation. Natural vegetation is a sensitive integrator of the total environment, and, in the hands of an ecologist who knows about farming as well, it can be a valuable guide to land use and its changes. Moreover, ecologists by training consider dynamic relations within the ecosystem. In regions dependent on extensive livestock systems, reconnaissance resource inventory could be focused on ecology.

A persuasive case for an ecological approach to resource mapping in general has been put forward, and demonstrated for a test area in Nigeria, by Moss (1968, 1969). It has not since been widely adopted, in part because the practical survey operations are not well defined. The principles of this approach, however, repay study and can be incorporated to a limited extent in land systems mapping.

Agro-ecological surveys. This approach directs attention to the actual and potential farming systems which are the main objects of reconnaissance surveys. 'Agro-ecological zones' refer to broad climatic regions suitable for certain crops or farming systems, as widely recognised within the country. The *Agricultural survey of Southern Rhodesia* (Vincent *et al.* 1961) was unusual for its time in combining an agro-ecological with an agro-economic survey.

Terrain analysis or classification. This is a form of mapping based largely or entirely on landforms with their associated geology and regolith cover. It employs parametric methods of landform description. It can be used for military and other purposes where vehicle access, trafficability, and related aspects are the object (Beckett *et al.* 1972, Mitchell 1973). Techniques of landform description and classification originating from terrain analysis have been incorporated into land systems survey. This method should not be confused with another of similar name, terrain analysis for forestry, which is applied at detailed or intensive scales (Rowan 1977).

Soil landscapes. This is a mapping unit that can be used if it is desired to carry out a survey at reconnaissance scale but specifically directed at soils. The soil landscape is an association of soils described and delineated by means of landforms. An example is the map at 1: 2000000 scale in the *Atlas of Australian soils* (CSIRO 1960–68).

Evaluation in reconnaissance surveys

Evaluation in many land systems surveys has undoubtedly been weak. It sometimes consists of a map showing something like 'high, moderate and low' potential for arable use, with potential for intensive and extensive pastoral use. To some extent this very generalised interpretation can be justified on the grounds that anything more specific would be inappropriate on the basis of reconnaissance survey. What is not defensible is the fact that it is sometimes apparent that the evaluation was carried out only in the post-fieldwork stage, as an office exercise.

This situation is a criticism of the way some surveys have been conducted but not of the approach itself. Wider possibilities for evaluation at reconnaissance scales may be illustrated by two examples. A survey of the Northern and Luapula Provinces of Zambia (Mansfield *et al.* 1975) included a land capability classification based on five factors of soil and three of relief, from which are derived capability classes I–V for rainfed arable farming; there is in addition an assessment of soil suitability for irrigation. The cartographic device adopted to show land capability at a scale of 1: 1000000 was to map 'percentage of land in classes I and II' and likewise in classes IV and V. The land system descriptions include proportional circles showing estimated proportions in each capability class together with additional interpretative information and a description of 'engineering land facets'. In one of the largest land system surveys ever conducted, that of Central Nigeria (Hill *et al.* 1978–79), the interpretative phase was based on suitabilities for eight individual crops, selected by the government. Suitability was assessed from climatic limitations, soil physical and chemical limitations and erosion hazard. This led to a map of 'crop options' at 1: 250000. There was a separate assessment of growth potential of forest reserves. The results of the survey were summarised in a map of 'agricultural development possibilities' in a simple and direct format.

Land systems and facets form a valid basis for soil engineering mapping for roads. There are three groups of parameters involved in such interpretation: features of landforms relevant to road layout (e.g. slope, drainage and flooding), soil engineering test data, and sources of constructional materials. Controlled studies have shown that engineering test values obtained by sampling on a given mapped land facet can be extrapolated, within confidence limits that can be established, to the remainder of that facet (e.g. Dowling 1968, Dowling & Beaven 1969). National data banks for the storage of geotechnical data, linked to landforms and geology, may be set up (National Institute for Transport and Road Research 1976).

The value of reconnaissance surveys

The main advantages of the land systems approach are speed and relative cheapness, integration of the different factors of the environment, and clear communication of results.

Through coverage of several square kilometres per working day, it becomes a realistic proposition to attempt complete coverage of a region or many entire countries in a period of the order of 5–10 years. This has been achieved, for example, for Lesotho, Malaŵi, Papua–New Guinea and nearly half Nigeria. From the point of view of development planning, this is a realistic time scale in which to obtain a basic resource inventory, generalised but comprehensive.

The integration achieved is only limited, as borne out by the separate accounts of each factor in map legend and text, but the same set of boundaries is used for all features. True integration is reached only at the stage of interpretation, when, by having the component factors set out side by side, the prospects for linking them into, say, a mechanised food farm or a ranching scheme can be judged.

Rapid communication of results is achieved through the clear style of presentation. There is only one map to comprehend instead of eight or more maps of factors. Through studying the block diagram, cross section and tabular description, anyone can grasp the essentials of a land system in 5–10 min. This aids comparison between one region and another, for example, 'This land system looks very similar to the Lobi area, where we already have a successful tobacco scheme.'

Do not expect high levels of prediction for individual land and soil attributes from land system surveys. Tests have shown quite wide ranges of variation for textural, physical and other properties within land facets, with coefficients of variation (p. 94) of the order of 25–50% or more (e.g. Mitchell *et al.* 1979). The highest value for effort from land systems surveys is obtained at reconnaissance or exploratory scales, which for comparatively little effort yield a considerable increase over no information at all. If the survey is to be taken to more intensive levels, then the ceiling of prediction level from surveys based on photo-interpretation is encountered (p. 96) and the balance of activities must be changed in favour of more field survey.

Disadvantages of land systems surveys are the high degree of generalisation, the variable and somewhat ill defined basis of the mapping units, the static nature of the information presented and weakness of the evaluation stage. Some of these weaknesses are not inherent in the approach but lie in the way in which it has been applied.

The degree of generalisation is an inevitable consequence of the scale and intensity of the survey, but is acceptable provided that it is recognised and the survey is not used for more detailed planning purposes. The fixed hierarchy of land system and facet is more of a problem to the surveyor than to the user, as also is the transitional nature of some boundaries; the inclusion on the same map of some boundaries based on landforms and others on vegetation is disturbing from a scientific point of view but works in practice.

Land system surveys present a somewhat static view of the environment as a set of relatively fixed resources available for use. Dynamic interactions between environmental factors and between the environment and land use receive only brief coverage. This is particularly unfortunate in surveys which are intended to be integrated. Now that this defect has been recognised, it would be possible to give greater attention during field survey to such dynamic aspects; examples are the soil moisture regime, as influenced by climate and available water capacity interacting with land use, or relations between fallow vegetation and land use intensity, including forest/grassland/fire interactions (Moss 1968, 1969). Whilst it is desirable in principle to attempt to describe such interactions, it is doubtful how much can be achieved within the time constraints of reconnaissance survey. Most such dynamic aspects require monitoring for a year or more, detailed local studies, or both.

Whether resource inventory at the reconnaissance scale should have priority call upon survey resources over more detailed project planning is a matter for individual countries to decide. There are no short-term gains to be seen from the application of reconnaissance surveys. The benefit is extended over time and comes in many ways. The first and most obvious is through identification and early stages of formulation of development projects. Secondly, and less easily definable, it provides a basis for achieving balanced development of resources, by whatever lights governments may wish. Thirdly, agriculturalists, foresters, planners and administrators find it a help to be able to look up an answer to day-to-day questions that arise on natural resources; the land systems map on the wall is more than a decoration, it is consulted.

The value of reconnaissance surveys in settled areas of developed countries is more questionable. Everyone knows already which areas are suited to arable farming, and which to livestock; the location of development schemes is likely to be the subject of local political lobbying, based on more detailed preparatory surveys. On the other hand, lack of national coverage of some kind leaves you without a scientific framework to which local studies can be related. Potential users who make enquiries inevitably lose interest if told that no information at all is available for their areas. There is also no proper basis on which to plan the national soil survey programme itself. So although open to the jibe of being an 'academic exercise', complete coverage of a country at reconnaissance scale does serve some scientific and planning purposes.

Further reading

Christian and Stewart (1968), Brink *et al.* (1966), Haantjens (1965a).
Examples of land systems surveys are: CSIRO Australia (1953–80, nos 1–30), Land Resources Development Centre (1966–80, nos 2, 3, 9, 19 and 29), Forster (1977), Murdoch *et al.* (1971), Scott *et al.* (1971), Mitchell and Howard (1978a, b).

Land Evaluation

Land evaluation is the process of estimating the potential of land for alternative kinds of use. These include productive uses, such as arable farming, livestock production and forestry, together with uses that provide services or other benefits, such as water catchment areas, recreation, tourism and wildlife conservation.

The basic feature of land evaluation is the comparison of the requirements of land use with the resources offered by the land. Fundamental to the evaluation procedures is the fact that different kinds of use have differing requirements. It is obvious that crop production, grazing by livestock, forestry and recreation call for different qualities of land, but there are also large variations in requirements within each of these major kinds of use. Thus cotton, sugar beet and dates can tolerate relatively high salinity levels whereas citrus and soft fruits are very sensitive. Land requirements are also affected by the technology of use; for example, basin irrigation needs land which is level or can be made so, whereas sprinkler and trickle methods do not.

Land evaluation needs information from three sources: land, land use and economics. Data on land are obtained by natural resource survey, including soil survey. Information on the ecological and technical requirements of different kinds of land use is obtained from agronomy, forestry and other relevant disciplines. If the results of an evaluation are required in purely physical terms, then the data drawn from economics need only concern broad features of the economic and social context, e.g. general wage levels, the extent of mechanisation, approximate size of land holdings. If the results are required in economic terms, then data on specific costs and prices are needed.

The demand for evaluation arose when it was appreciated that the mapping of natural resources alone did not provide sufficient guidance on how the land could be used and what would be the likely consequences. Natural resource surveys express their primary results in terms of the environmental factor mapped: soil maps show soils, vegetation maps are based on plant associations, climatic studies are expressed in terms of averages and variability of rainfall, temperature and other parameters. None of these as such indicates whether the land can be used to grow, say, sugar cane. To be of value in land planning and management, a further stage is needed, that of relating the features of soils, vegetation, climate, etc., to the requirements of different kinds of land use. This stage, in which the requirements of land use are compared with the qualities of land, thereby assessing the value of each type of land present for each kind of use considered, is the essence of land evaluation.

There is a substantial overlap between soil survey and land evaluation. Special-purpose soil surveys necessarily incorporate an element of evaluation for specified kinds of use, whilst general-purpose soil surveys often include evaluation of a generalised nature, e.g. potential for arable farming. Conversely, the process of land evaluation in the broader sense of the term incorporates the basic surveys from which it obtains data, including soil survey. Evaluation may also require other kinds of natural resource survey, for example surveys of geomorphology, climate, hydrology and vegetation. Thus evaluation for grazing on natural rangelands draws primarily upon ecological survey.

In theory (and as a student exercise) it is possible to base an evaluation upon a previous, published, soil survey and other information already available, although up to the present this practice has been infrequent. Even where the area of interest has been covered by soil survey, it is usually found that the data collected from general-purpose survey are not sufficiently specific to the requirements of the various kinds of land use of interest, and need at least to be supplemented by further information. If there is a general-purpose soil map of good quality, then it is a great saving in time and expense to take its mapping units and their boundaries as a basis and collect the necessary information for each unit, rather than to resurvey. In the United States, general-purpose soil surveys of counties, carried out by the Soil Conservation Service, have been used by consultant firms as the data base for evaluation assessments.

The reason why soil survey is so often the main basis for land evaluation is partly that arable farming is the major type of rural land use, and partly that environmental factors vary at different scales. Climate is often relatively uniform, or does not fall outside the tolerance limits of particular crops, over distances of tens or hundreds of kilometres; thus wheat can be grown over most of lowland Britain, groundnuts over northern Nigeria. Such areas of relative climatic uniformity are commonly called **agro-ecological zones.** Land development often takes place within the context of a single zone, and land management on a single farm invariably so. Where this is the case, the local pattern of variation between land of different qualities is set by landforms and soils, with the variation in hydrology and vegetation largely dependent on these factors. Thus a soil survey, provided that it incorporates slope phases and other major features of geomorphology and hydrology, is usually the primary basis for land evaluation.

As the term 'evaluation' is used in at least three other senses associated with planning or land development, it is necessary to clarify these distinctions. Land evaluation as discussed in this book refers to rural land, within which is included the urban fringe zone. **Urban land evaluation** involves the assessment of property, rental and other economic values of land and buildings within cities; whilst sharing some principles with rural evaluation, it has its own distinct objectives and procedures (Thomas 1973). **Project evaluation** is the stage in land development planning in which the economic viability, practicability and desirability of the project as a whole is assessed. Cost–benefit analysis usually plays a prominent part. Where the project is for rural land development (as distinct from urban or industrial projects), land evaluation forms a large and essential part of project evaluation, but is by no means the only consideration (Overseas Development Administration 1972, Hansen 1978). Finally, the term **evaluation** is also applied to *post facto* studies of development projects, the aim of which is to see how much went as planned and what went wrong, so as to learn from past mistakes. All US AID projects include provision for this type of evaluation (Cracknell 1978). None of these three uses of the term 'evaluation' is further considered in this book.

Definitions

Land comprises all elements of the physical environment to the extent that these influence potential for land use. Thus land not only refers to soil but also includes the relevant features of geology, landforms, climate and hydrology, the plant cover and fauna, including insects and micro-fauna associated with diseases.

The physical results of past human activity, such as vegetation clearance and reclamation from the sea, are included within the concept of land. Unfavourable consequences from past use, such as eroded soils and degraded vegetation, must also be included. Economic and social features, however, whilst taken into account in evaluation procedures, are not part of land.

A **land mapping unit** is a mapped area of land with specified characteristics. Land mapping units are defined and mapped by natural resource surveys, and form a basis for evaluation. Any kind of area which possesses a degree of homogeneity in physical characteristics may be employed as a land mapping unit. Thus soil associations, soil series or phases, geomorphological units of various kinds, soil–landform associations, units of vegetation mapping, or land systems and facets may be employed as appropriate to the purposes of the evaluation.

Where land has been altered by human activity, a working distinction is made between major and minor improvements. A **major land improvement** is one which involves a substantial and reasonably permanent improvement in the qualities of land, and which requires a large capital expenditure. The most common examples are irrigation schemes, land drainage on a regional scale, and reclamation from the sea. Once accomplished, there are continuing maintenance charges, but the land itself is more fitted to certain uses than formerly. **Minor land improvements** have a smaller effect, are less permanent, or do not require large capital investment; examples are field drainage or the reseeding of formerly unimproved grazing land. The distinction between major and minor land improvements is not clear cut, but a useful criterion is whether the works required are within the technical capability and financial resources of an individual farmer or landowner. Thus some improvements, e.g. land levelling, might be considered minor in developed countries but major in developing countries. However, even where it is within the means of the farmer, irrigation should usually be regarded as a major improvement on grounds of the magnitude of change in land qualities involved.

A second group of terms concerns land use. In the context of land evaluation this refers to possible kinds of use under consideration for the future. These may, of course, include the present uses.

A **major kind of land use** is one of the few major subdivisions of rural land use, such as rainfed agriculture, irrigated agriculture, grazing, forestry and recreation. It is convenient to have a term to refer to uses of land at such a level of generality, although difficult to define it other than by listing the uses (Table 8.1). Major kinds of land use are employed in evaluation studies of a qualitative or reconnaissance nature.

A **land utilisation type** is any use of the land defined in greater detail than a major kind of land use. The degree of detail necessary varies with the scale and intensity of the study. Thus a rainfed arable farming enterprise based on maize and tobacco constitutes a land utilisation type, as does any individual crop, tree species, or a particular kind of recreational park. If evaluation is to proceed beyond a generalised level, it is necessary to define the land utilisation types considered in some detail.

Two further terms cover situations in which two or more kinds of land use are practised in an area. **Multiple land use** consists of more than one kind of use simultaneously undertaken on the same land. Examples are livestock grazing within a tree-crop plantation, or a softwood forest reserve used also for recreation. **Compound land use** consists of more than one kind of use undertaken on areas of land which are treated in the evaluation as a single unit. Mixed arable–livestock farming is a compound land use, a requirement for which might be that an area should contain freely drained cropland and valley floor grassland in association.

Table 8.1   Major kinds of land use.*

rainfed arable farming (annual crops)
tree and shrub crops (perennial crops)
intensive, specialised agriculture (market gardening)
irrigated agriculture
swamp rice cultivation
grazing of natural pastures (ranching)
grazing of improved pastures
production from natural forests (logging)
forest plantations
recreation and tourism
wildlife conservation
water catchments
engineering works
military use

*The terms in parentheses are more descriptive and concise but less accurate (arable farming includes field perennial crops, grazing of natural pastures includes nomadic grazing). If still greater generalisation is called for, the two kinds of grazing may be grouped together, as also may recreation and wildlife conservation. Swamp rice cultivation has such distinctive requirements that it is kept separate. Instances of multiple use occur, e.g. forest plantations/water catchments.

Types of land evaluation

The results of land evaluation may be given in terms that are qualitative, quantitative physical, or economic. A **qualitative evaluation** is one in which the suitability of land for alternative purposes is expressed in qualitative terms only, such as highly, moderately or marginally suitable, or not suitable for a specified use. Economic considerations are necessarily present as a background for, if profit is thrown to the winds, bananas can be grown at the North Pole. There are, however, no calculations based on specific costs and prices, although the boundary between land assessed as suitable and not suitable for a given purpose is set at what is roughly estimated to be that between profit and loss.

Qualitative evaluation is employed mainly in surveys at a reconnaissance scale, or as a preliminary to more detailed investigations. Set against the generalised nature of the results is the fact that it permits the integration of many aspects of benefits, social and environmental as well as economic. Qualitative evaluation is of little value in settled, developed countries, where its use is likely to lead to a 'so what' reaction, the potential of land in these terms being already known by experience. This is far from being the case in sparsely settled areas, where qualitative evaluation indicates alternative development possibilities. It can also be used in settled parts of developing countries, since even if the land potential is already known to the local farming population (within their perceived horizons), it may not be known to planners and politicians.

The results of qualitative evaluation remain valid for many years, or until a major new technology is introduced.

A **quantitative physical evaluation** is one which provides quantitative estimates of the production or other benefits to be expected, e.g. crop yields, beef or wool production, rates of timber growth, recreational capacity. To do this it is necessary to specify the inputs also in quantitative form, e.g. tonnes of fertiliser, man-days of labour, pesticide treatments. Economics is again present mainly as a background, e.g. the general level of wages for labour and hence the labour intensities likely to prove practicable. Some approximate calculations of costs and prices are often made, in order to decide appropriate levels of inputs on which to base the estimates.

Quantitative physical evaluation is most frequently carried out as the basis for economic evaluation. It is sometimes appropriate to special-purpose evaluations such as the estimation of growth rates expected of different timber species (mean annual increments). The drawback with this type of evaluation is that it does not normally supply a basis for comparison between different forms of production. Production from tree species can be compared if their value as timber (or firewood) is similar, and different grain and root crops can be compared to some degree on the basis of calorific production. But there is no easy means of comparing a cubic metre of timber with a tonne of grain, and still less with a coachload of tourists, other than in economic terms. Where used as the basis for economic studies, however, the evaluation should always be presented in detail at the quantitative physical stage, so that the results can be reinterpreted using other economic assumptions should this prove necessary.

An **economic evaluation** is one which includes results given in terms of profit and loss, for each specified enterprise on each kind of land. Specific money values are applied to data from quantitative physical evaluation, thereby obtaining the cost of inputs and value of production. Whilst terms such as highly or moderately suitable, etc., are still employed, the boundaries between these classes are defined in economic terms. It should be stressed, however, that an economic evaluation is by no means exclusively confined to considerations of profit and loss. Other consequences, e.g. environmental and social, are also set out among the results, to be combined with the economic data as a basis for taking decisions.

Economic land evaluation is always required for project appraisal, for most planning decisions and for private investment. Through the use of money as a common denominator, it permits the comparison of different forms of production. Either market prices or shadow prices can be employed, at the wish of those commissioning the evaluation. A money value can also be placed on intangible benefits, such as unpolluted water, recreation or scenic value, although this must be done in the knowledge of the severe limitations of such artificial procedures. As cash-flow discounting is nearly always necessary, changes in assumptions about discount rates and project life can considerably affect the results. Economic evaluations are ephemeral, changing with variations in costs and prices; the rise in fertiliser costs from 1973 had the effect of transferring much land from marginal to not suitable, whereas the escalation in the price of coffee had the opposite effect. Despite these drawbacks, economic evaluation must precede decisions to invest, becoming more important with the magnitude of the investment.

A further distinction in types of evaluation is that between current and potential suitability. A classification of **current land suitability** refers to the value of the land in its present condition, without major improvements. Evaluations of current suitability may assume minor improvements as part of the specification of the land utilisation type. A classification of **potential land suitability** refers to the value of the land at some future date, if and when major land improvements have been carried out. An example is the evaluation of land at present in the tidal zone for rice production or other use, the assessment being made prior to, and as a basis for taking decisions upon, reclamation. Irrigation schemes invariably require an economic evaluation of potential land suitability before the decision whether to invest is made.

Purposes of land evaluation

The fundamental purpose of land evaluation is to predict the consequences of change. If a farmer is already growing maize or barley, or grazing livestock, he does not need formal procedures of land evaluation; the value of the land for these forms of production can be better assessed from records of his own costs, yields and returns. Similarly, foresters will use growth in the past, where such data are available, as a guide to that in the future. Land evaluation becomes necessary where change is contemplated. This may be a change in kind of use, such as bringing into production land formerly under natural vegetation, or establishing a recreational park; or it may be the introduction of a new technique, such as supplementary sprinkler irrigation, the introduction of mechanised farming in areas of manual and animal labour, or the use of direct drilling.

Prediction is needed of the suitability of the land for different forms of production, the inputs and management practices needed, the production or other benefits, and the consequences of such changes upon the environment. These include adverse consequences, such as the warning that certain land should not be cultivated owing to a severe hazard of soil erosion.

As with soil surveys, the detailed purposes of land evaluation vary with the physical, economic and social context, with the scale and intensity of the study, and with the aims of the users.

Purposes in less developed countries and sparsely settled developed countries

Land use changes in these planning environments take place mainly within the context of land development projects or programmes. There are three main levels of scale and intensity, which may form successive parts of development planning.

Resource inventory. Evaluation at a reconnaissance scale is the best way of indicating the development possibilities of large areas relatively quickly and cheaply. Land evaluation at this scale might enable developers to see, for example, where the best areas for large-scale food-crop production are to be found, or where there are 100 000 contiguous hectares of viable grazing land. Identification of alternative development projects can follow. Such evaluations are based on current suitability, and provide qualitative classification of suitabilities for major kinds of land use. They require a wider range of data than can be obtained from soil survey alone, and can conveniently be based on land systems survey.

Many developing countries have commissioned land evaluation studies of this nature as an initial guide to development possibilities; the *Land resource studies* series of the UK Land Resources Development Centre includes examples. Among developed countries, Canada and Australia have both surveyed large areas; evaluation forms a major component of the survey in Canada but has been subsidiary to land systems description in Australia.

Project feasibility. Once a possible development project has been identified, the next stage is a feasibility study, carried out before the decision to invest has been irretrievably taken. Land evaluation provides one of the main sources of data for such a study. The evaluation will usually refer to land utilisation types described in some degree of detail. A multipurpose land settlement or reorganisation scheme makes use of land evaluation as a basis for selection of areas for arable, grazing, forestry and other uses, as well as for more detailed planning. The economic land evaluation feeds into the economic appraisal of the project as a whole.

The evaluation may be of either current or potential suitability, according to whether an irrigation scheme or other major improvement is involved. Both quantitative physical and economic evaluations are required. The map scale used for the evaluation varies from semi-detailed to detailed, the latter range being more appropriate in cases of irrigation and other large capital investment.

Given the decision to proceed, further land evaluation studies may not be necessary at the project planning stage. If, however, the layout of individual farms, village land, or blocks of settlements is required, land capability classification at a detailed scale may be called for. The economics at the feasibility stage will often have been in generalised terms, and more detailed data are required for planning; these can sometimes be based on the same quantitative physical evaluation, with supplementary studies.

Farm planning. Every unit of management, whether it be a private or government farm, communal land, a livestock ranch or forest reserve, requires areas of land to be allocated to different purposes. The clearest illustrative case is the mixed arable–livestock farm, where there is a need for rotational arable land, winter and summer grazing, and space for roads, farm buildings and other structures. Where the productive use is more specialised, as in a softwood plantation, decisions are needed on which land to plant or not to plant, on selection of tree species, or on where different kinds of minor land improvements are needed. For farm layout, **land capability classification** (Ch. 9) has stood the test of time. For more specialised management purposes, including farm management, suitability for specified techniques or kinds of use will be needed.

Purposes in closely settled developed countries

Planning. Against the background of competition between alternative uses for the same land area, and pressures from the many interest groups concerned, land evaluation provides one of the most objective sets of data contributing towards planning decisions. A recurrent demand is for the conversion of agricultural land to urban and industrial uses. In Britain, land evaluation was required for planning once it became accepted that the best agricultural land should be protected where possible. A rapid survey of the country was called for, grading land from 1 (best) to 5 (poorest); although published on a 1:63360 scale, the methods employed were such that the evaluation can only be called reconnaissance (Agricultural Land Service 1966). Refinements to this classification are in progress, as well as an alternative classification based on soil survey.

Examples of other land use changes are the planting of former rough grazing land with forest and the establishment of a park or other recreational area in an urban fringe zone. Such changes call for the comparison of suitability between present and proposed uses, both defined in detail. Economic evaluation will most certainly be included but the assessment should by no means be confined to criteria expressed in money terms. Environmental impact and possibly social consequences of changes will be included.

Management. Evaluation is appropriate wherever land improvement or a major change in management practices is being considered. The successive stages involved may be illustrated by reference to a new management practice, the proposed introduction of supplementary irrigation.

A detailed soil survey is first required as a basis. This will be a special-purpose survey, giving particular attention to slope, drainage, soil texture, the presence of slowly permeable layers and other relevant characteristics. The field survey is supported by laboratory determinations, including soil water retention curves and the salinity of both soils and groundwater.

On the basis of these data, a qualitative evaluation of crop response to supplementary irrigation can be made. The user can also be alerted to hazards, such as surface waterlogging or runoff from slowly permeable soils, excessive percolation through sands, or danger of salinisation through raising of the groundwater.

The optimum water requirements and the effects of deficits for alternative crops can be estimated, and if long-term data for rainfall and potential evapotranspiration are available, then a quantitative physical evaluation can next be made. This will relate the expected return frequencies of droughts of specified degrees of severity to the improvements in crop growth to be expected from supplementary irrigation, calculated separately for each combination of crop and soil.

Finally, the economic justification can be calculated by comparing costs with benefits. The costs are those of installation, maintenance and operation of the irrigation system and additional fertiliser, pesticide and harvesting requirements. The benefits are derived by taking the predicted increases in yields, and/or the opportunity of growing more profitable crops, combined with projected commodity prices.

Principles

Land evaluation involves comparison between the requirements of the land use and the qualities of the land. Different kinds of land use have different optimum conditions and different limitations. Thus perennial crops require that soil moisture should remain above wilting point within the rooting zone through the year, annual crops do not; sorghum can survive short periods of desiccation better than maize can. Hence evaluation is only meaningful if the nature of the use to which it refers is specified. In qualitative evaluation at reconnaissance scale, it may be sufficient to refer just to a major kind of land use, e.g. annual crops, perennial crops, forest plantations. As the scale and intensity of the evaluation increase, so it becomes necessary to define and describe the land use in more detail.

Evaluation requires a comparison of benefits obtained with inputs needed. The benefits may either be production, as of crops, meat, wool, dairy produce or timber, or they may be services or intangible benefits, such as waste disposal, provision of recreation or conservation of wildlife. The inputs include material inputs, such as seed, fertiliser, protective chemicals, fuel (for powered traction) and fencing, as well as inputs of labour and provision of machinery.

Land alone rarely if ever possesses productive potential. Inputs of at least seed and labour are required for crop growth, grazing of natural vegetation cannot take place without livestock supervision, felling of natural forests requires labour and machinery, and the recreational value of a wild landscape can be maintained only by measures for its conservation. Conversely, almost any land can be used for any purpose provided sufficient inputs are supplied. Within a local region the difference between good and bad land for a particular crop often lies more in levels of inputs needed than in differences in crop yields. Through drainage, terracing, deep ploughing or supplementary irrigation, land on which there would otherwise be low yields or total crop failure can be brought into productive use. The land is only suitable for a given use if the expenditure on inputs is justified by the returns. For qualitative evaluation the inputs may sometimes be tacitly assumed as being at levels customary in the region, whilst for quantitative evaluation, and still more for economic evaluation, amounts must be specified in detail.

Evaluation is made in terms relevant to the conditions of the country or region concerned. For example, if you are carrying out a land evaluation of part of Bolivia, take the labour availability, wage rates, shortages and surpluses, and the political and social conditions of that country as the basis for assessment. The clearest difference caused by local conditions is that between high- and low-income countries; land which could be put to productive use where hand labour is usual may be unsuitable for that use in high-income countries; conversely, farmers able to call upon advanced technology and large sources of capital may be able to apply kinds of land use which low-income farmers cannot. A contrasting example illustrates the effect of differences in demand; land which in south-eastern England would be regarded as having extremely high scenic and recreational value would be considered very ordinary in the Rockies.

It follows that most evaluations are not of universal applicability. The principles remain the same in all circumstances, but the relevant land qualities, and their critical values for determining suitability classes, vary between countries and sometimes between regions. This does not mean that a worldwide evaluation, say of the world's capacity to produce maize, is impossible, but any such exercise must necessarily be very generalised and must make many simplifying and sometimes rather unrealistic assumptions. Evaluation systems applicable throughout a country are considerably less generalised, although still not applicable in detail without local modifications; the UK Soil Survey system of land capability which deems that Wales has almost no class 1 land is a case in point. A consequence is that one of the first stages in a land evaluation study is to determine the local physical, economic and social context.

Evaluation involves comparison between alternatives. It has been found by experience that if evaluation is made for only a single kind of land use then it loses much of its force. It is usually best to present two or more alternative kinds of use, with the consequences of each. These need not be different major kinds of use. Where the land is obviously best suited to, say, arable use, evaluation can be made for alternative crop rotations or different management systems. If those who commission a study make a call such as 'find land for tea growing' they should be gently persuaded, if possible, that it will be a much more efficient use of time and money if at least some other kinds of production are considered. There is a case on record in which an entire country was assessed for suitability for oil palm cultivation, with the finding that, if you want to grow oil palm, this is not the place to do it.

Where one specific change is being considered, say the provision of supplementary irrigation or where to dispose of urban waste, the alternatives take different forms. In the former example the choice lies between change and no change; evaluation of the consequences of continuing with present management practices must be made for comparison with the proposed irrigation. In the latter example there must be a rubbish dump (and it cannot be a sauna instead), so the alternatives are different sites.

At the end of Chapter 1 we listed some of the things that soil surveys cannot do, as a warning to those who might have overoptimistic hopes of their potential. Many of the same caveats apply to land evaluation. Thus you get what you pay for; that is, one cannot expect to obtain detailed estimates of the economic viability of different kinds of land use on the basis of a qualitative survey at reconnaissance scale. Hence some kind of nested survey plan may be called for, with reconnaissance surveys indicating where semi-detailed work would be appropriate, the latter giving guidance on sites where detailed investigations are necessary.

A particular restriction of land evaluation is that it cannot be in economic terms and also time-invariant. If the classification is based strictly on profit and loss, then it will quickly become inaccurate, and over a longer period substantially misleading, as relative costs and prices change. A consequence is that the quantitative physical data should be presented as a permanent record.

Above all, as is the case with soil survey, land evaluation cannot take decisions for the user. Evaluation presents the consequences, favourable and adverse, of various possible changes in use, as well as of continuing with the present use. The evaluation procedure as such stops there. If the person commissioning the survey requires firm land use recommendations then these can be provided, but they are not part of the evaluation and frequently involve wider considerations. Land evaluation cannot, and is not intended to, tell the user what to do.

Further reading

Stewart (1968), FAO (1974a), Olson (1974), Vink (1975), Young (1973b, 1974, 1976 Ch. 20), Beek (1981).

Land Capability Classification

'We don't need soil survey, just give us land classification', is a heartfelt cry not infrequently heard from land use planners. A general-purpose soil survey initially produces a map which can be interpreted for many different purposes. The user, however, wants the interpretation and not the soil map. It is unrealistic to expect anyone other than a soil surveyor to produce interpretations of a pedological soil map, couched as it is in abstruse terminology and containing many conventions and hidden assumptions. For farm planning and certain related activities, the system of land capability classification has been found by experience to meet the needs of users well. Originally devised for farm planning in the USA, (Klingebiel & Montgomery 1961) it has since been adapted and widely applied in other countries, developed and developing.

The main product of land capability classification is a map in which areas of land are put into capability classes ranging from I (best) to VIII (worst). The reason why any area is allocated to a given class is indicated by a letter suffix; thus subclass IIe indicates an erosion hazard, IIw a problem of excess water. Each class of land has the potential, or capability, for use in a prescribed number of ways, or with specified management techniques. Thus class I land can be put to arable use without soil conservation measures whilst classes II to IV require increasingly costly conservation practices; classes VI–VIII should not be put to arable use at all.

Capability classification enables the land on a farm to be allocated rationally to the different kinds of land use required – rotational arable, permanent grazing, woodland, etc. Whilst leaving as much choice as possible open to the farmer, there is a strong element of guidance on soil conservation needs. Although originally intended for the planning of individual farms, it has since been successfully applied in developing countries to the planning of village lands as a whole, as well as providing a basis for drawing up farm boundaries on newly settled land.

Concepts and assumptions

Two concepts basic to the system are those of capability and limitations. Both involve tacit assumptions.

Capability is the potential of the land for use in specified ways, or with specified management practices. There is an assumed sequence of uses built into the system, a kind of land use pecking order. In descending sequence of assumed desirability, this is as follows: (a) arable use for any crops and without soil conservation practices; (b) arable use with restrictions on choice of crops and/or with soil conservation practices; (c) grazing of improved pastures; (d) grazing of natural pastures or, at the same level, woodland; (e) and at the lowest level, recreation, wildlife conservation, water catchments and aesthetic purposes.

Land which is allocated to any particular capability class has the potential for the use specified for that class *and for all classes below it*. Thus class I land, whilst excellent for arable use, can equally be put to any of the other uses; class VI land is suited for improved pastures but also to any of the uses below this, whilst class VIII land can be used only for recreation, etc. (Table 9.1). The capability class does not necessarily indicate what is the best use for land, nor the most profitable. Land defined as suitable for arable might more profitably be put to grass or tree crops. It only indicates the range of uses to which each area could be put. A good measure of discretion is left to the farmer or to his adviser.

Limitations are land characteristics which have an adverse effect on capability. **Permanent limitations** are those which cannot easily be changed, at least by minor land improvements; they include slope angle, soil depth, liability to flooding and, in the original but only some adaptations of the system, climate. **Temporary limitations** can be removed or ameliorated by land management; examples are soil nutrient content and at least a minor degree of drainage impedance.

Land is classified mainly on the basis of permanent limitations. The general rule is that if any one limitation is of sufficient severity to lower the land to a given class it is allocated to that class, no matter how favourable all other characteristics may be. Thus it is no good having level land, well drained and free from flooding if it only has 10 cm of soil. In most adaptations of the system this allocation rule is applied throughout the classification, although the original states that classes I to IV are distinguished from each other by summation of the degree of limitations.

For the most part it is the negative features of land which are taken into account in assigning different types of land to capability classes. Soil erosion hazards, and hence conservation requirements, normally loom large.

Other explicit assumptions are as follows:

(a) A favourable ratio of output to inputs, based on long-term economic trends, is one of the criteria for allocating land to capability classes. Land which could be rendered cultivable by, say, stone clearance, but at a cost which experience shows cannot be repaid, may not be

Table 9.1 Land use alternatives of capability classes. Based on the definitions in the original US version of the system (Klingebiel & Montgomery 1961)

Capability class	Limitations	Management under cultivation		Capability					
		Choice of crops	Conservation practices	Cultivation	Pasture (improved)	Range (unimproved pasture)	Woodland	Wildlife food and cover	Recreation water supply, aesthetic
I	few	any	none	✓	✓	✓	✓	✓	✓
II	some	reduced or	moderate	✓	✓	✓	✓	✓	✓
III	severe	reduced and/or	special	✓	✓	✓	✓	✓	✓
IV	very severe	restricted and/or	very careful management	✓	✓	✓	✓	✓	✓
V	other than erosion				✓	✓	✓	✓	✓
VI	severe				✓	✓	✓	✓	✓
VII	very severe					✓	✓	✓	✓
VIII	very severe							✓	✓

placed in classes I–IV. Thus economics, in the form of the general level of costs and prices, does play a part.

(b) Management is assumed to be at 'a moderately high level . . . one that is practical and within the ability of a majority of the farmers and ranchers' (Klingebiel & Montgomery 1961, p. 4). This manner of definition, although intended for US conditions, has lent versatility to the system, enabling it to be applied in developing countries where the prevailing methods of management are very different from those of Western countries. The technical means, capital resources and management skills of the 'better' farmer under local conditions are taken as the basis for classification.

(c) Location and accessibility, for example distance to market, existence and condition of roads, are not taken into account. Remote land, say in a mountain valley, could still be put into class I.

Structure of the classification

Three categories are recognised: capability classes, subclasses and units. Where the classification is based upon soil survey, i.e. not upon direct survey for capability, the capability units are themselves groupings of soil mapping units. In practice the system is often applied without identifying capability units.

A **capability class** is a group of capability subclasses that have the same relative degree of limitation or hazard. Classes are indicated by roman numerals, the restrictions on kinds of land use and management increasing from class I to class VIII (Table 9.2).

The classes fall into two groups. Classes I–IV can be used for cultivation, whilst classes V–VIII cannot. The risk of soil erosion increases through classes I to IV, progressively reducing the choice of crops and requiring more expensive conservation practices and more careful management. Classes I–IV can conveniently be thought of as 'very good', 'good', 'moderate' and 'marginal' arable land, respectively. Class IV

Table 9.2 Structure of land capability classification.

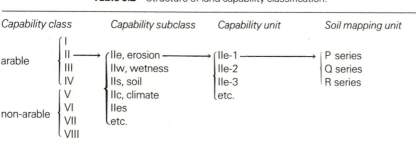

Capability class		Capability subclass	Capability unit	Soil mapping unit
arable	I			
	II →	IIe, erosion →	IIe-1 →	P series
	III	IIw, wetness	IIe-2	Q series
	IV	IIs, soil	IIe-3	R series
non-arable	V	IIc, climate	etc.	
	VI	IIes		
	VII	etc.		
	VIII			

should only be put to arable use if very carefully managed. Class V is allotted to land rendered unsuitable for cultivation by reasons other than erosion hazard, i.e. wetness, excessive stoniness. The main use of this class is for wet valley floor land.

Classes VI–VII are precluded from arable use by very severe permanent limitations; for the most part they consist of steeply sloping land. Class VI can be managed under improved pasture, class VII only under rough grazing or woodland, whilst class VIII cannot be used for commercial plant production of any kind.

The mapped extent of capability classes enables a farmer to see how much land can be put to arable and other uses if he so wishes, and where it lies.

A **capability subclass** is defined in the original system as a group of capability units that have the same major conservation problem. It may be defined alternatively as land which has the same kind of limitation. Four conservation problems, or kinds of limitation, are recognised in the original: e=erosion hazard, w=excess water, s=soil root zone limitations (depth, stoniness, etc.), and c=climatic limitations. Thus subclass IIe consists of land placed in class II on account of its erosion hazard, whilst subclass IIs has been placed there because of soil limitations.

In subsequent adaptations of the system, the number of subclasses has sometimes been increased, for example by recognising separately, soil depth, stoniness and salinity in place of a single soil root zone limitation, by subdividing wetness into high water table and flood hazard, or by adding a salinity limitation.

The mapped extent of subclasses enables the user to appreciate at a glance the location and extent of each particular kind of hazard, and therefore management problem.

A **capability unit** is a group of soil mapping units that have the same potential, limitations and management responses. Units are shown by arabic numbers, e.g. IIe-1, IIe-2. Soils within a capability unit can be used for the same crops, require similar conservation treatment and other management practices, and have comparable productive potential. Thus any differences between soil mapping units that are of little or no significance in management are eliminated by the grouping into capability units.

Survey procedures

Maps of land capability can be produced either by taking an existing detailed soil survey as the basis and collecting supplementary information, or by direct field survey of capability mapping units without bothering with the finer points of soil mapping. The first procedure is more common in settled, developed countries, the second in developing countries.

Land is allocated to capability classes on the basis of a **conversion table.** This shows, for each kind of limitation, the worst conditions that can be accepted within each class. For example, as a first approximation, soil erosion hazard is equated with slope angle. Taking into consideration local climate and, where available, farming experience, it might be decided that class I land should not exceed 1° slope, class II land 3°, class III land 6°, and so on. Similarly, effective soil depth might be decided as not less than 150 cm for class I, or 100 cm for class II. For every land characteristic regarded as a limitation, worst possible values for each of the eight land classes are decided. Some of these may be qualitatively expressed, e.g. flooding hazard as 'never', 'rare', 'infrequent', 'frequent', etc., although even approximate quantitative specifications ('less than once a year on average') are to be preferred where information is available.

It is apparent that erosion hazard is not adequately represented by slope angle alone; swelling clay soils can erode on 1°. The same kind of problem arises with other limitations. To cover such interactions it is necessary to resort to subdivisions in the conversion table. Thus soils might first be placed in three groups, e.g. sandy soils, loams and well structured clays, and swelling clays, with different critical slope angles allotted to each group. If the surveyor gives thought to possible interactions between individual land characteristics, such tables may become quite complex and secondary tables may be necessary. This is right and proper. Simplicity is desirable in the end-product of a survey but cannot be realistically expected in the process of interpretation.

Once the conversion table is drawn up, allocation of a given soil mapping unit to a capability class and subclass is routine. The unit is placed in whichever is the lowest class to which it is lowered by any limitation. If only one limitation causes it to be in that class, say excess water, then it belongs to the associated subclass, IIIw. If two limitations cause lowering to the same class, both are shown, e.g. IIIws.

Table 9.3 shows the conversion table in use in Malaŵi, in simplified form. Where set out in this way, the land class and subclass can be rapidly determined by a zig-zag method. Place a finger in the top left-hand box, i.e. class I, limitation number 1. Run it along to the right until the observed slope angle at the site is reached, say 3°; the site cannot then be higher than class III (locally CA). Keeping in this class, move down to the second limitation, evidence of past erosion. If such erosion is 'moderate' or 'nil' (as defined in detail in a secondary table), continue downwards to the third limitation; if it is 'severe', the land is irretrievably lowered to class IV. Continue in this way until the ninth limitation has been passed, when the final move downwards

Table 9.3 The Malawi system of land capability classification. Terms employed in limitations 2–5 and 9 are defined in subsidiary tables (not reproduced here).

	Limitation	A-Arable (AA)	B-Arable (BA)	C-Arable (CA)	D-Arable (DA)	Special Arable (SA)*	A-Non-arable (AN)	B-Non-arable (BN)	C-Non-arable (CN)	Wet (W)
Worst permissible value symbol in each class	1 slope (degrees)1	nil	2½	4½	6½	11	11	any	any	any
	2 past erosion	nil	moderate	moderate	severe	moderate	severe	severe	any	any
	3 wetness	nil	nil	short periods	considerable periods	nil	considerable periods	considerable periods	considerable periods	all or most of season
	4 surface hindrances (%)	10	10	25	50	10	50	50	any	any
	5 unfavourable surface conditions	porous	liable to capping	any	any	porous	liable to capping	any	any	any
Range of permissible values	slope (degrees)1	1	2½	2½ 6½	6½ 6½	11	6½ 11	11 any	any	any
	6 texture of top 20 cm	SCL-C	SL-HC	SCL-HC any SL-HC	SCL-HC SL-HC	SCL-HC	SL-HC SL-HC	any	any	any
	7 combinations of effective depth (cm)	90	90	50 25 50 25	25	50	50 90	25 50	any	any
......and......	8 upper subsoil texture	CL-C	SL-HC	SCL-HC any SL- HC SCL- HC CL- HC	any SCL-HC	SCL-HC	SL-HC SL-HC	any	any	any
	9 permeability within the profile	good	good–rapid	restricted–rapid	restricted–rapid	good	restricted–good	very restricted–rapid	any	any
Land capability class		A-Arable (AA)	B-Arable (BA)	C-Arable (CA)	D-Arable (DA)	Special Arable (SA)*	A-Non-arable (AN)	B-Non-arable (BN)	C-Non-arable (CN)	Wet (W)
USDA equivalent		I	II	III	IV	no equivalent	VI	VII	VIII	Vw

* The Special Arable class is restricted to areas with more than 1150 mm mean annual rainfall.

shows the capability class. Bifurcations occur from limitation 6 onwards.

Where there is a detailed soil survey in existence, it is possible to make a capability classification as a desk study but, except as a student exercise, this is undesirable. The purpose of the survey is not to produce a classification in the abstract but to make decisions about the kinds of use to which land can be put, and this is far better done in the field.

If a soil map exists, transfer it onto air photographs (if not already printed on them), take these into the field and by means of the conversion table allocate each soil mapping unit to a capability class. If the soil survey has been a good one it should not often be necessary to undertake the time-consuming process of surveying land class boundaries, although the rapidity with which slope angle varies may necessitate this.

If the land class indicated by the conversion table conflicts with what you judge to be its appropriate use and management, note down the details and ask a farmer and your senior co-evaluator to come to the site. If they agree, then the conversion table as applied to that region needs to be modified.

The alternative procedure, that of direct field survey, is perfectly satisfactory providing that land capability down to the subclass level is all that is wanted. As before, construction of a conversion table is the first step. By means of air photo-interpretation a substantial proportion of boundaries between class units, particularly those involving slope angle and drainage, can then be drawn in. Field observations are confined to determination of the critical limitations, e.g. effective soil depth, texture, without the need to identify soil series. As compared with soil survey at the same scale, this is a much quicker procedure. You cannot, however, map capability units in this way, since to do so requires identification of soil series and characterisation of their management responses.

Some countries have standard conversion tables, tested and modified by experience over the years, in which event the field surveyor can proceed straight to the mapping phase. Where no such table applicable to the country or region is in existence, the best way of compiling one is to start with an existing table from a similar agro-climatic zone. Go to an area with farming experience, try applying the table, and discuss the results with farmers. It will be found that the following modifications are necessary:

(a) Some land characteristics employed to determine capability classes in the system under test do not apply in your region; conversely, characteristics not included are of significance and need to be added.

(b) There are different interactions between characteristics, requiring the bifurcations or secondary tables to be changed.

(c) Almost certainly, the limiting values will not be in accord with local farming practice, and need to be changed. Two starting points are:

(i) place the lower limit of class I at the limit of what is regarded as really good land, and where even the local soil conservation service do not regard conservation measures as necessary

(ii) gather opinions on the worst possible land that can still be put to arable use; take the range of reasonable values offered and put this range as the lower limits of classes III and IV respectively.

The limit for class II is then put in by interpolation, and those for other classes by considering conditions for non-arable uses. There are no deep principles to be followed. Capability classification is an *ad hoc* system, relating farming experience to individual land characteristics as found in a particular physical environment and under prevailing local farming practices.

Thus two tasks of very different nature are needed to produce a land capability map: the drawing-up of a conversion table applicable to the region concerned, and mapping the distribution of capability units. These correspond respectively to the research and mapping phases of soil survey. The first is a task requiring much skill and judgement, knowledge of the interaction between environmental factors and, wherever possible, previous experience of local farmers. The second, the mapping phase, is by comparison fairly routine, and where appropriate can be placed in the hands of technical staff under professional supervision.

Using land capability classification

Farm planning

The purpose for which the system was devised, and to which it is best suited, is farm planning. A farmer has at his disposal a fixed area of land. He wishes to engage in one or more enterprises, e.g. grain crops, dairying, and choice of these is conditioned partly by the land available but more by the climate and market conditions. Each enterprise has certain land requirements; minimum areas may be needed for rotational arable, ley grass, permanent pasture, as well as farm service roads, buildings and possibly woodland. The capability map shows which land *can* be used for certain purposes, not which must be so used. Thus knowing that 80 ha of arable are needed, these can be blocked out from the higher land classes, perhaps adding on bits of class IV to make convenient field shapes.

Drawing up the farm plan can be regarded as the final stage in field survey. If it is for an existing farm, it is done in consultation with the farmer. If it is for new land settlement, the land use requirements must be assumed. The principal steps are as follows:

(1) decide upon the arable land
(2) add land for grazing, woodland, etc.
(3) if not already there, locate the central service point
(4) locate water supplies (wells, boreholes, channels, weirs)
(5) set out the farm service road system
(6) set out major conservation works (storm drains, waterways)
(7) identify in outline bunds or other soil conservation works which the farmer will construct himself.

This may be followed by discussion of land classes in relation to management, e.g. basic arable rotation(s), fertiliser needs, a stage that calls for additional information derived from soil survey. Detailed procedures lie beyond the scope of this book, and can be found in land use planning manuals (e.g. Shaxson *et al.* 1977, Department of Agriculture, Zambia 1977).

Whilst originally intended for large modern farms, of 100 ha and upwards, the system has been found of equal value in developing countries, where it is applied in three circumstances:

(a) On *individual farms,* usually of more progressive farmers who have asked for advice; there is scope for such planning even on farms of 10 ha.
(b) In *village land reorganisation;* the village land is first planned as a unit, then individual farm boundaries (or rights to use) are superimposed, ensuring that each management unit has a range of types of land.
(c) In *new land settlement;* requirements are specified, e.g. 6 ha arable, 4 ha dry-season grazing, etc. Prospective farm boundaries are then laid out, starting by finding the arable requirement and adding on blocks of other land. Requirements for individual crops, e.g. tobacco only on classes I and II land, can be taken into account.

Other supposed uses

Capability classification has, on occasion, been applied both in reconnaissance surveys for resource inventory and in project feasibility surveys. It is not well suited to either of these purposes. The omnibus nature of capability groupings and the arable bias of the system are not what is needed when weighing up ranching, forestry, irrigation, etc., against rainfed arable development. It may be useful for political and planning purposes to be able to make statements such as 'There are 32 500 ha of class I and II land in Western Province', but, if such information is called for, it can be derived as an office exercise from suitability maps for individual kinds of land use.

The other attempted use is in settled, developed countries where planning authorities need to know which is 'good agricultural land' in order to steer non-agricultural development away from it. Capability classification does not work well for this purpose either. Heavy, wet clays can be highly profitable under good pasture management, sands still more so under market gardening, yet neither are likely to make the highest capability classes. Economic suitability evaluation, made separately for each use and combined through money values, is better for the purpose.

Discussion

Features of land capability classification are that it attempts to provide a single-scale grading of land from 'best' to 'worst'; it assumes arable use to be the most desirable; it is strongly biased towards considerations of soil conservation; it is based on negative land features, the limitations; and it only takes economics into consideration as a background. The first three of these may be summarised by saying that this is essentially a grading of land for arable use.

The system is versatile, simple and easy to present. The versatility lies in the fact that it can be adapted to any physical environment, and to any level of farming technology. Jamaica, for example, is so mountainous that, to be realistic, far higher slope limits for arable land have to be specified than would be acceptable in most countries. The concept of limitations and its application via conversion tables calibrated by individual land characteristics, is simple in principle and where necessary allows it to be applied in the field by staff of technical level. The straightforward way in which the results can be presented is an important asset; by looking at the land classes and subclasses respectively, answers are given to the questions: 'How much good arable land is there, and where is it?' and 'Where are there problems of erosion, drainage, salinity, etc?'

It lends itself to local *ad hoc* modifications and, indeed, needs them if it is to work in practice. A nice neat conversion table, with all the values increasing logically, will never give results corresponding to farming judgement and practice. Good tables are those to which subdivisions and qualifications, e.g. 'sandy clay loam or heavier (sandy loam if rainfall exceeds 1200 mm)', have been added over the years. In Zambia, the arable land is first put into 'clays' or 'sandy soils', graded respectively into classes C1–C3 and S1–S4 ('S4 is used only for Barotse Sands'), and the non-arable land then assessed for grazing, as classes G1–G2, leaving the residuum available for woodlots.

The operation of the climatic limitation has always been found un-satisfactory. Crops vary widely in their tolerance of drought or other extremes, and so also does the degree of hazard which local farmers regard as acceptable. In the British system, *high* rainfall is treated as a limitation. If one assumes a certain crop, say maize, as the basis for the arable grading, then really good land for bullrush millet or other drought-resistant crop will be classed as non-arable. It is better to leave out the climatic limitation altogether, and handle it by working within a framework of agro-ecological zones.

Capability classification cannot distinguish between 'elite' soils, which have no limitations for general arable use, and 'unique' soils, those which are particularly suitable for certain specialised kinds of land use even though they may have limitations for the typical arable use of the area. Unique soils require specialised management, but under such management they can sometimes be more profitable than soils which would be placed in a higher capability class. The value of sandy soils for market gardening is an example; they are easily tilled in all weather conditions, warm up early in spring, but are likely to need supplementary irrigation.

The main disadvantage is the failure to classify land adequately for uses other than arable. Ranchers and foresters do not like being told they are restricted to classes V–VIII, nor is the differentiation between these at all adequate for their purposes. Capability classification should be used for the purpose for which it was designed, farm planning, for which it has stood the test of time.

Further reading

Klingebiel and Montgomery (1961) is the fundamental text; Bibby and Mackney (1969), Shaxson *et al.* (1977), Department of Agriculture, Zambia (1977), Thomas *et al.* (1976), Woode (1981).

Land Suitability Evaluation

Land suitability evaluation is the process of assessing the suitability of land for specified kinds of use. These may be major kinds of land use, such as rainfed agriculture, livestock production, forestry, etc.; or land utilisation types described in more detail, for example rainfed arable farming based on groundnuts and sorghum, irrigated rice production, or softwood plantations of Douglas fir. Suitability is assessed, classified and presented separately for each kind of use.

There is nothing new about the principle of suitability evaluation. From the earliest times, farmers have been deciding which crops are best for the land that they possess or, as settlers, where there is to be found land suited to the crops they wish to grow. This must often have been a process of trial and error; one may suppose, for example, that the well defined zones in which tea plantations occur were not found without failures in areas which proved to lie outside the climatic limits of the crop. In the era of modern planning it has always been recognised that irrigated agriculture has specialised land requirements calling for evaluation directed at that use. But evaluation procedures for other kinds of land use, apart from locally devised *ad hoc* methods, were developed only quite recently; as late as 1961 it was still necessary in a leading international journal to make the point that land cannot simply be graded on a scale from 'best' to 'worst', irrespective of the kind of use (Gibbons 1961).

Surveys in developing countries revealed shortcomings in land capability classification, and procedures were devised for comparing suitabilities of land for different uses. Examples are a system for use in New Guinea which provided separate suitability ratings for annual crops, tree crops, improved pastures and swamp rice production (Haantjens 1965b), and a *Manual of multipurpose land classification* developed for Iran (Mahler 1970). The initiative for developing some measure of standardisation of terminology and procedures was taken by the FAO through a series of international discussions from 1970 onwards, and the results are incorporated in *A framework for land evaluation* (FAO 1976). The outline which follows is based upon this publication, but includes additional details about evaluation procedures for specific crops and land utilisation types.

The results of a land evaluation survey are threefold as now discussed.

Descriptions of land utilisation types. These amplify their nature, in a greater or lesser degree of detail according to the intensity and purposes of the survey; thus the description of 'rainfed arable farming based on groundnuts and sorghum' might include approximate farm size, crop varieties, levels of fertilisers and other inputs, extent of mechanisation, etc.

Suitability maps. These show the suitabilities of each land mapping unit for each defined kind of land use. They might show on the one hand that a particular mapped area of land is highly suitable for softwood plantations, moderately suitable for cattle ranching, but not suitable for groundnut–sorghum farming; and on the other, that some land units are highly suitable for groundnut–sorghum farming, some moderately or marginally suitable, and others not suitable for that use. Such data can be presented either as a single map with a tabular legend or as a series of individual suitability maps (see Table 10.10 and Fig. 10.2, pp. 181–2).

Statements of the consequences, favourable and unfavourable, of applying each kind of land use to each area of land. These would include, for example, data such as estimated crop yields, meat production, or mean annual increments of timber; kinds and amounts of inputs required, such as fertilisers, labour, machinery; assessments of environmental impact and of social consequences; and in economic evaluation, estimated costs, benefits and profits. For land assessed as not suitable for a given use, reasons for this are given.

These results enable the organisation commissioning the survey to make choices. Information is provided on what farming systems or other kinds of land use are possible within the surveyed area, where the best land for each use occurs, and what are the likely consequences of the use. Other considerations lying outside the range of the evaluation may influence the final development decisions, but even if these should overrule the mapped suitabilities, then development will be undertaken with some knowledge of the likely outcome.

Structure of the classification

There are four categories or levels of classification: land suitability orders, classes, subclasses and units (Table 10.1). These suitability classes are assessed separately for each kind of land use under consideration, with respect to each land mapping unit in the survey area. The same classes are applied to qualitative, quantitative or economic land evaluation, and to assessment of current or potential land suitability (pp. 119–21).

Table 10.1 Structure of land suitability classification.

Order	Category Class	Subclass	Unit
S, suitable——————————→	S1 S2————————→ S3 etc.	S2m S2e————————→ S2me etc.	S2e–1 S2e–2 etc.
phase: Sc, conditionally suitable	Sc2	Sc2m	
N, not suitable	N1————————→ N2	N1m N1e etc.	

Definitions

Suitability orders

order S, suitable — Land on which sustained use of the kind under consideration is expected to yield benefits which justify the inputs, without unacceptable risk of damage to land resources

order N, not suitable — Land which has qualities that preclude sustained use of the kind under consideration

Suitability classes

class S1, highly suitable — Land having no significant limitations to sustained application of a given use, or only minor limitations that will not significantly reduce productivity or benefits and will not raise inputs above an acceptable level

class S2, moderately suitable — Land having limitations which in aggregate are moderately severe for sustained application of a given use; the limitations will reduce productivity or benefits and increase required inputs to the extent that the overall advantage to be gained from the use, although still attractive, will be appreciably inferior to that expected on class S1 land

class S3, marginally suitable — Land having limitations which in aggregate are severe for sustained application of a given use and will so reduce productivity or benefits, or increase required inputs, that this expenditure will be only marginally justified

class N1, currently not suitable — Land having limitations which may be surmountable in time but which cannot be corrected with existing knowledge at currently acceptable cost; the limitations are so severe as to preclude successful sustained use of the land in the given manner

class N2, permanently not suitable — Land having limitations which appear so severe as to preclude any possibilities of successful sustained use of the land in the given manner

NR, not relevant — Land which has not been assessed for a given use, because the application of the use to that area is precluded by the initial assumptions of the evaluation

Suitability orders. These separate land assessed as 'suitable' (S) from that which is 'not suitable' (N) for the use under consideration. The three main reasons why land may be classed as not suitable are that the proposed use is technically impracticable, e.g. cultivating very thin or rocky soils; is environmentally undesirable, e.g. would lead to severe soil erosion; or is economically unprofitable, the income from estimated production being less than the cost of the required inputs.

Suitability classes. These indicate degrees of suitability. Within the order 'suitable' the three classes, 'highly', 'moderately' and 'marginally' suitable, are defined in relative terms. The S1/S2 boundary, or lower limit of highly suitable land, should be set at the point where conditions have become clearly less than optimal: crop yields or other forms of production are slightly but definitely lowered, or inputs to counteract the effects of a limitation become needed. Highly suitable land is not 'perfect' land for the use in question, but could be described as 'the best that might reasonably be hoped for'. The S2/S3 boundary, dividing moderately from marginally suitable land, should separate land which, whilst it has some limitations, is quite clearly suited to the use, from land which is still considered to be suited to the use but only by a small technical, economic or environmental 'safety margin'. Note, however, that marginally suitable land lies wholly within the order suitable and is not intended to straddle the border with 'not suitable' land.

Of the two classes within the order 'not suitable', N1, indicating 'currently not suitable', refers to land on which the use under consideration is technically possible but not economic; at present prices the cost of inputs needed to overcome the limitations would exceed the cost of production. Changes in the relative prices of the product and inputs, or advances in technology, e.g. new drought-resistant crop varieties, can result in upgrading of N1 land. N2, indicating 'permanently not suitable', is applied to land on which it is unlikely that any foreseeable change in technical or economic conditions would render it viable for the use. The N2 class is widely applied to steep slopes, swamps, rock outcrops and arid areas.

The boundary between S3 and N1 is defined in economic terms, and is variable with time, according to changes in relative costs and prices. That between N1 and N2 is a physical boundary and relatively permanent. Thus the large relative rise in the price of coffee in the mid-1970s led to areas of land formerly classed as N1 being upgraded into S3. A rise in fertiliser prices without a corresponding increase in the market price of crops could lead to downgrading of land from S3 to N1 or from S2 to S3.

A phase of 'conditionally suitable' can be applied in cases where land is not suitable for a given use in its present condition but might be made suitable by some local modification to the land or to management practices. The *Framework for land evaluation* (FAO 1976 p. 21) lays down stipulations designed to avoid excessive use of this device. As conditional suitability is confusing to users of maps, it is better to avoid it entirely if possible.

The symbol NR, indicating 'not relevant', is used in maps and tables where the basic assumptions of the evaluation are such that there is no question of certain areas of land being placed under the given use. If, for example, it has been made clear that farmers will not be turned off their land, then there is no purpose in assessing the suitability for a national park or livestock ranch on land which is already densely settled. Provided such basic assumptions have been made clear, this device can be used extensively, with considerable saving of survey time and expense.

Suitability subclasses. Suitability subclasses indicate kinds of limitations, e.g. moisture deficiency, erosion hazard. They are indicated by lowercase letters placed after the class symbol, e.g. S2m, S2e. There are no subclasses to S1. There is no limit to the number of subclass symbols that may be employed in a particular survey. These symbols are not at present standardised, but 'm' and 'e' as defined above, plus 'd' for drainage limitations and 'n' for soil nutrient deficiencies might usefully be adopted for regular use.

Suitability units. These are divisions of subclasses that differ from each other in detailed aspects of their production characteristics or management requirements. They are numbered successively, e.g. S2d-1, S2d-2. Thus there might be two types of land assigned to S2 on grounds of drainage, on one of which it was better to counteract this limitation by tile drains and on the other by open ditches. The definition is very similar to that of capability units in land capability classification; land in a single suitability unit has similar productive potential and requires similar management practices. Units are mainly used in surveys at the detailed or farm planning scale; at smaller scales the classification is normally only to subclass level.

For the common case of land evaluation for specific crops under rainfed agriculture, supplementary definitions of suitability classes have been devised (Table 10.2). These are in terms of two parallel sets of criteria: the amount by which crop yields will be reduced in the absence of inputs specific to a land quality or limitation, and the inputs or special management practices needed to overcome a limitation. There are at present very few land qualities for which the quantitative information needed to apply these criteria precisely is available: salinity tolerances of crops are an exception, for which data from controlled experimental conditions are available (Richards 1954, FAO 1979a pp. 24–5).

Table 10.2 Supplementary definitions of suitability classes employed for assessment in terms of individual land qualities.

Class	Definition in terms of yields:	Definition in terms of inputs:
	expected crop yields, as a percentage* of yields under optimal conditions, in the absence of inputs specific to the land quality considered	inputs or management practices, specific to the land quality considered, necessary to achieve yields of >80% of those under optimal conditions
S1, highly suitable	>80%	none
S2, moderately suitable	40–80%	inputs needed, which are likely to be both practicable and economic
S3, marginally suitable	20–40%	inputs needed, which are practicable but only economic under favourable circumstances
N, not suitable	<20%	limitation can rarely or never be overcome by inputs or management practices

*The crop yield percentages are approximate guidelines only, and are conceived in terms of Third World conditions; for commercial agriculture, a substantially lesser yield reduction may render production uneconomic and thus land 'not suitable'.

Carrying out a land suitability evaluation survey

The sequence of activities in conducting a suitability evaluation is shown in simplified schematic form in Figure 10.1 and in more detail in Table 10.3. As with a soil survey, the evaluation begins with *initial consultations* between those commissioning the survey and those responsible for its execution. The first need is to establish the objectives of the evaluation. The data already available are reviewed, and any assumptions which are to be made are discussed and agreed upon, for example, the extent to which existing rights of land users are to be taken into account. This leads to *planning the evaluation*.

The *field survey* consists of two parallel sets of activities: studies directed towards the identification and description of land use, and surveys of the available resources of the land. It is fundamental to suitability evaluation that consideration of the various possible uses of the land is given equal attention to that given to the basic surveys of soil, landforms, climate, etc., and is studied more or less at the same time. In theory, if not always in practice, as much survey effort is devoted to finding the best land management practices for each area as is devoted to soil and other resource surveys.

Taking first the activities directed towards land use, the *kinds of land use* are defined and described. These will be set first by the objectives of the survey and secondly by the general physical nature of the area. The

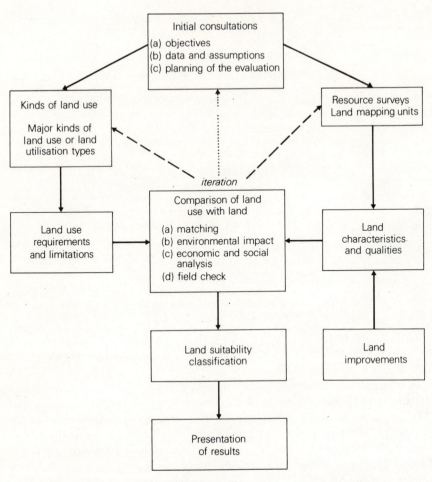

Figure 10.1 Schematic representation of activities in land evaluation.

kinds of land use are initially defined in very general terms, e.g. coffee farming, dairying, and are amplified and refined as the survey proceeds. Description of the kinds of use is followed by determination of the *land use requirements and limitations*; these are the climatic, moisture, soil, slope and other requirements for each kind of use.

Simultaneously, the basic *natural resource surveys* are commenced, leading to production of the maps and other resource data on which the evaluation is based; these could include a land systems or soil–landform map, climatic data, vegetation types or other mapping units appropriate to the purposes of the survey. For each of these land mapping units the relevant *land qualities and characteristics* to be used in assessing suitability

Table 10.3   Procedures in land evaluation.

Phase	Activities related to land use	General activities	Activities related to land
		Initial consultations objectives; assumptions	
pre-field or planning phase	land utilisation types to be considered; data needed for assessment for land utilisation types	context of the study area; data required	available data on land
		Planning of the evaluation planning of surveys; staff and timing; models, problem/solution	
field survey phase	Kinds of land use study of present and possible future land utilisation types, including inputs, produce and their relations requirements and limitations of land utilisation types	interim reviews including matching	Surveys of land basic surveys of resources; land mapping units; land characteristics and qualities; land improvements
		Comparison of land use with land matching; environmental impact assessment; economic and social analysis; field check	
		Review of interim results (discussions with principals)	
	(modifications to land utilisation types if necessary)		(additional data collection if necessary)
		final stage of matching	
post-field or results phase	land utilisation types: descriptions, input/produce relations	Land suitability classification Preparation of results maps of land suitability; report; cartography and printing; presentation of results	(maps and accounts of basic resources)
post-evaluation	applications of the results to land use planning and management		

are measured or estimated. Consideration is then given to *land improvements*, ways in which the existing land qualities can be modified so as to meet more closely the requirements of the uses.

The information collected by the resource surveys is that likely to be needed to assess suitability for the provisionally defined land utilisation types. Thus, if it is clear that livestock production will be important, pasture resource surveys will be included. As the study progresses, frequent contacts are maintained between these two sets of activities, so that by a process of iteration, or successive refinement, the specifications of kinds of land use and their requirements are repeatedly modified in the light of information gained from surveys of the land. Iteration may include modifying the specified inputs or in other ways revising the descriptions of land utilisation types, or modifying the land improvements. It can occasionally happen that the original objectives of the study are shown to be unattainable, e.g. a survey for smallholder tea production in a region which proves to have little land suited to this purpose; in this case the iteration process includes reference back to the governmental or other organisation which requested the survey and modification of the objectives.

The two sets of activities are brought together in the *comparison of land use with land*. The first step is that of matching, in which the requirements of the various kinds of use are compared with the qualities of the land. This matching procedure is followed by economic and social analysis and a study of environmental impact. The comparison should include a *field check*, in which the areas provisionally classified as suitable for various uses are reviewed in the field by farmers, foresters, etc, together with those responsible for the classification.

The *land suitability classification* is then finalised, having been proceeding by successive approximations through the later parts of the survey. This is followed by *presentation of results*, including map preparation and report writing.

The essence of these procedures is the comparison between the qualities of the land and the requirements of the various kinds of use to which it might be suited. This is a major difference from the earlier approach to land evaluation, in which the resource surveys were completed first, and the resulting soil and other maps regarded as a fixed basis on which studies of land potential were built.

Initial consultations

Matters to be discussed during the initial consultations between client and surveyor are the objectives of the evaluation, basic assumptions or constraints, the information that will be required to achieve the objectives, and the planning of the evaluation.

The possible *objectives* can be grouped on a similar basis as for soil surveys: multi-purpose and special-purpose. A general-purpose land evaluation assesses the suitability of an area for all relevant forms of use. These include both existing uses and new ones, for example the introduction of new crops. At a reconnaissance scale such a survey may be made in terms of major kinds of land use, but usually it is better to amplify these at least to a limited degree into land utilisation types. By no means all the kinds of use will be given at the start of the survey, since one of the aims of a multi-purpose evaluation is to identify, investigate and describe potential new uses.

In a special-purpose evaluation the kinds of land use to be considered are restricted and at least partly stated in the objectives. Examples in the context of developing countries are to find areas suitable to smallholder tea production, to evaluate suitability for mechanised government food farms, or to evaluate rangeland as a basis for introducing some form of control on grazing. Examples from developed, settled countries might be to compare suitabilities of upland areas for either hill sheep farming or forestry plantations, or to compare alternative sites for a recreation park in an urban fringe zone.

The objective need not always be to produce maps showing discrete suitability classes. A survey aimed at extending, say, banana production to new areas could be presented simply in terms of estimated yields and production costs for each land mapping unit. The comparison of sites for a recreation park could present the consequences, favourable and unfavourable, of each alternative, without attempting a synthesis into suitability classes, since the final decision will in any case involve considerations other than those of land suitability.

The objectives will further determine whether the evaluation is to be one of current land suitability, or potential suitability in the event of some major land improvement being completed, e.g. a regional drainage scheme. The survey team will discuss with the clients whether the evaluation is to be in qualitative, quantitative physical or economic terms, and also the relative weighting they wish to be assigned to different criteria: return on capital invested, production per unit area in economic terms, income per capita, food production, settlement density, environmental impact, social effects, political consequences, etc.

The *data* and *assumptions* on which the evaluation is to be based are also clarified during these discussions. The boundaries of the area to be surveyed, and whether these boundaries may or may not be modified in the light of early findings of the study, are decided. An important decision is whether location and accessibility are to be taken into account, and if so in what manner. It is also necessary to be clear about the social, institutional and political constraints which underlie land use planning in the area. A common example is whether the rights of existing owners or land users are inviolate or can resettlement (developing countries) or compulsory purchase orders (developed countries) be considered; this can greatly affect the land areas and kinds of use which are not assessed but mapped as 'not relevant' because change in use is precluded. The descriptions of land utilisation types are also affected by the social and political context, e.g. whether farms are to be operated individually, communally or by the state.

The *planning of the evaluation* follows similar lines as that outlined for soil survey in Chapter 2 insofar as it is a logistic exercise, involving staffing, times taken for the different kinds of surveys, transport and accommodation, scheduling of the various activities, and costs. The differences are, first, that the range of basic surveys may extend more widely beyond landforms and soils, e.g. to include forest inventory, pasture resource survey or other vegetation studies. Secondly, parallel to the resource surveys are the studies of land utilisation types; on a large team project these will be carried out by agronomists, livestock production specialists, foresters, etc., although in a small survey some of this information may be collected by the soil surveyors. Where the evaluation is to be in economic terms, a third stream of economic data collection has to be added. To schedule these activities so that the various kinds of information come together at the right time requires careful planning and a clear view in advance of what will be needed and in what form. The circumstances of different surveys vary so widely that no generally applicable sequence of activities can be laid down; any necessary soil survey, however, should be started early, simply because it takes longer to complete.

Owing to the interaction between different activities in land evaluation, it is desirable for as many as possible of the survey team to be there for as much time as possible. This principle conflicts with the need to reduce costs by phased employment of specialist staff. As a minimum, at least one soil surveyor, one agronomist and one economist, in addition to the project manager, should be there from start to finish of the survey.

As a means of synthesising the initial discussions, it is useful at this stage to construct *models of the problem* and *its proposed solution*. In these models, the objectives as outlined by the client are clarified and elaborated; the kinds of information that will be required to achieve these objectives are listed, and an estimate made of the methods of survey, time and cost needed to obtain that information; and specimen results of the evaluation are presented in dummy form, i.e. using assumed data. In effect the survey team says to the client: 'Given that this is what you wish to know, here is how we propose to achieve it and this is what the results will look like; will results of this kind satisfactorily achieve your objectives?'

Land utilisation types

In the procedures of land evaluation, land utilisation types play a balancing role to that of land mapping units. In some surveys, as much effort is devoted to the details of land utilisation types as that directed towards resource surveys; a corresponding amount of space in the survey report may be taken up by descriptions of the land utilisation types.

In practice, the relative emphasis varies and there are two distinct situations. In the first, the land utilisation types are described in only a generalised manner, and are taken as fixed early in the survey. For example, smallholder coffee production or mechanised food farms based on maize might be identified as possible uses in some part of the area, and the field survey effort would be directed towards evaluating land suitability for these generalised kinds of use. This practice is appropriate for surveys at reconnaissance scales, designed for resource inventory and project location. In the most highly generalised case, evaluation is for major kinds of land use.

In the second situation, appropriate for semi-detailed and detailed scale surveys, the land utilisation types are described in detail, are subject to successive refinement in the course of the study, and these descriptions in themselves form a major output of the evaluation. At the start of the survey, the land utilisation types are identified in a provisional and generalised manner. As the survey proceeds they are progressively refined, often by the addition of quantitative detail. The information used to achieve this refinement is drawn from studies of agriculture, livestock production, forestry, farm system studies and economic studies as appropriate.

A further method of modifying the land utilisation types is through the repeated process of comparison with the land qualities as found by resource survey. Suppose, for example, that mechanised food farms based on maize were initially identified as a likely use. As the resource survey progressed, it might become apparent that areas well suited to mechanised cereal production were very limited in extent; it could then be reconsidered whether the same objective, that of food surplus production, could be achieved by a more labour-intensive farming system based on ox-drawn implements. Alternatively, if much of the area were shown to have a substantial drought hazard for maize, production systems based on drought-resistant crops could be formulated. These examples involve rather drastic modifications, but the same can apply to details of farming systems. Suppose smallholder rubber production on 3 ha plots had provisionally been identified. Yield estimates based on soil survey might show that this holding size was insufficient to meet the target farm income for the area; if labour constraints permitted, the holding size could be increased, with consequential modifications to other details of this land utilisation type.

The land utilisation types employed can include those already practised in the study area, those not present in the area but practised in other parts of the country, and those not currently found in the country but being considered for introduction. In the first two cases, descriptions will be based initially on farm system or other studies of existing practices. In developing countries, two land utilisation types based on the same form of production will often be given, an 'unimproved' type based on existing practices and an improved type synthesised from experimental data, recommendations of agricultural advisory services and the practices of more advanced farmers.

The purposes of land utilisation type descriptions are twofold. In the first place, they form an output from the evaluation in their own right. The various possible uses have been investigated, modified and elaborated in the light of environmental, economic and other circumstances of the area. Their descriptions form a starting point for implementation, whether by project planning or other means of initiation or through advisory services. The second purpose is that land utilisation type descriptions are the basis for determining the requirements and limitations of the uses. These could include, for example, the ecological requirements of each of the crops in a farming system, land requirements for mechanisation, or a specified minimum amount of dry-season grazing land. Not every detail of the land utilisation type description has implications for land requirements, but many have direct or indirect implications.

The *physical, economic and social setting* forms a background to all the land utilisation types of an area. To avoid repetition, this is described at the outset. It includes such information as the broad climatic zone, major landform region, density of settlement, general levels of income, and the social and political setting of the country, e.g. private freehold land ownership, communal village farming, state-controlled farming. The setting includes the distinctions between developed and developing economies and between settled and empty areas, which are fundamental to land use planning (p. 4). Sometimes there will be two or more distinct economic and social settings, corresponding to sectors of the economy, e.g. traditional village agriculture and estate agriculture.

The following outline method of description can be used for the description of most agricultural land utilisation types and for forestry and horticulture. Modifications in detail are needed as between rainfed agriculture, irrigated agriculture, livestock systems and forestry. For such distinctive uses as national parks, water catchment/conservation areas, etc., more substantial modifications will be needed. The attributes for description are listed below, and an example is given in Table 10.4.

Produce. This includes goods (e.g. kinds of crops, meat, dairy products, timber) and services or other intangible benefits (e.g. recreational facilities, wildlife conservation, regulation of river flow).

Market orientation. This can be classed as subsistence, subsistence with subsidiary commercial, commercial with subsidiary subsistence, or commercial production. Types classed as subsistence may include cash sales of up to 20% total production, and conversely commercial production may include up to 20% subsistence.

Capital intensity. This is described qualitatively as high, medium or low capital intensity; quantitatively, give capital investment per hectare and recurrent annual costs per hectare.

Labour intensity. This is described qualitatively as high, medium or low labour intensity. It is often the converse of capital intensity. Quantitatively, give labour in man-months per hectare.

Technical knowledge and attitudes. In many developed countries this may be taken for granted and listed under the setting. In the developing world, levels of literacy, general education, agricultural education and skills, and receptiveness to innovation can be important differentiating features of land utilisation types.

Power. The main distinctions are between production largely or entirely by human labour, by animal power in conjunction with human labour, and by tractors and other fuel-driven machinery. Quantitatively, it is possible to convert all power inputs into joules per hectare and to express them as percentages of man, animal and machine power (Pimental and Pimental 1979).

Mechanisation and implements. The basic distinctions are between fully mechanised farming or other production, various forms of partly mechanised production including intermediate technology, and non-mechanised production. Give machinery or implements used for the main operations, e.g. cultivations, sowing, weeding, harvesting, farm transport.

Size and configuration of land holdings. Give range of areas of typical farms, ranches, forest plantations, etc., in hectares. Indicate if holdings are other than single blocks of normal shape, e.g. if fragmented, or in linear strips from interfluve crest to valley floor.

Land tenure. This is the legal or customary manner in which ownership or rights to use of land are held. The following is a broad classification, which will need to be amplified with details of local practices.

(a) *Private ownership* (freehold): (i) family farm, private estate, ranch, woodland, etc.; (ii) corporately owned estate, ranch, woodland, etc.
(b) *Tenancy:* (i) cash rent tenancy; (ii) labour tenancy; (iii) sharecropping.

Table 10.4   Example of the description of a land utilisation type.

Large-scale irrigated sugar cane farming, Ethiopia

Major kind of land use. Irrigated agriculture: field perennial crops.

Summary. Irrigated cropping of sugar cane by state-operated commercial farms of greater than 500 ha; high capital intensity, medium labour intensity, motor-driven machinery supplemented by manual labour; an advanced technology farming system with a high level of inputs.

Setting. This use is appropriate for alluvial floors of the Awash and other larger rivers at 400–1200 m altitude. These areas have a semi-arid to savanna climate (Köppen BShw to Aw) with mean annual rainfall of 300 to 650 mm. The land is naturally thorn scrub, used for nomadic grazing. Under irrigation, sugar cane can be grown on a wide range of soil types, each requiring special management practices. Initiation of this kind of development requires high initial investment, and the subsequent level of returns must be sufficient to pay off the amortisation costs. Skilled engineering studies and design are essential, coupled with careful land selection.

Description

Produce. Sugar cane *(Saccharum officinarum)* grown entirely under irrigation.

Market orientation. 100% commercial production.

Capital intensity. High capital intensity. Capital investment on farms exceeds Birr 1000 (£250) per hectare. Recurrent costs exceed Birr 200 (£50) per hectare.

Labour intensity. Medium labour intensity, 0.25–2.5 man-months per hectare per year. Whilst some operations are mechanised, labour-intensive methods are used for planting and cane cutting.

Technical knowledge and attitudes. Farms are operated by managers and professional staff with degree or diploma-level agricultural education. Technical and supervisory staff are required, plus moderately large numbers of both semi-skilled and unskilled labour.

Power. Motor-driven machinery, supplemented by manual labour.

Mechanisation and implements. Operations carried out by machinery include land preparation, ridging, fertiliser and insecticide applications and removal of the harvested crop from fields. Manual operations include planting, weeding with hand hoes and cane cutting with machetes.

Size and configuration of land holdings. Large farms in excess of 500 ha, laid out in regularly shaped blocks, bounded by sloping 'not suitable' (N2) land.

Land tenure. State farms, owned and operated as government enterprises.

Infrastructure requirements. Ready access to processing factory, preferably on farm site. Supply of improved varieties of plant material, access to specialist services including agronomy, soil science, entomology. Good road transport essential.

Material inputs. High level of inputs. Modern methods with advanced technology and large capital resources. Crop varieties: improved high-yielding varieties as selected for low–medium altitudes in Ethiopia. Fertilisers applied near to levels of maximum economic return. Sugar cane has a high requirement for N and K but relatively low P; approximate applications of

---

(c) *Communal ownership:* (i) cooperative (collective) farming; (ii) village land with rights to cultivate; (iii) common land (arable, grazing or woodland).

(d) *State ownership:* (i) state farm, ranch; (ii) forest reserve.

Infrastructure requirements. These include, for example, access to processing factories, sawmills, special advisory services (e.g. entomology). The

Table 10.4 (contd)

elements are N 100–200 kg ha^{-1}, P 20–90 kg ha^{-1}, K 125–160 kg ha^{-1}, for a 100 t ha^{-1} yield. Levels of N increased with ratoon crops to encourage vegetative growth. Heavy soils can be improved by mill waste organic matter. Crop protection: in soils with pH greater than 8.0 protect against ratoon stunting disease. Possible nematode problem on sandy soils.

Water inputs and practices. A carefully controlled irrigation system based on pumping from river. Water applications by furrow and siphon. During vegetative growth apply approximately 1500 m^3 ha^{-1} at 21 day intervals on soils with high available water capacity, smaller amounts at 8 day intervals on sandy soils. During establishment, frequent light irrigations; during stem elongation, increase depth; during ripening, increase intervals between applications until these are stopped to bring crop to maturity.

Cropping characteristics. Farming system based on medium-term field perennial crop with life of 3–8 years depending on land suitability. Cultivation factor and cropping index both exceed 70%. No crop rotation. Period from planting to first harvest 15–18 months. Harvests from ratoon crops continue for up to 3–8 years. Frequency of harvesting and number of ratoons which can be harvested before replanting becomes necessary are both higher on highly suitable (S1) soils than on moderately suitable (S2) soils.

Livestock characteristics. No livestock.

Cultivation practices. Land preparation: ploughing and ridging; row spacing 1.1–1.4 m, number of setts 21 000–35 000 per hectare. Setts planted in furrows and ridged up after 3 months. Soil conservation measures are not required on the level land. Fertiliser applications: apply total P and K in furrows at planting, N within 3 months of planting. Harvesting: burn crop before harvesting to facilitate cutting and removal of leaves for processing. Cut by hand. Transport stem rapidly to processing factory to minimise loss in sucrose content. Salinisation hazard: ensure adequate drainage and include a leaching requirement in water application, particularly in more arid climates or where incipient salt accumulation is detected.

Yields and production. Under good management, yield of first crop 100–175 t ha^{-1} cane with 10–16% recoverable sucrose. Yields decline with successive ratoon crops. Allowing for yield decline and soil rest and replanting period, production will average at least 50 000 t cane per year from a 500 ha farm.

Economic information (£/ha yr)

fixed costs	40 (including amortisation of capital)
variable costs	50–70, lower on S1 than on S2 land
value of production	120–150, higher on S1 than on S2 land
gross margin	50–100
net farm income	10–60
income levels	not applicable

For a capital-intensive land utilisation type of this kind, such summary data are only indicative of approximate levels of costs and returns.

degree of importance of access to good roads varies between different production systems, e.g. high for sugar cane, lower for cattle ranching.

Material inputs. For generalised descriptive purposes, three levels of inputs may be used, defined in terms of arable farming as follows:

(a) *Low inputs:* traditional methods of farming; no use of artificial fertilisers or transported organic manure.
(b) *Intermediate inputs:* methods practised by farmers who follow the advice of agricultural extension services but who have limited technical knowledge and/or capital resources; improved agricultural techniques; fertilisers at levels of the order of 50–100 kg ha^{-1} (combined weight of nutrients expressed as elements) and/or practicable amounts of organic manures.
(c) *High inputs:* modern methods with advanced technology and high capital resources; fertilisers at levels of maximum economic return; chemical weed and pest control; adequate soil conservation measures.

The detailed description of inputs to rainfed agricultural systems includes crop varieties, types and amounts of fertilisers, organic manures and composts, and pesticides or other crop protection inputs. Modifications for livestock production and forestry are apparent.

Water inputs and practices. These are applicable primarily to irrigated agriculture, but also to rainfed systems that employ supplementary irrigation. Amounts of water, methods of supply, distribution and application, and timing of applications all need to be given.

Cropping characteristics. For arable systems based on annual crops, the relative frequency of cultivation compared with fallow, grass ley or other soil rest periods, the number of crops per year, and the crop rotations are fundamental characteristics. The **cultivation factor** R is the number of years under cultivation as a percentage of the total cultivation/non-cultivation cycle, given by

$$R(\%) = \frac{A}{A+F+L} \times 100$$

where R is the cultivation factor, A is the number of years of arable use (i.e. in which at least one crop is taken), F is the number of years of fallow and L is the number of years of ley or other non-arable use. Systems with $R<30\%$ are described as shifting cultivation, $R=30–70\%$ as semi-permanent cultivation and $R>70\%$ as permanent cultivation (Ruthenberg 1980, FAO 1974b). The **cropping index** C is the number of crops harvested in relation to years in the cropping cycle, given as a percentage. Where there is no multiple cropping, the cropping index is identical with the cultivation index. Where double or triple cropping is practised, the cropping index rises above 100%. **Crop rotations** are described by giving the basic arable rotation, e.g. tobacco–maize–groundnuts–maize–4 years' grass/legume ley. Areas cropped for a typical holding are given, and systems of mixed cropping and intercropping described.

Livestock characteristics. Corresponding to the cropping characteristics, the fundamental descriptive features for livestock production systems are the types and numbers of livestock, the livestock intensity, and the degree, if any, of nomadism. The **livestock intensity** is the number of livestock units per square kilometre of grazing land. As defined in a land utilisation type, it must not exceed the carrying capacity as determined by resource surveys. Where present, livestock systems may be classified as total nomadism, semi-nomadism or transhumance (for definition, see Ruthenburg 1980). Where not specified, non-nomadic livestock practices may be tacitly assumed. This descriptive heading can also be used for the livestock component of mixed or predominantly arable farming.

Cultivation practices. In detailed surveys, these can be given at some length, including the following:

(a) land preparation, including clearance;
(b) cultivations;
(c) planting practices, including nurseries, transplanting, timing of planting;
(d) fertiliser application: timing and methods of application;
(e) weeding: timing, methods;
(f) crop protection practices, e.g. spraying;
(g) harvesting; for perennials, including frequency and timing;
(h) processing.

Livestock production practices, Forestry production practices. These involve equivalent technical details to those for cultivation practices, given for systems based on livestock or forestry and, where of sufficient importance, for the livestock component and woodlots of arable systems.

Yields and production. The estimated amounts of crops, meat, dairy products, timber or other produce may be expressed both as production per unit area and as production for a typical farm or other management unit. For crops, this will be in terms of crop yields per hectare and production from a farm of specified cultivated area, the latter taking into account cultivation intensity and cropping intensity. For livestock production, meat and/or milk output in kilograms per hectare is given; for forestry, give estimated mean annual increments of timber in cubic metres per hectare.

It is not strictly possible to estimate yields or other production for a land utilisation type in isolation, but only in relation to a given land mapping unit. Since crop yields can rarely be estimated at all precisely, a convenient method is to give estimated yields for S1, S2 and perhaps S3 land, and possibly also in relation to different levels of fertiliser inputs, for example as follows:

	Fertiliser input kg ha^{-1}	Estimated yield kg ha^{-1}
S1 land	200	5000–7000
	100	4000–5000
S2 land	200	3000–5000
	etc.	

Economic information. For economic land classification, the economics of farming systems will be assessed in detail. This is discussed further in Chapter 11. A certain amount of basic economic information is, however, an essential part of the description of a land utilisation type. The main parameters to be estimated are:

(a) *fixed costs:* farm overheads and other costs which cannot be attributed to a specific crop;
(b) *variable costs:* costs attributable to the cultivation of a specific crop;
(c) *value of production;*
(d) *gross margin:* the value of output (yield×price) minus the variable costs;
(e) *net farm income:* the total gross margin for all crops, minus the fixed costs;
(f) *income levels:* approximate income per capita of the farming population.

Natural resource surveys

There are two main functions of the basic natural resource surveys in land evaluation: to divide the study area into a number of relatively homogeneous units, and to provide the information necessary to evaluate the suitability of each of these units for the kinds of land use under consideration. Thus the products of the resource surveys are, first, one or more maps showing land mapping units, e.g. land systems, soil series, agro-climatic zones, vegetation types; and, secondly, information on the relevant land characteristics and land qualities of each of these units.

Resource surveys are an integral part of an evaluation, not an external activity which supplies information to it. This distinction is not merely one of semantics. The central concept of suitability evaluation is that the various activities are directed towards assessment of land for specified kinds of use; for this to be the case, the resource data collected need to be directed towards the requirements of those uses. To treat the resource surveys as a separate activity would be to revert to the older and discredited approach to evaluation, that of first describing the physical environment in as much detail as possible *in vacuo,* and only subsequently giving thought to what use might be made of its resources. Hence the resource survey activities should be planned in the light of the provisionally identified kinds of land use; for example, in a semi-arid region likely to be dependent on livestock grazing, survey effort would be directed towards pasture resource surveys and the determination of livestock carrying capacities.

There is one apparent exception, in that in an area already covered by a good general-purpose soil survey it is possible to envisage a land evaluation which draws its resource data from already published material, without primary field surveys. Except as a student exercise this is rarely done, although there have been evaluation studies by consultants in the USA which drew heavily upon the wealth of resource data contained in the 1: 20 000 county soil surveys. More often, it is possible to base an evaluation on previously surveyed land mapping units, collecting the further data needed to evaluate these units for the given uses, but without the need to resurvey boundaries. This can be done because, owing to the fundamental controls of climate, landforms and soil parent materials, the boundaries between land mapping units for landforms, hydrology, soils and vegetation show a fair measure of coincidence, e.g. passing from free to impeded drainage at valley floor margins, or the well defined break in many tropical landscapes between hillslope and pediment. As world coverage by land system and general-purpose soil surveys progresses, this practice is liable to become more common; there is an increase in survey efficiency, since the effort that would otherwise have been needed to map boundaries can be directed towards collecting information related to land use.

The kinds of basic surveys needed will vary widely with the kinds of land use under consideration. For multi-purpose evaluation at the reconnaissance scale, a land systems survey is an excellent basis, this being in fact a set of specialised studies which employ a common set of mapping units. At semi-detailed and detailed scales, a soil or soil–landform survey is invariably necessary for multi-purpose evaluation and for all special-purpose evaluations that involve arable use. On the other hand, an evaluation directed specifically at forestry by extraction from natural forests would be based on forest inventory, soil engineering properties for road construction and economic information, without need for the agriculturally orientated soil survey. The more closely defined and specialised the purpose (e.g. a comparison of alternative sites for the disposal of toxic wastes), the more specialised and purpose-directed is the information collected.

Leaving aside evaluations of highly specialised purposes, the following are the kinds of natural resource surveys most likely to be needed in a land evaluation study.

Land systems survey. These are necessary for evaluations at reconnaissance scale and are based on air photo-interpretation and/or satellite imagery, in conjunction with field surveys of landforms, hydrology, climate, soils and vegetation.

Landform survey. Landform maps can serve as the basis for other resource studies, particularly in dry climates (e.g. Cooke & Doornkamp 1974 Ch. 14, Brunsden *et al.* 1979).

Engineering geology. This includes, for example, rock, regolith and landform properties for roads, availability of road-making materials. Systematic geological mapping is rarely part of an evaluation, although supplementary geological observations are often necessary as an adjunct to soil survey (cf. also hydrogeology, below).

Climatic studies. These involve mainly agro-climatology, and are of particular importance in areas of marginal moisture availability, both for irrigated land use and for dry farming.

Hydrological studies. These include studies of surface water resources (river regimes, flooding) and groundwater resources or hydrogeology. They are a major component in irrigation surveys, but can also be important for domestic and/or industrial water supplies.

Soil survey. Soil survey is the most widely required basis for land evaluation. In addition to standard methods of survey, studies of soil moisture properties are often of particular importance in evaluation.

Vegetation surveys. The two main applied types are pasture resource surveys and forest inventory. Availability of firewood may be important. In the hands of an ecologist with long experience of an area, ecological survey is arguably as good as soil survey as a basis for diagnosing general land use potential.

Surveys of fauna and disease. Such surveys involve insect vectors of human and livestock diseases, endemic diseases, predators (e.g. locust,

Quelea bird hazard); in special circumstances they involve a wildlife inventory.

As discussed earlier for soil survey, the information needed to map environmental distributions efficiently is not the same as that needed to evaluate for land use. A parallel example is that of pasture resource inventory. The information needed concerns amounts and seasonal distribution of dry matter production, digestible protein, etc., but to define mapping units and to delineate their boundaries calls for some combination of vegetation physiognomy and species frequency according to established principles of vegetation mapping. In the conduct of field activities, however, distribution mapping and the collection of information on relevant land characteristics are for the most part done at the same time. For special-purpose evaluations, the kinds of land use can affect the mapping units. In tropical rain forest, for example, the species frequency and hence value as timber can sometimes show surprisingly little variation across a range of soil types which have substantially different agricultural potentials; different mapping units would be needed for a survey directed towards forest exploitation from one directed at clearance for agriculture.

Whatever the circumstances, the requirements of the land use should be provisionally identified at the outset or at an early stage of resource surveys, in order that field survey effort can be directed towards collecting relevant information and excluding that which will not be needed. In principle, as the studies of land utilisation types progress, further refinements to the land characteristics needed may be called for; but this should not be overdone if the goodwill of the resource survey team is to be retained!

The manner of presentation of data from resource surveys will vary with circumstances, but should generally contain the following three elements:

(1) One basic map at the fundamental scale of the survey, showing the land mapping units employed for evaluation (soil or soil–landform units, vegetation units, land systems, etc.): this map is printed at a high cartographic standard, and forms a major output from the evaluation in its own right; it may have a longer life of utility than the evaluations based upon it.

(2) A set of maps of individual factors of the environment: climate, soils, vegetation, etc.: these can be on a smaller scale than the basic map, often conveniently half the scale, and need not be of the same cartographic specifications.

(3) Tabular and textual information on the land characteristics and land qualities of the mapping units: it is essential that such information should be compactly but clearly presented, since it permits reinter-

pretation in the light of changes in the economic circumstances or basic assumptions.

Studies of natural resources are one set of basic surveys that contribute to an evaluation. The second is the collection of economic information, discussed in the following chapter. For two reasons, this should be scheduled to start at about the same time as resource surveys. First, the studies necessary for an economic evaluation take about the same amount of time as the most time-consuming of the resource studies, namely soil survey. Secondly, feedback from interim studies of markets, prices and other information can prevent wasted effort in resource survey by limiting the kinds of information collected or even indicating that some part of the original survey area can be excluded.

Land qualities and land characteristics

The requirements of given types of land use are compared with the properties of mapped areas of land by means of land qualities and characteristics. It is decided, for example, that for mechanised maize production, the limits of 'highly suitable' land will be set at a growing season of 120–180 days, a slope angle of not more than 6°, a soil depth of over 120 cm and a topsoil with no more than 5% stones. For coffee production, the limits will be different: a longer growing season, deeper soil, but a higher limit of acceptable slope angle. Similar values are estimated as the limits of other suitability classes. These climatic, land-form and soil properties are determined for each of the land mapping units. Comparison between requirements of the land use and properties of the land is the first step in suitability classification. Before describing the next step in survey procedures, a discussion of the distinction between land qualities and characteristics is necessary.

The requirements of land use can be expressed in terms of land characteristics, land qualities, or a mixture of these. A **land characteristic** is an attribute of land that can be measured or estimated. Examples of land characteristics are mean annual rainfall, slope angle, soil drainage class, effective soil depth, topsoil texture, soil available water capacity, pH, and soil nitrogen percentage. A **land quality** is an attribute of land which acts in a distinct manner in its influence on the suitability of the land for a specific kind of use. Examples of land qualities are temperature regime, moisture availability, drainage, nutrient supply, rooting conditions, erosion hazard, and potential for mechanisation.

This distinction may be illustrated by comparing slope angle, a land characteristic, with erosion hazard, a land quality. Slope angle is a single and measurable property, and is thus a land characteristic. It can affect land use in several different ways: higher slope angles increase the erosion

162

hazard, decrease the potential for mechanisation and reduce access within the production unit (e.g. harvest roads). Erosion hazard is a property which has an identifiable and distinctive effect upon land use, and is thus a land quality. It is influenced not only by slope angle but also by slope length, rainfall intensity, and soil texture, structure and infiltration capacity, that is, by at least six land characteristics. The quality of erosion hazard results from the interaction of these characteristics.

There are other cases in which a land quality can be measured or estimated by a single land characteristic. Consider the quality of drainage. This affects land use in a distinct way, in that with the exception of rice and a few other specialised crops, most plants require oxygen in the rooting zone. A mild degree of drainage impedance reduces growth and crop yield, severe impedance results in the death of the plant; crops vary in their ability to withstand poor drainage. The most direct way to measure drainage conditions would be to monitor redox potential within the rooting zone throughout the growing period, but this is impracticable except under experimental conditions. For practical land evaluation, use has to be made of some land characteristic that is more easily measured or estimated; possibilities are depth to the water table at some period of the year, depth at which soil mottling commences, or soil drainage class. This last characteristic is usually the best to use, particularly as the same definitions of drainage classes are adopted in nearly all soil profile description manuals.

The above examples refer to arable kinds of land use, but the distinction between characteristics and qualities applies equally to livestock production and forestry. Thus for livestock ranching, two important land qualities are the nutritive value of natural pastures and the availability of drinking water. The former can be assessed in terms of a range of characteristics, directly by rates of dry matter production and their protein content at different seasons, indirectly by species composition of pastures, or still more indirectly by estimating some relation to climate. Availability of drinking water could be assessed in terms of distance to a source of perennial surface water, or of geological strata yielding groundwater, depending on whether the description of the land utilisation type includes provision for the drilling of boreholes.

Land characteristics are simpler to use, and in a local context they can provide a valid basis for estimating suitability classes. The main problem is that no account is taken of interaction between different characteristics. The case of erosion hazard has been noted above. For another example, consider the moisture requirements of crops. The crudest way to assess requirements is in terms of mean annual rainfall; but this interacts with potential evapotranspiration, as well as with soil available water capacity and thus texture and profile depth. In a small region it may be acceptable to state land use requirements in terms such as 'over 800 mm per year=highly suitable', or '600–800 mm=moderately suitable', etc. But even in that region, the criteria may require qualification such as 'except on sands and loamy sands' and may become invalid at different altitudes and temperatures.

Certain characteristics, for example soil texture, can affect use in several different ways, in some cases having both favourable and unfavourable effects. Thus sandy textures tend to reduce moisture and nutrient availability, but to have favourable effects with respect to rooting conditions and workability; heavy clays favour moisture availability but have adverse effects upon workability and potential for mechanisation.

A consequence of the failure to take account of interactions is that tables showing suitability ratings in terms of land characteristics are applicable only to the area for which they were drawn up. For example, a soil available water capacity of 10% over 1 m depth might be regarded as suitable for maize in the moister parts of the savanna zone but only marginally suitable or not suitable towards the drier margins of that zone.

Land qualities take account of such interactions, and at least in theory do not vary from place to place. Thus a particular cultivar of maize has a specific moisture requirement for optimum growth; this requirement can be provided by various combinations of rainfall, potential evapotranspiration and soil moisture storage. In addition, the employment of land qualities serves to direct attention to the land use; drainage, moisture availability, nutrient availability, erosion hazard and conditions for ripening all influence crop production in a distinctive way. There are also considerably fewer land qualities than characteristics.

To summarise, advantages of using land characteristics as a basis for evaluation are that they are simpler to use and direct, permitting a direct link between the observed value of the characteristic and the suitability rating. Disadvantages are the very large number of land characteristics, the fact that it is not always clear which effect on the use is being assessed and, most importantly, the failure to take account of interactions. Advantages of using land qualities are, first, that they are fewer in number, secondly, that they direct attention to the effect upon the land use and, thirdly, that they take account of interactions between environmental factors. The main disadvantage is that of greater complexity, in that they require an intervening stage of converting characteristics into qualities.

There is no hard-and-fast rule over this decision, which can be affected both by the circumstances of the survey and by personal preference. As a general rule it is better to start by assessing land use requirements in terms of land qualities. This directs attention to the ways in which the various kinds of use can be favourably or adversely affected. It is in any case necessary to decide which land characteristics are to be used to measure or estimate the qualities. If it is then found that, within the survey area, single characteristics provide a valid basis for assessing suitabilities, then these characteristics can be employed directly. Single characteristics are more likely to be valid in surveys lying within a restricted range of environments, e.g. a single climatic type.

Table 10.5 lists the land qualities that may affect land utilisation types belonging to rainfed agriculture, including assessment for individual crops, together with land characteristics that can be used for their measurement or estimation. Qualities 1–8 are related primarily to climatic requirements and limitations, 9–11 to water needs or excess, 12–19 to soil requirements and limitations, and 20 and 21 are hazards related to combination of factors. The final group, qualities 22–26, are related to land management and inputs; these affect other forms of use besides rainfed agriculture. Discussions of the nature of each quality, its effects and the methods of measurement are contained in the *Guidelines on land evaluation for rainfed agriculture* (FAO in preparation).

By no means all the qualities listed will be applicable to a given survey; the method of selection is discussed in the following section. In some cases, alternative characteristics for use in assessing a quality are given, allowing choice on grounds of availability of data. In some cases, conversion tables are employed as a means of combining the effects of several characteristics; Table 10.6 is an example. Less comprehensive lists of land qualities related to two other major kinds of land use, livestock production and forestry, are given in Table 10.7.

Requirements of the land use

Having described the land utilisation types, the next step is to determine the properties of land that will be used in suitability assessment. These can be expressed as *requirements* of the land use or as *limitations*. Most limitations are requirements expressed in a negative sense; thus good rooting conditions are a requirement for crops, whereas poor rooting conditions, caused by either shallow soils, coarse massive structure or excessive stones, are a limitation. For each land utilisation type, there are four steps:

(1) select the land qualities that are relevant to that land use within the survey area;
(2) decide the land characteristics to be used to measure or estimate each of these qualities;
(3) for each quality, determine the values which will form the boundaries of suitability classes;
(4) determine how ratings based on individual qualities are to be combined into overall suitabilities.

Table 10.5 Land qualities for rainfed agriculture.

Reference no.	Land quality	Subdivision	Land characteristics which may be used to measure or estimate the quality
1	radiation regime	(a) radiation requirements	Mean daily sunshine in growing season* (h day^{-1})
		(b) day length	Day length at floral initiation (h)
2	temperature regime		Mean temperature in growing season (°C); coldest and/or hottest months of growing season (°C)
3	growing period		Calculated growing period (days)†
4	air humidity as affecting growth		Mean relative humidity of least humid month in growing season (RH %)
5	conditions for ripening		Period of successive days rainless and with specified minimum sunshine hours and/or temperature days
6	conditions affecting post-harvest operations		Varies with crop, e.g. humidity of month following harvest
7	conditions affecting timing of production		Varies with crop and area, e.g. earliest date specified soil temperature reached
8	climatic hazards	(a) frost	Frequency of occurrence of damaging frosts in growing season
		(b) storm	Frequency of occurrence of damaging storms in growing season
9	moisture availability	(a) total moisture	Relative evapotranspiration deficit‡; total for growing period; number of humid months, rainfall greater than potential evapotranspiration; length of dry season, rainfall less than specified amount; etc.
		(b) critical periods	Relative evapotranspiration deficit, critical period for crop
		(c) drought hazard	Probability of rainfall less than specified amount, for growing, season, year, or critical period
10	drainage (oxygen availability to roots)		Soil drainage class; depth to soil mottling; depth to water table at specified period; vegetation indicators
11	flood hazard		Period of inundation during growing season (days); frequency of occurrence of damaging floods
12	nutrient availability		(i) Nutrient levels by topsoil analysis, N, P, K, other. (ii) Indicators of nutrient availability and/or renewability: pH, ratio Fe_2O_3/clay, weatherable minerals percentage, total (reserve) P, K. (iii) Fertility capability classification§, presence of condition modifiers, a, h, i, x, k
13	nutrient retention		Cation exchange capacity; total exchangeable bases; texture class

14	rooting conditions		Soil effective depth (cm); degree of limitation to root penetration, based on texture, structure and consistence; bulk density
15	workability		Degree of limitation to workability based on topsoil texture, structure and consistence; topsoil texture class
16	conditions affecting germination or establishment		Varies with crop and area, e.g. soil conditions for seedbeds
17	excess of salts	(a) salinity	Electrical conductivity of saturation extract (mS cm^{-1}); total soluble salts (ppm)
		(b) sodium alkalinity	Exchangeable sodium percentage; sodium absorption ratio
18	toxicities	(a) Al; $CaCO_3$, $CaSO_4$; Mn; acid sulphate	pH, Al saturation; percentage $CaCO_3$, $CaSO_4$ in root zone, depth to calcrete, gypsum; presence of/depth to actual or potential acid sulphate horizon, etc.
19	physical degradation hazard		Index of rainfall erosivity, index of crusting¶; observed signs of crusting
20	erosion hazard	(a) water erosion	Potential soil loss as calculated by the universal soil loss equation or the FAO methodology‖; slope angle in relation to specified soil texture groups
		(b) wind erosion	Potential soil loss as calculated by the FAO methodology‖
21	pests and diseases		Properties of climate or soil affecting incidence, e.g. high humidities
22	land preparation or clearance requirements	(a) land preparation	Varies with crop and area
		(b) vegetation clearance	
23	potential for mechanisation		Degree of limitation to mechanisation (see Table 10.6)
24	access within the production unit		Degree of terrain limitations, based on relative relief, slope angle, presence of landsliding, swamps, stream channels and cracking clays
25	size of potential management units		Minimum size of acceptable units (ha)
26	location	(a) existing access	Distance from tarmac/earth road
		(b) potential access	Index of accessibility, based on slope, relative relief, frequency of stream channels and distance

*Growing season: approximate period, to nearest month, of crop growth; equals whole year for perennials.
†Growing period: calculated period when temperatures exceed minimum for growth and moisture is available within rooting zone; for calculation see FAO (1978a pp. 33–8).

‡Relative evapotranspiration deficit is given by $(1 - ETa/ETm)$ where ETa=amount of water actually transpired by the crop, ETm=amount that would be transpired if available water were not limiting; for calculation see Doorenbos and Pruitt (1977).
§Fertility capability classification, see Buol and Cuoto (1981).
¶Index of rainfall erosivity, index of crusting, see FAO (1979b).
‖Wischmeier and Smith (1965); FAO (1979b).

Table 10.6　Example of a conversion table: limitations to mechanisation.

Land characteristic	Degree of limitation to mechanisation				
	1 Nil	2 Slight	3 Moderate	4 Severe	5 Very severe
slope angle (degrees)	5	10	18	35	any
(%)	9	18	32	70	any
rock hindrances (outcrops and boulders) (%)	1	4	10	25	any
stones, topsoil (%)	1	5	15	40	any
Heavy clay	absent	absent	present	present	present

Selection of land qualities is based on three criteria: the quality has an effect upon the land use; critical values, such as might adversely affect the use, occur in the survey area; and there is some practicable means of collecting information about the quality. Some qualities affect most kinds of land use, e.g. access within the production unit. Many others differ between major kinds of land use; nearly all forms of arable agriculture are influenced by growing period, moisture availability, drainage, nutrient supply and erosion hazard, and all forms of livestock production are influenced by availability of drinking water. Others are more specific, e.g. conditions for ripening are not applicable to rubber. The second criterion, whether the quality is significant within the study area, con-

Table 10.7　Examples of land qualities.

Land qualities related to livestock production (natural and/or improved pastures)
　　nutritive value of natural pastures
　　nutritive value of improved pastures
　　resistance to degradation of vegetation
　　resistance to soil erosion under grazing conditions
　　toxicity of grazing land
　　availability of drinking water for livestock
　　climatic hardships affecting livestock
　　endemic pests and diseases
　　access, size of units, location: see qualities 24–26 in Table 10.5

Land qualities related to forestry (natural forests and/or plantations)
　　types and volumes of existing timber species
　　pests and diseases affecting trees
　　climatic hazards: windthrow, forest fire
　　many qualities similar to those affecting crop growth, as in Table 10.5 applied to tree growth, e.g. temperature regime, moisture availability, drainage, nutrient availability, rooting conditions
　　land preparation, mechanisation, access, size of units location: see qualities 22–26 in Table 10.5

siderably reduces the number of qualities to be considered. Thus maize can be affected adversely by excess of salts, moisture deficiency and erosion hazard; but salts can be ignored except in arid or coastal areas, and moisture deficiency is unimportant in areas with annual rainfall exceeding 1200 mm. Similarly for livestock production, availability of drinking water can be taken for granted in areas with piped supplies but is often critically important in the semi-arid tropical zone. The criterion of whether there is some means of collecting information on a quality should only be used as a last resort, since, if the quality is believed to have important effects, some means of estimating it, even if indirectly, should be found. Thus in a reconnaissance survey of a large area it may be impossible to carry out enough soil analyses to measure nutrient availability directly; rather than ignore this important quality, it must be estimated from field profile description.

The *significance* of qualities is assessed as 'important', indicating that it requires special attention in the survey; 'significant', indicating that it requires consideration; or 'subordinate', indicating that it can be largely or wholly omitted from consideration. To make this assessment, rate each quality as follows:

(a) *effects upon the use:* large; moderate; slight; nil or inapplicable
(b) *occurrence of critical values in the study area:* frequent; infrequent; rare or never
(c) *practicability of obtaining information:* obtainable; unobtainable.

The significance is then given as:

(a) *important:* large, frequent, obtainable
(b) *significant:* large, infrequent, obtainable; moderate, frequent, obtainable
(c) *significant* or *subordinate* (choice to be made for each survey): moderate, infrequent, obtainable
(d) *subordinate:* slight and/or rare and/or unobtainable.

The qualities rated as significant and important for each kind of land use are then combined, and form the set of qualities on which information is required. This selection procedure greatly reduces the number of qualities to be considered and thus the information to be collected. There have been surveys of quite extensive areas for a variety of kinds of arable land use which have employed no more than eight qualities (e.g. Mansfield *et al*, 1975–7).

Having selected the relevant land qualities, next decide how each is to be measured or estimated. Rooting conditions, for example, depend on soil effective depth, grade, size and type of structure, and stoniness. Ideally a conversion table should be constructed, taking all these aspects into consideration, but in some areas it may be satisfactory to employ effective depth alone. For arable land use, it will be necessary in particular to decide how moisture availability and nutrient availability are to be estimated. For each, there are refined methods, accurate but requiring much information, or more approximate but quicker and cheaper methods. For livestock production, it must be decided whether the nutritive value of pastures is to be determined by taking cuttings at monthly intervals for a year on each land mapping unit, or estimated indirectly from vegetation composition and ecological experience. This step leads to production of a list of land characteristics on which information is needed from field survey.

Now comes the most difficult part of a land evaluation survey. For each land quality, as estimated by one or more land characteristics, the values that are to form the boundaries between suitability classes must be determined. Consider the example of maize cultivation and the land quality rooting conditions, as measured in terms of soil effective depth. The limit of Highly Suitable land might be set at an effective depth of 120 cm, Moderately Suitable at 70 cm and Not Suitable at 20 cm. If soil structure and stoniness were also taken into account, similar limits could be added, e.g. Highly Suitable with less than 5% stones throughout the rooting zone, or Not Suitable with over 30% stones and gravel for more than 50 cm horizon thickness.

The criteria employed in setting such limits have been noted in the discussion of suitability classes above (p. 143). The order of procedure is as follows:

(1) Decide on the limit or limits of Highly Suitable (S1) land. This is set at the value where the effect of a limitation begins to become clearly noticeable, through lowering of yield or other production, desirability of inputs, or both. Highly suitable land is not optimal, but is reasonably considered by an experienced farmer or other user to be very good land for the use.

(2) Decide on the limit or limits of Not Suitable (N) land. This is set at the value where the effect of a limitation is so severe as greatly to reduce the yield or other production, or to require inputs which would almost certainly be uneconomic. Not Suitable land is such that an experienced farmer or other user would unhesitatingly reject it for the use. Note that for rating of individual qualities, only one class of Not Suitable, equivalent to Permanently Not Suitable (N2), is employed.

(3) The limit between Moderately Suitable and Marginally Suitable land (S2 and S3) is then set in one of two ways, either by simple interpolation, halfway between the S1/S2 and S3/N limits, or by judging a value at which an element of doubt as to suitability enters. An

experienced farmer would say of land with S3 properties, 'Well, I suppose it could be used but I wouldn't like to.'

For some characteristics, e.g. soil depth and slope angle, there will be only one limiting value to each class. For others, e.g. pH, or in some cases temperature, upper and lower limits need to be set. Many characteristics require limits defined in terms of discrete classes, e.g. soil drainage classes, which might be set at S1=well drained; S2=moderately well, imperfectly and somewhat excessively drained; S3=excessively drained; and N=poorly and very poorly drained.

At present, there are few standard tables setting out suitability limits for defined land utilisation types. Even for the simple case of individual crops, little of the vast amount of agronomic experimental work has been directed at determining such limits, and there are few standard tables available. An exception is salinity limits, which have been determined in relation to percentage reduction in crop yield (Richards 1954, FAO 1979a). The FAO is currently attempting to compile such tables for individual crops. The practice at present is to get hold of a previous land evaluation survey for similar kinds of land use and with a broadly similar environment, look at the limits employed therein, and discuss with agronomists, etc., in what ways they need to be modified for the uses and area under consideration.

Most statements in books on crops are in qualitative and vague form, such as 'prefers deep, well drained loams but can be grown on a wide range of textures', or 'yields best with high temperatures and abundant sunshine'. For crop requirements, the sources given in Table 10.8 can be consulted, although these too are partly qualitative. Table 10.9 is an example of such a table, giving climatic, soil and water requirements for crops. Accounts of crop requirements in text form include Purseglove

Table 10.8 Sources for information on crop requirements.

Source	Table nos	Notes
Vink (1975)	36	soil and water requirements
Young (1976)	33	soil requirements
Arens (1977)	1, 2	sugar cane, bananas; in terms of land characteristics; quantitative
FAO (1978) see Table 10.9	3, 4, 8, 9	climate and soil; especially growing periods, and ratings of FAO soil units
Doorenbos and Kassam (1979)	2	authoritative on water requirements; includes also climate and soil
Kassam (1980)	4, 10	an extension of FAO (1978) to other crops
Sys and Riquier (1980)	8–10	soil requirements; including ratings of FAO soil units

Table 10.9 Climatic, soil and water requirements for crops. From Doorenbos and Kassam (1979). For definition of growing period, see Table 10.5, footnote 't'. ky=yield response factor to water deficit, the yield decrease per unit of relative evapotranspiration deficit (Table 10.5, footnote '‡'). For quantitative information on salinity, see FAO (1979a).

Crop	Total growing period (days)	Temperature requirements for growth (°C): optimum (range)	Day length requirements for flowering	Specific climatic constraints and/or requirements
alfalfa	100–365	24–26 (10–30)	day neutral	sensitive to frost; cutting interval related to temp.; requires low humidity in warm climates
banana	300–365	25–30 (15–35)	day neutral	sensitive to frost; temp.<8°C for longer periods causes serious damage; requires high RH, wind <4 m s^{-1}
bean	fresh: 60–90 dry: 90–120	15–20 (10–27)	short day/ day neutral	sensitive to frost, excessive rain, hot weather
citrus	240–365	23–30 (13–35)	day neutral	sensitive to frost (dormant trees less), strong wind, high humidity; cool winter or short dry period preferred
cotton	150–180	20–30 (16–35)	short day/ day neutral	sensitive to frost; strong or cold winds; temp. req. for boll development 27–32°C (18–38); dry ripening period required
grape	180–270	20–25 (15–30)		resistant to frost during dormancy (down to −18°C) but sensitive during growth; long, warm to hot, dry summer and cool winter preferred/required
groundnut	90–140	22–28 (18–33)	day neutral	sensitive to frost; for germination temp. >20°C
maize	100–140+	24–30 (15–35)	day neutral/ short day	sensitive to frost; for germination temp. >10°C; cool temp. causes problem for ripening
olive	210–300	20–25 (15–35)		sensitive to frost (dormant trees less); low winter temp. (<10°C) required for flower bud initiation
onion	100–140 (+30–35 in nursery)	15–20 (10–25)	long day/ day neutral	tolerant to frost; low temp. (<14–16°C) required for flower initiation; no extreme temp. or excessive rain
pea	fresh: 65–100 dry: 85–120	15–18 (10–23)	day neutral	slight frost tolerance when young
pepper	120–150	18–23 (15–27)	short day/ day neutral	sensitive to frost

Table 10.9   (contd)

Soil requirements	Sensitivity to salinity	Water requirements (mm) in growing period	Sensitivity to water supply (ky)
deep, medium-textured,well drained, pH=6.5–7.5	moderately sensitive	800–1600	low to medium-high (0.7–1.1)
deep, well drained loam without stagnant water; pH=5–7	sensitive	1200–2200	high (1.2–1.35)
deep, friable soil, well drained and aerated; opt. pH=5.5–6.0	sensitive	300–500	medium-high (1.15)
deep, well aerated, light- to medium-textured soils, free from stagnant water; pH=5–8	sensitive	900–1200	low to medium-high (0.8–1.1)
deep, medium- to heavy-textured soils; pH=5.5–8.0 with optimum pH =7.0–8.0	tolerant	700–1300	medium-low (0.85)
well drained, light soils are preferred	moderately sensitive	500–1200	medium-low (0.85)
well drained, friable, medium-textured soil with loose topsoil; pH=5.5–7.0	moderately sensitive	500–700	low (0.7)
well drained and aerated soils with deep water table and without waterlogging; optimum pH=5.0–7.0	moderately sensitive	500–800	high (1.25)
deep, well drained soils free from waterlogging	moderately tolerant	600–800	low
medium-textured soil; pH=6.0–7.0	sensitive	350–550	medium-high (1.1)
well drained and aerated soils; pH=5.5–6.5	sensitive	350–500	medium-high (1.15)
light- to medium-textured soils; pH=5.5–7.0	moderately sensitive	600–900	medium-high (1.1)

Table 10.9   (contd)

Crop	Total growing period (days)	Temperature requirements for growth (°C): optimum (range)	Day length requirements for flowering	Specific climatic constraints and/or requirements
pineapple	365	22–26 (18–30)	short day	sensitive to frost; requires high humidity; quality affected by temperature
potato	100–150	15–20 (10–25)	long day/ day neutral	sensitive to frost; night temp. <15°C required for good tuber initiation
rice	90–150	22–30 (18–35)	short day/ day neutral	sensitive to frost; cool temp. causes head sterility; small difference in day and night temp. is preferred
sorghum	100–140+	24–30 (15–35)	short day/ day neutral	sensitive to frost; for germination temp. >10°C; cool temp. causes head sterility
soybean	100–130	20–25 (18–30)	short day/ day neutral	sensitive to frost; for some varieties temp. >24°C required for flowering
sugar beet	160–200	18–22 (10–30)	long day	tolerant to light frost; toward harvest mean daily temp. <10°C for high sugar yield
sugar cane	270–365	22–30 (15–35)	short day/ day neutral	sensitive to frost; during ripening cool (10–20°C), dry, sunny weather is required
sunflower	90–130	18–25 (15–30)	short day/ day neutral	sensitive to frost
tobacco	90–120 (+40–60 in nursery	20–30 (15–35)	short day/ day neutral	sensitive to frost
wheat	spring: 100–130 winter: 180–250	15–20 (10–25)	day neutral/ long day	spring wheat: sensitive to frost; winter wheat: resistant to frost during dormancy (>−18°C), sensitive during post-dormancy period; requires a cold period for flowering during early growth. For both, dry period required for ripening

Table 10.9 (contd)

Soil requirements	Sensitivity to salinity	Water requirements (mm) in growing period	Sensitivity to water supply (ky)
sandy loam with low lime content; pH=4.5–6.5		700–1000	low
well drained, aerated and porous soils; pH=5.6	moderately sensitive	500–700	medium-high (1.1)
heavy soils preferred for low percolation losses, high tolerance to O_2 deficit; pH=5.5–6.0	moderately sensitive	450–700	high
light to medium/heavy soils relatively tolerant to periodic waterlogging, pH=6–8	moderately tolerant	450–650	medium-low (0.9)
wide range of soil except sandy, well drained; pH=6–6.5	moderately tolerant	450–700	medium-low (0.85)
medium- to slightly heavy-textured soils, friable and well drained; pH=6–7	tolerant	550–750	low to medium-low (0.7–1.1)
deep, well aerated with ground water deeper than 1.5–2 m but rel. tolerant to periodic high water tables and O_2 deficit; pH=5–8.5; optimum pH=6.5	moderately sensitive	1500–2500	high (1.2)
fairly deep soils; pH=6–7.5	moderately tolerant	600–1000	medium-low (0.95)
quality of leaf depends on soil texture; pH=5–6.5	sensitive	400–600	medium-low (0.9)
medium texture is preferred; relatively tolerant to high water table; pH=6–8	moderately tolerant	450–650	medium-high (spring 1.15, winter 1.0)

(1968, 1972), Arnon (1972), Young (1976, Ch. 16) and books on individual crops in the Longman 'Tropical agriculture' series.

The next step is to combine suitability ratings of individual land qualities into an overall suitability for the land use in question. Thus maize–groundnut farming will combine suitabilities for these two crops, whereas mechanised maize farming will combine requirements for maize with requirements for mechanisation. No hard-and-fast rules can be given for such combinations; the following are possible methods.

(a) *Limiting conditions.* This is the procedure (as usually employed in land capability classification) of taking the lowest individual rating as limiting to the overall suitability. Thus land rated S1 on rooting conditions, S1 on erosion hazard, but S3 on moisture availability would be assessed overall as S3. The principle of limiting conditions should always be followed where a Significant (or Important) quality is rated as Not Suitable, for it is no use having, say, excellent moisture and nutrient conditions if the land is subject to frequent flooding. For any quality classed as Important, a single limiting value which separates higher suitability classes will sometimes also be taken as limiting.

(b) *Arithmetic procedures.* Where large numbers of land units and uses have to be classified, it is possible to devise additive formulae, on the lines of, e.g.

$$S1+S1+S2=\text{overall } S1,$$
$$S1+S2+S2=S2,$$
$$\text{etc.}$$

Weightings for whether a quality is important or only significant can be incorporated. Additive methods of this nature work quite well in the higher suitability range, where several favourable conditions can compensate for one limitation which is less than ideal but not severe. There have also been attempts at productivity ratings based on multiplication of individual ratings, converted to percentages, but these give poor results if applied outside the areas for which they were devised.

(c) *Subjective combinations.* The surveyor, preferably in consultation with the farmer, agronomist, forester, etc., summarises the various combinations of conditions which occur, and judges how they should be assessed for overall suitability.

(d) *By reference to economics.* Economic evaluation is carried out for the various land units; by retrospective comparison of these results with the land qualities, ratings of the latter are derived.

The method of limiting conditions is the easiest to use, and should always be used for a single severe, i.e. N, limitation. Arithmetic procedures may be necessary when a very large number of land units (or single site observations) are to be evaluated, in order that two surveyors shall achieve the same result. They will in any case be necessary if this step is to be carried out by computer; the constraint that N ratings are limiting is then incorporated. Subjective combination is best wherever the number of units and uses to be considered is small, and where there is experience of the use in the survey area or a similar environment. Retrospective rating based on economic calculations is possible only in economic evaluations; this method gives the interesting possibility of putting a monetary value on, for example, a centimetre of soil thickness or rainfall.

The kinds of limitation that cause lowering of suitabilities are the basis for allocating subclasses. Any land unit placed in a suitability class other than S1 by reason of, say, limitations to moisture availability is placed in subclass S2m, S3m, N1m or N2m. It is left open whether separate subclasses are distinguished for every kind of limitation, or whether they are grouped, e.g. limitations related to moisture, soil, climate, pasture resources, etc.

Observed production data

In addition to using requirements expressed in terms of land qualities, observed production data can be an important source of information. Depending on the major kind of land use, this consists of crop yields, observed livestock carrying capacities or production of meat, etc., or mean annual increments of tree species. Crop yield and livestock records may be obtained from experimental stations, demonstration sites, marketing board records or existing farms, whereas timber increments may be obtained from existing forest site trials. The *Framework for land evaluation* (FAO 1976) lists observed crop yields, grassland productivity and timber increments as land qualities; in view of their very different nature, this is confusing, and observed production is better regarded as a distinct and additional source of information to be used in suitability classification.

Observed crop yields or other production data can be used in two ways: as a means of 'calibrating' land qualities by noting actual production in conjunction with observed climatic data and soil observations, and retrospectively as a check on suitability assessments based on such qualities. Clearly this source of information will be of most use in settled areas. Occasionally it can form the major basis for classification; if there already exists, for example, a network of forestry trial sites covering most types of environment present, evaluation as such can be based largely on records from these sites, using soil survey to define the mapping units within which the trials occur, and to map the extent of similar land.

Observed crop yields are often less useful than might appear. It is an unfortunate but undeniable fact that yields are affected considerably more by differences in management than by soil and other land conditions. In developing countries, yield differences between farms may be as much as three- to fivefold (e.g. Young & Goldsmith 1977). In developed countries with advanced farming methods, the best and worst managed farms typically obtain yields 30–40% above and below the average, a range about equal to that between good and bad years for rainfall. Yield data are of little use without details of management, including crop varieties, fertilisers, weeding and date of planting. Besides this, there is not often a rainfall gauge on or close to the farm and, as a general rule, rainfall variations have more effect on yields than do soil differences.

These reservations notwithstanding, observed crop yields or other production data are a far more realistic type of information than ratings based on land qualities, and should be put to full use where they exist.

Land improvements

Where a change in land use is being considered, it is uncommon for the land to be left exactly in its existing condition. Its qualities will be improved so as to match better the requirements of the proposed use. A major land improvement, such as an irrigation scheme, forms part of the basic assumptions, and the evaluation is then treated as one of potential suitability (p. 121). Minor land improvements are an element in evaluation of current land suitability.

Towards the later part of the basic resource surveys, following the first stage of comparison with land use requirements and leading on into the matching process (see below), consideration is given to possible land improvements. Field drainage, land levelling or grading, construction of bunds or other works for soil conservation, or reseeding of pastures are examples of such improvements. These require initial labour and other inputs, followed by continuing costs of maintenance; they therefore involve both capital and recurrent costs. In some circumstances, land improvements can very substantially reduce the gap between land use requirements and existing land qualities, and thus raise the suitability classification.

Comparison of land use with land

A stage is reached at which the land utilisation types have been described, their requirements determined, suitability class limits for these requirements have been set, the land units have been mapped, and the necessary information collected for each unit. Suitability assessment is then made by comparison of land use with land, or more precisely comparison of the requirements of each defined kind of land use with the qualities of each mapped area of land. There are four steps to such comparison: matching, assessment of environmental impact, economic and social analysis, and the field check.

Matching in its simplest form is the comparison of suitability class limits with conditions on each mapped area of land. This is a more or less automatic process, and yields suitabilities of each land unit for each kind of use. If carried out by computer, such maps can be printed directly. Surveys in which the land utilisation types are taken as fixed will stop at this point. Matching in the deeper sense of the term, however, involves considerably more. Where it is found that the land is not well suited to the utilisation types as originally defined, two kinds of modification may be made in order to match the land use to the land more closely: to the land utilisation type, or to the land. Modifications to the descriptions of land utilisation types often involve changes in the defined inputs; examples are adding provision for supplementary sprinkler irrigation, changing the levels of fertiliser application, changing the numbers of livestock in a mixed farming system, or changing the farm size so as to improve the economic return. In livestock production, stocking rates could be changed or provision made for increased supplementary feeds. In forestry, new tree species could be sought if there proved to be areas not well suited to any of those initially considered. Changes to the land are brought about by land improvements, as discussed above. The object of the matching process is to bring the needs of the land use more closely into harmony with the resources of the environment, and in so doing to raise the suitability classification.

Following matching comes consideration of **environmental impact.** In theory this should already have been taken into account, through suitability limits for soil erosion, vegetation degradation hazard, etc. As a precautionary measure, however, it is as well to give it specific consideration, employing appropriate experts in a large team project. Off-site effects, e.g. on river regimes, are included in this review. Many evaluations will not employ the full procedures of environmental impact analysis (Munn 1979), although in principle this should be done. Such specific study serves on the one hand to reassure the clients or sponsoring organisation that environmental impact has been given attention, and on the other it is a further check against the huge financial losses that can occur when something goes seriously wrong.

Economic and social analysis can be at two levels. In economic evaluations the full procedures outlined in the next chapter will be employed. Even where the evaluation is qualitative, it is still necessary to give some consideration to both social and economic consequences of the various types of land use. Social considerations include consequences for population density, settlement, or any enforced movements of people. Some simplified economic analysis should also be carried through, to ensure that the qualitatively based suitabilities do not make economic nonsense.

At this stage it may be possible to isolate the class of N1, representing 'currently not suitable'. Qualitative evaluations can strictly only employ the classes S1, S2, S3 and N, the limit between S3 and N being only an approximation, since this boundary is defined in economic terms. In practice there is often an appreciable range of land in the S3 class, and the simplified economic analysis carried out as a check on qualitative evaluation may allow it to be apportioned provisionally between S3 and N1.

The **field check,** possibly carried out concurrently with economic and social analysis, is a further means of confirming the soundness of the results. The precise details of soil depth, rainfall, slope angle, etc., are for the moment put aside. Taking the descriptions of land utilisation types and the mapped suitabilities, the surveyor accompanied by an agronomist or other expert visits a selection of the sites in each suitability class, and discusses whether the results are in accord with common sense and experience. If the opinions of people already living there can be obtained, so much the better. A field check is particularly important if the classification has been carried out by relatively automatic methods, and is essential if it has been computerised. If the results of the field check do not agree with experienced judgement, some of the criteria or limiting values will need to be changed.

Presentation of results

The objectives of a land suitability evaluation normally contain three main elements: definitions and descriptions of land utilisation types suited to the survey area; a map with supporting data showing the kinds of land present and their distribution; and an assessment of the suitabilities of each land utilisation type for each kind of land.

Normally the results include maps and tables in terms of discrete suitability classes; they need not invariably be in this form (p. 149), but to simplify discussion the normal case will be assumed.

There are two ways of presenting mapped suitability classes. In the first, the land units are presented as a single map on the basic scale of the survey. Either on this same sheet or on a second map at the same scale, the suitabilities are shown in the form of a tabular legend, in the form illustrated in Table 10.10. Such a legend can be looked at in two ways. By reading horizontally across, the various alternative uses of any particular land mapping unit can be seen. Thus the Lilongwe unit is highly suitable

Table 10.10 Legend to a land suitability map. Qualitative current suitability for major kinds of land use, Dedza District, Malawi. From Young and Goldsmith (1977).

Land mapping unit	Annual crops	Perennial crops	Livestock production	Forestry, natural woodlands	Forestry, plantations	Tourism and conservation
				Major kind of land use		
Lilongwe	S1	N2	S2	NR	S2‡	NR
Mkwinda	S1	N2	S2	NR	S2‡	NR
Thiwi	S3	N2	S2	S2	S2	NR
Linthipe	S2	N2	S2	NR	S2‡	NR
Chiphazi	S2	N1	S3	NR	S1	NR
Bembeke	S2/S3	S3	S3	S2	S1	NR
Dedza Mt.	N2	N1/N2	S2	S3	S1	S2
dambo	N2	N2	S1	NR	N2	NR
valley floor	N2*	N2	S2	NR	N2	NR
hill	N2	N2	S3†	S2	N1	S3
crag	N2	N2	N2	N2	N2	S2

*S2 for vegetables
†S2 as component in multiple use.
‡Relevant for small fuelwood plantations only.

for annual crops, moderately suitable for livestock production and forestry plantations, and not suitable for perennial crops; it has not been assessed for forestry based on natural woodlands nor for tourism, since these uses were ruled out of question for this land unit during the initial discussions. Looking vertically down a suitability table, the areas most suitable for any kind of land use can be picked out; thus the best areas for annual crops are the Lilongwe and Mkwinda units, and the best for forestry plantation are the Chiphazi, Bembeke and Dedza units.

The second means of cartographic presentation is a series of suitability maps, one for each kind of land use. Figure 10.2 illustrates this for major kinds of land use, and the same method can be used for land utilisation types. Subclass letter symbols can be added. If such maps are coloured, this method is visually striking and effective for presentation. They need not be on as large a scale as the basic map of land units; in Figure 10.2 a pattern of two kinds of valley floors and hills is too complex to map at this scale, and so is represented by single areas called 'dambo', 'valley floor', 'hill' and 'crag'.

Taking as an example a survey on the basic scale of 1: 50 000, the best combination of maps is the following:

(a) A *land resources map,* showing the basic land mapping units (e.g. soil–landform units, soils), at 1: 50 000. The legend includes data on parent materials, landforms, drainage, soils, climate, vegetation, and other resource information.

Land Suitability Evaluation

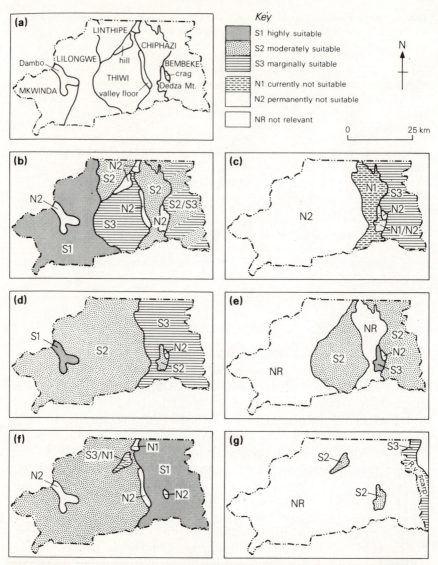

Figure 10.2 Land suitability maps. Qualitative current suitability for major kinds of land use, Dedza District, Malawi. (a) Land mapping units; dambo is broad valley floor grassland. (b)–(g) Suitability maps: (b) arable farming, annual crops; (c) arable farming, perennial crops; (d) livestock production; (e) forestry, natural woodland; (f) forestry, plantations; (g) tourism and conservation. From Young and Goldsmith (1977).

(b) A *land suitability map*, showing suitabilities for the defined kinds of land use, also at 1: 50 000. The legend is in tabular form similar to Table 10.10.

(c) A *series of individual suitability maps*, for each land utilisation type separately, as in Figure 10.2. The scale of these can range from half the basic scale, e.g. 1: 100 000, to still smaller, e.g. 1: 250 000.

As with soil surveys, the content of the evaluation report will vary widely with the objectives and circumstances of the survey. In particular, the relative amount of space devoted to the description of land utilisation types will vary according to the two different situations noted on p. 151 and the space devoted to economic analysis will depend on whether it is an economic evaluation. Given these variations in emphasis, the report should include the following sections:

- Summary
- Objectives
- Initial assumptions
- The setting
  The physical environment (general description)
  The economic and social setting
- Land utilisation types
  Summary list and definitions
  Detailed descriptions, including inputs
- Requirements of the land use: the physical criteria used as a basis for suitability classification
- The basic resource surveys; with reference to the land resources maps
- Economic and social analysis
- Environmental impact
- Results of the suitability classification; with reference to the land suitability map or maps
- Discussion of results

The types of basic resource surveys conducted and an outline of their results are always included. Whether detailed environmental information is given in this section of the report will depend on how lengthy it is. If, as is often the case, a considerable amount of climatic, soil and similar information has been collected, details of this should be given in an appendix or in a separate volume. The section on requirements of the land use may also be presented selectively; some of the considerable volume of conversion tables should be relegated to an appendix, although those most directly related to the assessed suitabilities can appear in the main text. As with soil surveys, the results of a large evaluation should be presented as a summary volume followed by more detailed reports.

The desirability of a readable and so necessarily selective presentation does not mean that data on which detailed evaluation has been based should be discarded. The details should be placed on record, in appendices or supplementary volumes, for two reasons. First, as backup material to the survey itself, enabling an independent assessor to verify or dispute the results. Secondly, many of the basic data have a longer useful life than the final suitability assessments. This applies not only to the natural resource data but also to the physical criteria employed to assess suitabilities. In economic evaluations, in particular, many data are subsumed in the calculation of costs and returns which form the main basis of the final evaluation. As economic calculations have a short life, it is important to place on permanent record the quantitative physical data used as a basis. This permits reappraisal in changed economic circumstances. Pressure to leave such basic data in typescript form on files should be resisted. In practice such material is unusable by anyone other than the authors; it should be written up in an orderly and fully explained form, and it should be printed or at least mimeographed and bound.

Discussion

Whilst complex in detail, land suitability evalution is straightforward in principle: describe the possible kinds of land use, estimate their land requirements, and survey the area to map the distribution of these requirements. This could be done without recourse to the foregoing terminology, which is employed as a means of giving some measure of standardisation to the concepts employed. The US Bureau of Reclamation (USBR) land classification for irrigation (p. 241), devised many years earlier, closely follows the procedures of a special-purpose economic suitability classification; USBR classes 1 to 3 correspond to suitability classes S1 to S2, class 4 could be regarded as conditionally suitable, class 5 as N1 and class 6 as N2.

Space has not allowed all of the stages to be illustrated by examples. To gain a deeper understanding of the concepts and procedures, start by following through the details of a published land suitability report. Then take another region and carry out an evaluation in simplified form; as a training exercise, this can be done with information drawn from existing soil surveys and other published sources, simulating additional data where necessary.

One further concept, the **land use system** provides a summary of suitability evaluation and illustrates the interdependence of the different components. A land use system (Fig. 10.3) consists of a land utilisation type applied to a land mapping unit. The former has land requirements, the latter possesses land qualities, and the functioning of the system is controlled by the relationships between these. Associated with the system are inputs, land improvements and outputs.

Every component in a land use system interacts with the others. As a schematic example, let the land utilisation type be maize cultivation and the land mapping unit be an area of gleyic luvisols (FAO–Unesco 1974) with impeded drainage, on gentle slopes under a 900 mm rainfall. If the inputs consisted of improved seed, adequate labour, etc., and 200 kg ha^{-1} of fertiliser, but without land improvements in the form of drainage, the output might be 200 kg ha^{-1} of maize. A change in any one of these variables causes changes in others. Lowering the fertiliser input will lower the crop yield. Adding a land improvement in the form of field drainage will raise it. If the land mapping unit were not luvisols but less fertile arenosols, the output would be lower, but could be raised by a larger fertiliser input. All such changes affect the economics of the system. The concept of a functionally interdependent land use system has wide-ranging consequences, particularly when considered in the light of the matching process. It is far removed from the earlier approach of 'resource mapping first, evaluation afterwards'. A discussion of some implications of this concept is given by Beek (1978).

Two problems require investigation. The first is to determine quantitative limits for rating land qualities, applied to individual crops. This is partly a matter of controlled experimental work, though fundamental questions may arise over how such limits can be expressed.

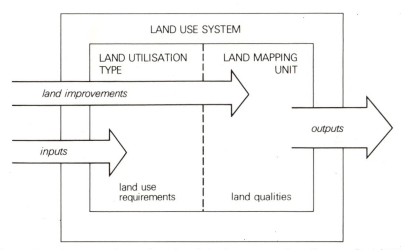

Figure 10.3 Diagrammatic representation of a land use system. Based in part on Beek (1978).

The second problem is that the integration of economic analysis with suitability assessments made in terms of physical factors has not been very fully achieved; in most surveys the economic analysis appears to have been carried out in large measure independently of the physical evaluation.

It is by the test of practical utility in land use planning and management that any system of land evaluation must stand or fall. From this viewpoint, suitability evaluation is far superior to land capability classification for most purposes; capability classification is effective only for farm planning, and then at a rather elementary scale. Suitability evaluation puts forward alternative possibilities for changes in land use, whether major new uses or changes in detail, presents the consequences of such changes for each part of the surveyed area, and so provides evidence contributing to planning, management and investment decisions. The approach has been most fully tested, applied and proven in developing countries. In principle it should also be applicable to settled and developed areas, and it has been applied on a trial basis to farming systems in the Netherlands. To what extent the approach can prove useful in some of the major planning decisions of developed countries, such as competition in hill lands between grazing and forestry uses, or siting of areas for recreation or conservation, could usefully be investigated.

Further reading

FAO (1976) is the fundamental text; Beek (1978), Agricultural Development and Advisory Service (1977), Young and Goldsmith (1977), Sys (1978), Beek (1981). *Guidelines on land evaluation for rainfed agriculture* and *Guidelines on land evaluation for irrigated agriculture* are in preparation by FAO.

The Economics of
Land Evaluation

The principle of economic land suitability evaluation is simple: cost the inputs, price the benefits, and calculate the net returns in money terms. The detailed procedures are lengthy, although not unduly complex, in that the successive steps follow in logical succession. The calculations are, however, by no means merely a matter of putting a price on physical quantities and making a routine calculation. Decisions have to be made at several stages about the manner of pricing, rates of discounting, costs and returns, external factors to be included, and which economic yardsticks to use for interpreting the results. These decisions call for careful judgement, since they have an equal or greater effect upon the results than that of qualities of the land.

It can be said with some truth that there is no such thing as the economics of land evaluation, but only general principles of economics applied to comparison between areas of land under different kinds of use. In economic terms, land evaluation consists of gross margin analysis of farming systems or other production units followed by discounted cash-flow analysis. Land, with labour and capital, is one of the factors of production, and land evaluation calls for the partial isolation of this factor or its treatment as an independent variable. By keeping all 'non-land' variables constant, it is possible to obtain economic measures which compare the suitabilities of different types of land for one defined use, or those of different uses on one type of land.

Two kinds of result can be obtained from economic evaluation: whether farms or other production units will make a profit year by year, and whether capital investment on land improvements will be justified. Gross margin analysis is a matter of taking a farmer's annual income from sales of produce, subtracting production costs and overheads, and obtaining the resulting profit or loss. Land suitability classes can be defined in terms of levels of income, either per hectare or per capita, e.g. $S1 > £200$ ha^{-1}, $S2$ £100–200 ha^{-1}. It is only by economic analysis that the $S3/N1$ boundary can be accurately determined, since there is no abrupt change in physical land characteristics or plant growth at this point, merely the margin between profit and loss. Gross margin analysis is the appropriate basis for land suitability determination wherever capital investment is not involved, since it is relatively objective.

Where substantial capital investment is involved, as in regional drainage schemes or other major land improvements, this investment must be analysed by setting the initial cost of the improvements against the increased production in future years. There is no unique way of comparing expenditure today with gains in the future. The procedure for doing so involves reducing a future cost or benefit to some lower figure, termed its present value, by a process of discounting, approximately the reverse of interest (Appendix B). The general term for this procedure is discounted cash-flow analysis. When carried out by farmers and private businessmen it is limited to financial accounting, in terms of private profit and loss, and commercial rates of interest are taken as the basis for discounting. When employed by governments for publicly financed projects it is called social cost–benefit analysis; external costs and benefits to the community at large are included in addition to commercial profitability, and a lower 'social' discount rate is used. These procedures produce three measures of value:

(a) *net present value:* the present value of benefits minus the present value of costs, arguably the most useful and robust measure;
(b) *benefit–cost ratio:* the present value of benefits divided by the present value of costs;
(c) *internal rate of return:* the rate of discounting at which the present value of benefits becomes equal to the present value of costs.

These measures can be used in various ways: to see whether a particular land improvement is commercially sound; to see whether it is 'socially' beneficial, i.e. to the community as a whole; to compare the economic consequences of investment on two or more different areas of land; and to compare the economic consequences of a land improvement with those of leaving the land in its present condition. Cost–benefit analysis is less precise and objective than gross margin analysis, involving a number of rather arbitrary assumptions, but it is wider in scope. It enables some account to be taken of social equity as well as economic efficiency. For instance the cost to the community at large of environmental degradation by soil erosion or salinisation can be taken into account, e.g. by reducing the discount rate thereby giving greater weighting to long-term costs. A possible result of cost–benefit analysis of an individual project is that it might be profitable to the individual farmers (as shown by gross margin analysis) but not profitable to the community as a whole.

Economic land evaluation is not the same as project appraisal, although in the context of rural development schemes the distinction can become blurred. Ideally, good land evaluation should take into consideration all aspects of a proposed development project. In practice, the focus of land evaluation is differences between areas of land, that of project evaluation on the overall feasibility or profitability of the enterprise.

The results of physical evaluation are used in economic evaluation in two ways: as a means of selecting the range of alternatives to be analysed, and as a source of data on inputs and production. Where the selection of kinds of land use is based on qualitative evaluation, further work is needed to convert data on the more promising alternatives into quantitative physical terms.

In settled, developed countries, the necessary quantitative data on inputs and costs will sometimes be available from published sources or government records. University departments of agricultural economics may have on-going studies of farm economics (e.g. Thompson & Sturrock 1976). In developing countries, farm system studies may be necessary. A sample of farmers carrying out different production enterprises is selected and records made of their activities, how long these take, and what material inputs are used. As such studies are often carried out by newly recruited junior staff, who in the course of weekly visits build up a working relationship with farmers on what it would be best to record in order to please their employer, the reliability of the results is not always what it might be.

There are two ways of combining physical with economic evaluation. In the **two-stage approach,** evaluation is first carried out in physical terms, and the results then subjected to economic analysis. In the **parallel approach,** physical and economic analysis proceed concurrently with more or less continuous interchange of data, leading to a single combined set of results. The two-stage approach is more straightforward, possessing a clearcut sequence of activities; it also allows economic attention to be selective, assessing only those land utilisation types found by physical evaluation to be the most promising. This makes the two-stage approach preferable in surveys involving a wide range of uses and types of land, although the saving of economists' time may be lost in a waste of resource surveyors' time, spent in assessing areas which are subsequently shown to be uneconomic for development. The parallel approach leads to a more concise concentration of survey activities, and when skilfully handled it can produce the results needed in a shorter time. It is preferable when the range of land types and uses is limited, and the problem concentrated on relatively few alternatives. The parallel approach can only be successfully operated by a team experienced in working together and with a mutual understanding of, and respect for, each other's methods. An *ad hoc* team of soil surveyors, agronomists and economists, such as might be thrown together by a multinational recruitment process, would do better to stick to the two-stage approach.

Even in a two-stage evaluation, it is well to phase in staffing and activities in economics early. Farm system studies take a minimum of one year, and other economic data collection activities are also time-consuming. In practice the economists can estimate in advance the kind of data that will be required. If the 'two-stage' approach is taken literally, finishing physical activities before starting on economic analysis, it will take much longer before results are obtained.

Procedures

By reason of its more clearcut sequence of operations, the two-stage approach will be described. To avoid repeated qualifications the examples quoted are based largely on arable farming. For readers not familiar with discounted cash-flow analysis an outline is given in Appendix B.

The sequence of activities in economic land evaluation can be outlined in terms of two stages: gross margin analysis followed by discounted cash-flow or cost–benefit analysis.

Gross margin analysis

The aim of gross margin analysis is to investigate the profitability of a farming system to the farmer. This is done by first considering individual crops or other farming enterprises (e.g. beef production, dairy production) and then combining these into farming systems. The steps in outline are as follows:

(1) Select the more promising land use alternatives, i.e. crops or other enterprises, using results of physical land evaluation. This selection may include (i) choosing the few most suitable kinds of use from among the larger number initially considered for each land mapping unit; (ii) choosing only the better-suited land mapping units for each kind of land use, e.g. deciding to analyse S1 and S2 land only, or to include also S3 land; (iii) deciding to analyse only for certain levels of inputs (p. 156), e.g. high inputs in developed countries, intermediate inputs ('improved traditional' farming) in developing countries.

(2) Estimate the recurrent inputs in physical terms, for each selected land use and land suitability class. These include both material inputs (seed, fertilisers, pesticides, machinery, fuel, traction animals, etc.) and non-material inputs, particularly the labour requirements of each farming operation. The necessary inputs will frequently be larger on lower suitability classes and may differ

between subclasses, e.g. S2m (m=moisture availability) requiring supplementary irrigation, S2n (n=nutrient availability) requiring higher fertiliser inputs than S1 land. This is the most time-consuming step, requiring considered estimates of hundreds of quantities and occupying many pages of tables.

(3) Estimate production in quantitative physical terms. In arable farming this means crop yield estimates, one of the most difficult tasks in land evaluation and yet fundamental to economic analysis. However hesitant they may feel, the soil surveyor and the agronomist together should make the best estimates they can, otherwise the economist will be forced to do so. Close inspection of published economic studies sometimes reveals some hair-raising assumptions, such as 'yields on S2 land are assumed to be 67% of those on S1 land, on S3 land 33%'! For other major kinds of land use, similar estimates are made of production of meat, dairy products, timber, etc.

(4) Ascertain prices of all inputs and products. This includes material and non-material inputs, particularly labour costs. Estimates of future price trends will usually be necessary, particularly for the relative prices of products and inputs, e.g. crop prices compared with fertiliser and fuel costs.

(5) Estimate the fixed costs of farms or other production units. Fixed costs are those which either cannot be attributed to a specific farming enterprise (e.g. upkeep of farm buildings) or do not vary in proportion to the size of that enterprise.

(6) Carry out gross margin analysis of farms or other production units, combining data from steps (1)–(5) in the following sequence:
   (a) For each selected land use enterprise, e.g. each individual crop, combine the recurrent inputs and estimated production with the prices of inputs and products. Inputs multiplied by their costs are the **variable costs**. The **gross margin** of an enterprise is the output (yield × price) minus the variable costs. At this stage, different crop rotations or other combinations of enterprises may be compared, leading to selection of more favourable rotations within the farming system, and thus to improvements in the descriptions of land utilisation types.
   (b) Combine the gross margins for each enterprise in proportion to their area of land occupied, and subtract the fixed costs. This gives the **net farm income,** the profit (or loss) that the farmer will make. For a land utilisation type to be economically viable, the net farm income must exceed an assumed target income, or normal profit.

Table 11.1 gives an example of the calculation of gross margin and net farm income, with the details reduced to a highly simplified form. There are three land units, 'fertile soil', 'sandy soil' and 'imperfectly drained soil'; all are assumed to be gently sloping and with a tropical savanna-type climate favourable for annual crops. Two crops are considered, maize and tobacco, both grown by smallholders at the intermediate level of inputs with high labour and low capital intensities. Maize is assumed to require more fertiliser than does tobacco, and through the matching process it has been estimated that the sandy soil requires more fertiliser than does the fertile soil. Given such inputs, the yield of tobacco is identical on these two soils but that of maize somewhat lower on the sandy soil. Yields of both crops are considerably depressed on the imperfectly drained area, but can be raised to the level of the fertile soil by installation of drainage; in the context of smallholders with low capital resources, installation of drainage works must be financed by outside capital and so is considered a major land improvement. Seed, protective chemicals, depreciation on implements and other inputs are summarised as 'variable costs other than fertiliser' and fixed costs; the variable costs of tobacco are substantially higher than those of maize. Gross margins on each crop are obtained from the value of production (yield × price) less the variable costs (fertiliser × price, plus other variable costs).

Tobacco is the more profitable crop on all land units, but a labour constraint in non-mechanised smallholder farming sets the maximum area for this crop at 1 ha. One farming system is considered, a 5 ha farm with 2 ha maize, 1 ha tobacco, 2 ha rotational fallow and a 1 ha woodlot. Gross margins for the farm are obtained by combining those for the two crops, and fixed costs are subtracted to give net farm income, by farm and per hectare. The gross margins are given per hectare cultivated, the net farm income per hectare of total land.

These results can be interpreted in two ways: which is the best land for each crop and which is the better use of each land unit. Taking the gross margins, for maize the order of suitability is fertile soil>sandy soil >imperfectly drained soil. For tobacco, the fertile and sandy soils give similar returns but the imperfectly drained land, if unimproved, is not suitable. If economic suitability classes for crops were to be defined with boundaries at gross margins of S1/S2=£200 ha⁻¹, S2/S3=£100 ha⁻¹, S3/N1=£50 ha⁻¹ (to allow for fixed costs), suitability classes would become:

	Maize	Tobacco
fertile soil	S2	S1
sandy soil	S2	S1
imperfectly drained soil	S3	N1

Table 11.1 Schematic calculation of gross margin and net farm income.

Land unit	Fertile soil		Sandy soil		Imperfectly drained soil			
land improvements	nil		nil		nil		drainage	
land use	maize	tobacco	maize	tobacco	maize	tobacco	maize	tobacco
fertiliser inputs (kg/ha)	200	100	400	200	200	100	200	100
crop yield (kg/ha)	5000	1500	4500	1500	2000	300	5000	1500
prices: fertiliser (£/100 kg)	12	12	12	12	12	12	12	12
crop (£/tonne)	40	200	40	200	40	200	40	200
variable costs other than fertiliser (£/ha)	20	60	20	60	20	60	20	60
fixed costs (£/ha)	30	30	30	30	30	30	30	30
value of production (£/ha)	200	300	180	300	80	60	200	300
variable costs (£/ha)	−44	−72	−68	−84	−44	−72	−44	−72
gross margin (£/ha)	156	228	112	216	56	−12	156	228
farm of 5 ha; 2 ha maize, 1 ha tobacco, 1 ha fallow, 1 ha woodlot:								
gross margin (£/farm)	540		440		100		540	
fixed costs (£/farm)	−150		−150		−150		−200*	
net farm income (£/farm)	390		290		−50		340	
(£/ha)	78		58		−10		68	

*Includes £50 for maintenance of drainage works.

If a target income of £250 per farm is assumed, the 5 ha farm considered is clearly viable for the fertile soil but marginal for the sandy soil. On the latter, consideration could be given to increasing the area of tobacco at the expense of maize, necessitating added costs of hired labour. This farming system is not viable on the imperfectly drained area in its present condition, although maize alone could be grown at a low income. If drained, however, despite added maintenance costs this land could be converted to profitable production (here artificially assumed to be the same as on the fertile soil) if the capital costs of drainage were to be written off.

The case given here for imperfectly drained land could be applied to other kinds of limitation. Suppose, for example, the limitation were one of erosion hazard; there would be little or no short-term effect on production, but cultivation of maize and tobacco on unimproved land would be rejected on grounds of environmental impact with effects on long-term productivity. The capital and maintenance costs of soil conservation measures would be substituted for those of drainage works without altering the principle of the calculations.

Discounted cash-flow analysis

Analysis of land use enterprises in which the costs of land improvements and other capital expenditure are not large in relation to the recurrent cash flows will not usually be taken beyond gross margin analysis. Where capital costs are substantial it is necessary to proceed to the further stage of discounted cash-flow analysis, the aim of which is to set initial capital expenditure against the gains derived from it over future years. Discounted cash-flow analysis cannot normally be applied to individual land use enterprises but only to farms or other production units. It commences with the six steps of gross margin analysis, with the following in addition.

(7) Estimate the necessary land improvements in physical terms, e.g. cubic metres of earth to be moved, metres of drainage channel to be dug. Inputs for land improvements are often the main cause of cost differences between suitability classes and subclasses; S1 land may require no land improvements, S2e (e=erosion hazard) land requires bunding, S3e requires terracing, S2d (d=drainage) requires field drains, S3d more substantial drainage works, etc. Land improvements will also differ as between kinds of land use on the same land, e.g. perennial forage crops may not need physical conservation works, rice needs levelling but not drainage,etc.

(8) Make the necessary economic assumptions. At this point practice differs according to whether it is assumed that the cost of land

improvements is to be paid for by the farmer himself. In developed countries the farmer may be expected to meet them by repayment of bank loans; in this case, subsequent analysis is based on real prices and the commercial interest rate. In developing countries land improvement costs will nearly always be met by the community, i.e. government and financing agency, and further economic calculations are based on 'social' cost–benefit analysis. The necessary assumptions include (cf. Hansen 1978, Overseas Development Administration 1972):

(a) Prices: real or 'shadow', reflecting costs to the community arising from e.g. fertiliser subsidies, foreign currency shortages, etc.
(b) Labour: to reflect opportunity costs. In particular, should the labour of the farmer and his family be costed?
(c) The 'social' discount rate. This is the rate of discounting, lower than the various commercial rates, employed for public projects. Discussion of the justification for its use lies beyond the scope of this book, but it is intended *inter alia* to reduce the influence of price inflation and to incorporate a long-term view of the interests of the community, taken by the government on behalf of the people. Most governments lay down a test rate of discount, in recent years usually between 5 and 10%, to be used in comparing public projects.
(d) The 'project life'. This has nothing to do with when the project is expected to end, but is an arbitrary cut-off point, usually taken as 20, 25, 30 or occasionally 50 years; benefits received after this time are excluded from the analysis. This is done partly for accounting convenience, but partly on the grounds that it is unreal to make assumptions about conditions further into the future, when technology or other circumstances may have changed radically.

Such assumptions can make just as much difference to the apparent economic viability of a kind of land use as can variations in land qualities. In particular, the 'social' discount rate is a highly arbitrary assumption, but can have massive apparent effects on the results obtained in uses involving high initial capital expenditure (e.g. irrigation schemes) or delayed returns (e.g. long-term perennial crops, forestry plantations).

(9) Allocate the cash flows of inputs and production by year. Capital costs of smaller land improvements may all be allocated to year zero, and thus not discounted. In larger schemes, capital improvements will be spread over several years. Benefits generally build up, e.g. as

new land is brought into use. A state is reached at which capital works are completed, recurrent costs and production are both steady, and therefore net annual excess of production over costs is steady.

(10) Discount costs and benefits, calculate their present values, and obtain the parameters of cost–benefit analysis (net present value, benefit–cost ratio and internal rate of return).

It is then possible to proceed to further refinements of economic analysis, some of which fall more within the realm of project appraisal than of land evaluation. One modification which may be especially relevant on marginal land is to analyse for selected levels of risk, e.g. to repeat the economic calculations on the basis of input and production estimates for rainfalls to be expected one year in five, in 10, etc.

These procedures may be illustrated by taking the example of the imperfectly drained land used in Table 11.1 and carrying out a cost–benefit analysis of land improvement by drainage works (Table 11.2a). The capital cost of the works is taken as £500, the recurrent annual maintenance cost as £50. Using a 'social' rather than a commercial basis, the discount rate is taken as 5% and the assumed project life 20 years. The annual value of benefits is taken from the gross margins in Table 11.1; in the case of maize, they are given first as compared with not using the land at all and secondly as the increase over the gross margin without drainage. Details of the calculation for tobacco are given in Table 11.2b, first using annual discount factors and secondly by the quicker method using tables of cumulative present value.

The results (Table 11.2c) show that for tobacco cultivation, land improvement by drainage works is well justified, with a net present value of £1344 ha^{-1}, and a benefit–cost ratio of 2.2; indeed, the internal rate of return of 30% would justify such improvements on a commercial accounting basis. For maize alone the benefit–cost ratio is only just above unity, and would not justify undertaking drainage for this crop alone. The 5 ha farm is also not a good proposition, the returns being below those for maize alone owing to the added cost of drainage of rotational fallow. To justify draining this land, a rotation with a greater proportion of tobacco (or other high-value crops) is desirable. Such modifications as this are part of the matching process when economic analysis is integrated into the evaluation.

Table 11.2 Discounted cash-flow analysis of improving imperfectly drained land by drainage.

(a) Data.

land unit	fertile soil, imperfectly drained
land improvements	drainage
economic assumptions	discount rate 5%, project life 20 yr
cost of land improvements (drainage):	
capital (£/ha)	500
recurrent (£/ha)	50
annual value of benefits:	
tobacco (£/ha)	198
maize (compared with non-use) (£/ha)	156
maize (less 'without-drainage' benefits) (£/ha)	100
5 ha farm; 2 ha maize, 1 ha tobacco,	
1 ha fallow, 1 ha woodlot (£/farm)	398
(£/ha)	80

(b) Details of calculation for tobacco.

Year	Costs (£)	Benefits (£)	Discount factor	Present value Costs (£)	Present value Benefits (£)	Present value Benefits−costs (£)
0	500	0	1.000	500	0	−500
1	50	198	0.952	48	188	140
2	50	198	0.907	45	180	135
3	50	198	0.864	43	171	128
⋮	⋮	⋮				
20	50	198	0.377	19	75	56
1–20	–	–	–	1123	2467	1344

Or using tables of cumulative present value:	£
present value of recurrent costs, years 1−20=£50×12.46=	623
capital costs	500
present value of costs	1123
present value of benefits, years 1−20=£198×12.56=	2467

(c) Results.

	Tobacco	Maize (compared with non-use	Maize (less 'without-drainage')	5 ha farm (less 'without-drainage')
present value of benefits, B (£/ha)	2467	1944	1246	992
present value of costs, C (£/ha)	1123	1123	1123	898*
net present value (=$B-C$) (£/ha)	1344	821	123	94
benefit−cost ratio (=B/C)	2.20	1.73	1.11	1.10
internal rate of return (%)	30	21	9	8

*Assuming rotational fallow land drained, but not woodlot.

Applications

Results of economic evaluation

In comparing different types of economic evaluation there is a spectrum, extending from more precise but narrowly based accounting to economic analysis which is less precise but includes broader considerations. Most precise is gross margin analysis, which gives exact data for the profit-ability of the enterprises concerned but tells policy makers nothing else. Cost–benefit analysis can be equally precise so long as it is concerned only with economic efficiency – the most profitable use of available capital. Social cost–benefit analysis is arguably more relevant to public decision making but, by incorporating assumptions about, for example, social equity and land degradation, it is inevitably less precise and the results depend to a large extent on the assumptions. Space does not permit further discussion of these aspects, but they cannot be ignored in land evaluation. In particular, the financial and economic basis within which an evaluation is to be carried out must be decided upon, and the nature of this basis made clear in the presentation of results.

Three features of economic land evaluation should be made clear. First, it is time-dependent. The results vary with changes in relative costs and prices. Short-term fluctuations can be reduced by taking average prices over a period of time, but long-term trends are hard to anticipate. There is no way around this problem, which is simply one way of saying that investment is a risky business.

Secondly, economic evaluation does not provide a single, unique measure of land suitability. Gross margins may be expressed either *per capita* or per unit area of land, with very contrasting results where differ-ent major kinds of land use are concerned. Once capital investment is included, cost–benefit analysis yields three different measures, each of which can give widely different values according to the discount rate adopted, 'project life' and other assumptions.

Thirdly, economic evaluation is not simply a matter of calculation from fixed data but involves assumptions. The element of assumption and judgement is least for gross margins, for analysis on a commercial basis and with paid labour, and is greatest for social cost–benefit analysis of capital investment in developing countries with family labour and absence of a free market. In particular, both the 'social' discount rate and the assumed 'project life' are arbitrary values.

For these reasons, it is better to use gross margins as a basis for land suitability classification where possible, namely when land improve-ments are not essential or not costly in relation to annual production. Suitability class limits are set at values of gross margin per hectare, putting the S3/N1 limit above zero to allow for fixed costs. Permanently not suitable land, N2, does not have an economic upper limit, since it will previously have been allocated to that class on qualitative grounds. Where capital investment is involved, as in particular in irrigation schemes, it is still preferable to conduct the land evaluation initially in terms of repayment capacity, as gross margins and net income on an annual basis. This relatively firm figure can later be subjected to the less objective process of discounting for a project as a whole rather than for individual areas of land. There are circumstances, however, in which discounting for individual land use systems cannot be avoided.

Because of these features of uncertainty, and in part artificiality, economic analysis should never be taken as the only guide to land use decisions. For example, forestry plantations can rarely be justified in narrowly economic terms, yet people will still need wood. In irrigation schemes, salinisation and progressive abandonment of the entire project area commencing in 30 years time would have almost no effect on its benefit–cost ratio, since the present value of benefits so far in the future is low even at 'social' discount rates. Variations in discount rates or 'project life' can often have a greater effect on the results of economic analysis than that of differences in land qualities. This may seem distressing to the soil surveyor, who feels that at a touch of the calculator, all his hard work on permeabilities and crop yield estimates appears to be changed.

The answer to this problem is that economic analysis is not the sole criterion of land suitability. Where investment is concerned, it needs to be justified in economic terms, but not on this basis alone.

A danger in economic evaluation is that by defining suitability classes in economic terms, with their appearance of quantitative objectivity, other aspects which affect suitability may be lost from sight. Non-economists sometimes assume in their innocence that by turning to economics you obtain a firmly based, objective, unique and invariant measure of land suitability; those who have worked through the procedures know better.

Economic analysis in physical evaluation

In qualitative and quantitative physical evaluations it is very desirable, following the initial suitability classification in physical terms, to carry out some generalised economic analyses, possibly on a sample basis. This is to ensure that the assessed suitabilities at least broadly correspond with economic realities.

Such generalised economic calculations will necessarily stop at gross margin analysis, since the procedures of cost–benefit analysis do not lend themselves to generalised treatment. Farm variable costs may be obtained as a single estimate, rather than being calculated from individual inputs; fixed costs may be ignored. Crop yield or other production estimates remain necessary; prices of products can be the present farm-gate prices rather than future projections.

If the results should suggest that one land utilisation type on S2 land (for that use) is currently a better farming proposition than another on S1 land, this does not necessarily mean that the physical evaluation must be started all over again. Not only are economic calculations short-lived, but there are more grounds for assessing suitability than profit to the farmer.

Combining measures of land suitability

Physical land evaluation is directed towards matching the ecological and technological requirements of land use with the qualities of land, aided by inputs and land improvements. Economic considerations are impli-cit: for example, in high-income countries, labour-intensive methods of production are simply omitted from consideration, without calculation of precise costs and returns. In economic land evaluation, profitability or other economic measures are the primary criteria of suitability. The influence of physical land qualities is subsumed in the monetary values assigned to the costs of inputs and production. In addition to these physical and economic criteria, environmental impact at the very least places constraints upon suitable forms of land use, whilst a range of demographic and social factors may also be relevant. It remains to con-sider how these different criteria can be combined.

Any or all of the following criteria might reasonably be employed, in various circumstances, in assessing the suitability of different areas of land for specified kinds of use.

Physical criteria
(a) *Physical suitability:* degree of correspondence between ecological and technical requirements for the use with qualities of the land.
(b) *Physical production per unit area:* production of basic subsistence carbohydrate (expressed in calories), or of meat, timber, etc. Com-parisons are only possible between products of similar kind, e.g. different tree species for firewood plantations in terms of mean annual increment multiplied by calorific values.
(c) *Physical production per capita,* similarly to (b).
(d) *Environmental impact:* other than as already taken into account under physical suitability. Off-site effects may be included at this stage, e.g. eutrophication of inland waters, effects on stream sediment loads.

Economic criteria
(a) *Income per capita:* at full production, from gross margin analysis.
(b) *Income per unit area,* similarly to (a).

(c) Measures of *return on capital invested:* net present value, benefit–cost ratio or internal rate of return, each calculated either on a commercial basis or by including a variety of broader aspects into social cost–benefit analysis.

Demographic and social criteria
(a) *Population-supporting capacity:* population per unit area. Sometimes as capacity for new land settlement.
(b) *Population displacements.*
(c) *Social consequences.*

Table 11.3 gives an example based on Central Malaŵi. The Thiwi land system is the kind of marginal land on which much development planning takes place: it is climatically suitable for annual crops but moderately sloping and with sandy soils of low inherent fertility. Annual crops give the highest income per hectare and the highest population-supporting capacity (the latter important in its own right in this region), but have a negative environmental impact through soil erosion. Coffee growing was not economically viable at the time of the survey, although with the rise in coffee prices it has since become so. Livestock ranching has a higher income per capita than arable use and is environmentally acceptable, but is highly unfavourable in terms of income per unit area and population-supporting capacity. Forest plantations are moderately favourable on all counts. The best decision for this area is probably to allot part to a forest reserve (with the added benefit of serving the firewood needs of an adjacent more fertile land system under arable use) and the remainder to mixed arable–livestock farming.

One method of combining diverse criteria is by means of a goals achievement matrix. First, select objectives or 'goals', that is, the results of land use change which are considered to be desirable in the area. Assign relative weightings to each of these objectives, the weightings adding up to unity; thus, food production per unit area might be assigned a high importance in developing countries with a food deficit. Estimate the extent to which each land use system will fulfil each selected objective. Where already expressed numerically, e.g. economic and demographic criteria, convert the most favourable land use system to a value of 100 and scale off others accordingly; where not initially numerical (e.g. environmental impact, social effects), estimate in relative terms from 0 (highly undesirable) to 100. For each land use system, multiply the relative percentage to which it achieves each goal by the weighting attached to that goal and add the products. The result is a measure of the degree to which each land use system fulfils the selected objectives. Table 11.4 shows this technique applied to the same example given in Table

Table 11.3 Quantitative current suitability: comparison of different land utilisation types on the Thiwi land unit, Dedza District, Malaŵi. From Young and Goldsmith (1977).

Major kind of land use	Land utilisation type	Net income (£) per hectare	Net income (£) per capita	Population density per km²	Environmental impact
annual crops	with livestock, improved management, 1.6 ha farms	113	36	312	Moderate
annual crops	no livestock, improved management, 3.0 ha farms	50	30	167	Moderate
perennial crops	coffee, 1.6 ha farms, improved management	−10	−16	156	Low
livestock	ranching	2.3	75	3	Low
forest plantations		63	51	63	Low

Table 11.4 Goals achievement matrix applied to the Thiwi land unit. Data derived from Table 11.3.

(a) As per cent of best.

Land utilisation type	Return per hectare	Return per capita	Population density	Environmental impact	Total
annuals/livestock, 1.6 ha	100	48	100	70	
annuals only, 3.0 ha	44	40	54	60	
ranching	2	100	1	90	
forest plantations	56	68	40	100	
weighting	0.3	0.2	0.3	0.2	1.0

(b) Weighted data.

Land utilisation type	Return per hectare	Return per capita	Population density	Environmental impact	Total
annuals/livestock, 1.6 ha	30	10	30	14	84
annuals only, 3.0 ha	13	8	16	12	49
ranching	1	20	1	18	39
forest plantations	17	14	12	20	63

11.3. Mixed annuals-with-livestock farming fulfils 84% of the objectives, ranching just under half this value.

Having shown the existence of this technique, it should be said that it is not usually a good way to arrive at decisions. The first results obtained will usually be at variance with a subjective feeling of what is the right decision, and will need adjustment by altering the weightings or by other means. Moreover there are thresholds, for example, of environmental degradation or profitability to the farmer, at which particular uses are completely ruled out, regardless of their fulfilment of other object- ives. But the method does serve to draw attention to the subjective weightings which are in fact being applied, and it can be employed as a means of presentation, to demonstrate results arrived at by other methods.

Wider aspects of economic and social analysis

There is a wide range of economic and social considerations which can affect land suitability for particular kinds of use. This applies not only to physical but also equally to economic evaluations; farm gross margins and other measures of profitability outlined above are by no means the whole of economic analysis, added to which there are considerations broadly related to effects on people which may be called for convenience 'social analysis'.

The following aspects therefore apply to all kinds of evaluation. They are listed in approximate order from economic to social, but there is no clearcut division.

(1) *Markets.* These may have been considered as part of the initial dis- cussions. Even so, if your survey has just discovered that there are 300 000 ha highly suitable for, say, cashew nuts, the danger of flood- ing the market needs to be pointed out.

(2) *Labour.* Analysis of labour requirements may be based on the same listing of inputs as that employed in step (2) of economic analysis. Labour constraints may call for the modification of land utilisation types, for example, reduction in the area allotted to profitable but labour-intensive crops, or modification of cropping patterns to ease peak seasonal labour demands of annual crops.

(3) *Transport.* If not already taken into account under the land quality location, consideration can be given to means of transporting inputs from their points of supply and products to local markets or ports of export. A useful technique is to add actual or potential accessibility as a kind of overlay to suitabilities initially determined irrespective of location.

(4) *Population.* Proposed changes in land use will usually have conse- quences for the population density of an area, and sometimes for settlement or displacement of people. In developing countries, potential for support of population, or for land settlement, can be a major criterion in decisions on land use.

(5) *Subsistence requirements.* In developing countries there is a need to consider, over and above the stated production from land utilisation

types, whether the pattern of proposed changes will make provision for firewood and domestic timber, grazing, or other village subsistence requirements.

(6) *Land tenure.* In developed and settled areas, legal rights to land ownership or use are frequently a major constraint to planning. In developing countries, quasi-legal customary rights, e.g. to communal grazing, can have equally important implications.

(7) *Minority groups.* Proposed land use changes may affect the interests of minority groups, for example, nomadic people.

There are still further aspects, such as political considerations, which may affect the final decisions taken. Although in a sense consequences of land use changes, these may reasonably be held to lie beyond the remit of land evaluation.

It is a far cry from effective soil depth to repayment capacity and population displacement but all are part of land evaluation. The two foundation stones of the structure are description of land qualities and assessment of the requirements of land use; of these, the former is at present the more solid. Spanning them, through the matching process, is qualitative land evaluation. This gives its results in terms of whether plants will grow or animals flourish. For the early stages of planning, this serves valuable purposes, particularly in ruling out the least favourable alternatives and selecting the most promising for further consideration. Quantitative evaluation gives a more clearly defined set of results, and forces the surveyor to be precise over inputs and to estimate amounts of production. Results from this stage will be subject to change with developments in technology, but the uptake of such changes is usually slow. Economic evaluation rests on quantitative physical data and combines them with prices and assumptions to give the information needed before making investments, namely whether the proposed use will pay. This is a major addition to the evaluation procedure but not the final one, for adverse environmental, demographic or other social effects may render unacceptable an otherwise profitable enterprise. All these are part of the process of land evaluation, contributing at different stages and according to the circumstances of surveys to the varied objectives of land use planning and management.

Further reading

See Dasgupta *et al.* (1972), Hansen (1978), Makin *et al.* (1976, Pt 8) and Overseas Development Administration (1972).

There is little published as yet on the economics of land evaluation, other than what is included in the *Framework for land evaluation* (FAO 1976). The references given cover project appraisal, within which are included techniques employed in economic land evaluation.

Automatic Data Handling

Soil information systems

Although applicable to any collection of soil data, the term soil information system (SIS) has come to refer to data stored in computerised form. A soil information system is based on the data for a large number of soil profiles, coded in a standardised form, usually input on cards and stored on magnetic tape. It can then be processed in any desired manner within the system and output as tables and maps, which can be directly supplied to the user or printed in a soil memoir. A number of national surveys have established soil information systems, the largest being those of the USA and Canada. Now that access to computer facilities is so widely available, including by means of microprocessors, it is quite possible for firms and individuals to set up their own systems.

Establishing a soil information system

Soil profile descriptions lend themselves readily to storage in coded form. There are five or more groups of data: location, site description, field profile description, analytical data and one or more sets of performance data (agricultural, engineering, etc.). It is convenient to treat each group as an array, one-dimensional for location, site and performance, two-dimensional for profile description and analytical data where values for each horizon are required. For example using Fortran, the site description could be input as an integer array ISITE (I), where ISITE (1) refers to class of parent material, ISITE (2) to mean annual rainfall, and so on. Similarly profile data could be stored as an array IPROF (I, J) where J=1 refers to data for the first horizon, J=2 the second, etc.; the first value stored under I should be the depth to the base of the horizon, which allows data to be retrieved for any chosen depth. Integer codes are convenient for site and profile data, real numbers for analytical data.

Sets of coded values are established for each soil property except those which are already in numerical form, as analytical data, rainfall, etc. Thus each parent material class must be allocated a number. Composite soil properties are stored as separate variables, e.g. Munsell hue, value and chroma, or grade, size and type of structure. For example, size of structural aggregates may be coded: fine=1, medium=2, coarse=3 and very coarse=4. Examples of codings are given in the field handbooks for the UK (Hodgson 1974) and Canada (Dumanski 1978). Letter symbols, e.g. texture classes, horizon designations, can be stored as such but are more convenient to process if allotted a number. Analytical data are input in their actual values. It is essential to establish a convention for distinguishing between 'zero', 'not applicable' and 'no data'; that is, to differentiate between variables which have a value of 0 (e.g. slope angle of 0°), circumstances where particular variables are not applicable (e.g. size of structure in a structureless horizon), and instances where, deliberately or accidentally, values were not recorded.

The surveyor in the field often records features which fall outside standard profile description (and therefore codings), such as unusual profile features, points of emphasis, or such comments as 'Darker than typical Able Series, probably because low on slope'. A substantial amount of space should be left for storing such matter in verbal form (Fortran A format).

Having been input as number codes, the information can be output as words. By taking some trouble with the conversion program the result can be made to look very much like a normal profile description (e.g. Webster *et al.* 1976). On the other hand, line printer tables in which each horizon is one line and every variable is in a column are if anything easier for a reader to take in than the conventional form.

Input of soil boundaries in digitised form is a much slower and more expensive process, and it is doubtful whether it has a cost advantage over manual recording. The cost rises rapidly with increase in the length of boundary and number of separate delineations.

If it is known that a soil information system will be used, the codes should be drawn up prior to field survey and printed on forms used for fieldwork. For example, structure could be directly recorded as '5. 2. 4' instead of the conventional 'wk med bl'. This is not merely to save time and avoid errors in coding; by indicating the nature of the Procrustean bed into which the greater part of the description is being forced, it draws the surveyor's attention to the need to record exceptional or significant features in addition to the coded values.

Uses of soil information systems

Data retrieval. This is simply a service to users, outside and within a survey organisation. It is possibly the most useful of all applications. Anyone needing soil information for a given area fills in location and kind of information sought on a preprinted form; this is punched onto a card, and all available information of that area is quickly and cheaply printed. An example on a large scale is the annually revised list of all soil series in the USA, classified by Soil I Taxonomy.

Classification. The criteria for a soil class, whether a series or higher categorical level, can readily be put into computerised form. In Fortran this is achieved by a sequence of IF statements, constructing a net such that, e.g. if the hue is 2.5 YR or redder, if the texture within 20–50 cm depth is sandy clay or clay, and if the structural grade moderate or strong, etc., the profile falls out at the bottom as Lilongwe Series. It is not necessary for all limiting values to be rigid; conditional situations can be built in on the lines of, for example, if the hue is 5 YR, the profile is still acceptable as Lilongwe Series provided the structural grade is strong.

Such a system takes a considerable time to set up, not least to discover, and to put into the program all the tacit assumptions that you have made. Once established, it allows any new profile to be instantly classified on a uniform basis (including output as 'Unclassified; no data for . . .'). A particular advantage over manual methods is that if the classification is changed, all recorded profiles can be reclassified. A related application is to set up a modal profile, with confidence limits for range of variation, for any set of profiles subjectively assigned to a group.

Parametric mapping. The values for any selected soil property or set of properties can be output directly on the line printer or graph plotter in map form using letters or symbols. Programs are available for drawing isolines around such geographically located values. This output can either be employed directly in presentation or used to trace off hand-drawn maps. Output of this nature is simple and cheap. Automated cartography, whereby fair-drawn coloured maps are produced, is a considerably more complex undertaking, requiring the services of a specialist organisation.

Quantitative techniques. Most of the methods of quantitative analysis, listed below, require a data base in computerised form.

Soil survey interpretation. Although not yet widely developed, the application of automatic data handling to the relations between soil properties and performance has considerable potential. The US SIS contains large amounts of interpretative data, related both to engineering properties and a variety of potential evaluations, e.g. suitability for picnic sites, sewage disposal. There is a particular opportunity to build up stores of information that will lead towards models of crop performance in relation to soil properties; it is worth noting that this can only be achieved if climatic data are recorded in just as much detail as those for soil. A great advantage of automated systems in this respect is the capacity constantly to update and revise as new information becomes available. Applications in land evaluation are further discussed below.

When to use automatic data handling

It has been well said that a task which by old-fashioned manual means would have taken six months can be accomplished with the aid of a computer in as little as a year. For the inexperienced surveyor to decide, for reasons of prestige, that all his results must be stored, processed and output by computer is a sure way of wasting his time and other people's money. Fortunately the mystique of computers, with its accompanying danger that the ignorant will suppose their results to be necessarily superior, is gradually being put into proper perspective in Western countries, and it is to be hoped that the developing world does not go through a phase of making this assumption. On many soil surveys it is entirely satisfactory to store profile descriptions on handwritten sheets, sort and tabulate by hand, and present results as a manually drawn map, and there is nothing to be gained from the substantial extra time needed to computerise the information.

The situation is different when two conditions are fulfilled: the number of profiles to be handled runs into thousands, and the survey organisation concerned possesses an established soil information system with staff to operate it. In these circumstances the mass-handling and rapid retrieval facilities made available can both save time and increase availability of information (the quantity of data now forever lost in filing cabinets is enormous). The manner in which interpretative data are tabulated in the county volumes of the US Soil Survey illustrates this favourable situation.

One problem with automatic processing is that computer programs are less able than human intelligence to cope with incomplete data. This forces the field surveyor to record all details for every profile.

Whether to set up, or employ, a soil information system is one of the decisions to be made in planning a survey programme. As with data processing in other fields, the computer may best be regarded as a slave. When, in the course of planning a survey it becomes clear that tasks are going to arise that call for large amounts of routine work, then use automatic handling for these tasks. This takes care of dull, repetitive jobs, releasing time for the many aspects of a survey that are much more effectively done by human intelligence.

Techniques for quantitative analysis of soils information

A large number of techniques of statistical analysis have been applied to soils, occasionally in the course of soil survey although mostly as research. They do not for the most part fall into the realm of practical soil survey. These techniques are reviewed by Norris (1970) and Webster

(1978a). The following list gives a very brief indication of what each technique is designed to do; further details can be found in the publications listed.

(a) *Scales of spatial variation*. Of possible use in the research stage of soil survey. See p. 92.

(b) *The predictive ability of a soil map*. See p. 95.

(c) *Analysis of variance*. See p. 96. This technique can be extended to groups of soil properties by the use of Wilks's criterion (Webster 1971).

(d) *Describing a media profile for a soil series and confidence limits for its variation*. This can be achieved from a set of profiles previously selected as typical of the series.

(e) *Calculating the potential economic benefit of soil survey*. See p. 101.

(f) *Determining the optimum locations for soil boundaries*. (Webster 1978b). This technique is far too time-consuming for routine application in soil survey.

(g) *Correlations between individual soil properties, or between soil and environment*. Such relationships are readily obtained from a soil information system.

(h) *Multiple regression*. 'Explains' (in a statistical sense only) one variable in terms of others, e.g. pH in terms of rainfall, parent material and drainage.

(i) *Numerical classification*. Descending classification, by a series of present/absent or less than/greater than criteria, has long been a feature of the Australian soil classification system (Northcote *et al.* 1971). There are several complex methods for statistical classification, the most common of which is similarity analysis; a large number of profiles are progressively grouped according to increasing similarity, producing a dendritic 'tree' (e.g. Moore *et al.* 1972; Cuanalo & Webster, 1970). The higher-level divisions in this can be used to indicate where taxonomic divisions can be drawn. A major problem of this approach is that the addition of new profiles produces a different classification.

(j) *Principal component analysis*. This, the most commonly used of the techniques of ordination, rearranges the many variables of a soil profile into a set of mutually perpendicular axes, like the two axes on a simple regression graph but in many dimensions; the result may be envisaged as a sort of multidimensional porcupine, the spines of which are cigar and rugby-football shaped clusters of points. This technique can provide insight into which groups of properties are and are not associated with each other, for example the early discovery that gleys had little in common apart from the properties directly associated with reducing conditions.

(k) *Canonical correlation.* An extension of multiple regression, which treats the relations not between single variables but between two or more sets of measurements made on the same individuals.

(l) *Multiple discriminant analysis.* A form of classification which, instead of initially grouping most similar individuals, takes as its starting point the (multidimensional) space which maximally separates two groups whilst minimising their within-group variation. This could be used to construct groups in which the value 1–*RV* (p. 96) was at a minimum.

(m) *Kriging.* A form of weighted local averaging, in which the soil properties at an unknown point are predicted from those at surrounding points (Burgess & Webster 1980). The first stage is to derive functions giving how each soil property varies with distance; this is done by comparing points observed at different distances apart and plotting semi-variance against distance (a semi-variogram). These functions are used to derive the weighting to be attached to observations at various distances from the point for which information is required. Observed values of soil properties for surrounding points are given appropriate weightings, and the results combined into a best estimate for the required point. By a further stage of calculation, isopleth maps for individual properties can be produced. This is an extreme form of treating soil as a continuum as opposed to treating it as homogeneous units separated by boundaries. It thus could be applicable in areas where the natural landscape exhibits gradual change, e.g. drift-covered plains with little topographic expression.

Automated methods in land evaluation

The potential gains from applying automated methods to land evaluation are probably greater than for their use in the handling of soils data alone. In soil information systems, the techniques consist fundamentally of different methods of treating sets of multivariate data which describe one entity, the soil profile, and in combining and comparing these sets in various ways. In land evaluation, the fundamental operation is one of comparison between two sets of data, the qualities of the land and the requirements of different kinds of land use. This basic feature opens up possibilities for the development of functional relationships between these two sets of data, for example of estimating crop yields or livestock-carrying capacity from information on climate, soils and vegetation. Up to the present, this potential has been little explored.

Land capability classification systems are readily turned into computer programs. The basic procedure of using a conversion table (Table 9.3, p. 134), that of starting in the top left-hand corner and moving right or

Table 12.1 Example of output from a computerised land capability classification. From Young and Goldsmith (1977).

Site no.	Soil management unit	Soil series	Land capability class	Gradient	Wetness	Outcrops, boulders	Topsoil texture	Effective depth	Subsoil texture	Permeability	Operative limitation
							Values of limitations				
1	Lilongwe	Lilongwe	1	0	0	0	3	0	6	2	–
2	Lilongwe	Lilongwe	2	1	0	0	3	0	6	2	gradient
5	Lilongwe	Mwanjema	4	1	2	0	3	0	6	2	wetness
6	Lilongwe	Kandiani	3	0	1	0	2	0	5	2	wetness
8	dambo	Mbabzi	9	0	3	0	6	0	6	5	wetness
14	Lilongwe	Kandiani	1	0	0	0	3	0	5	2	–
31	Thiwi	Jalira	7	1	0	0	2	3	1	5	eff. depth

downwards according to a series of questions of the form 'Is the value of X greater/less than N?', can immediately be programmed in Fortran by a series of IF and GO TO statements. Any subdivisions in the table, e.g. different slope angles according to soil texture, are handled by nested questions. Each time a question results in the land class being lowered, the code number of the limitation which caused that lowering is recorded. At the end, the observation site has been allotted to a capability class and subclass, and the kind of limitation which caused it to be in that class, the operative limitation, has been recorded. If wished, the values of all the limitations for that site can be stored and output (Table 12.1). Each observation site is treated successively and, as in soils data alone, its location is recorded by coordinates. Wherever the information necessary to assess any limitation is missing the site is recorded as 'insufficient data'. The resulting land classes can be output by the graph plotter directly as symbols on a map at any desired scale (Fig. 12.1). If the classiffication scheme is changed the complete set of observation sites can be reclassified by altering the program and applying it to the same original data, stored on tape.

For land suitability evaluation based on land qualities, the principle is similar but there are two main stages (Fig. 12.2). First the basic data, recorded in the form of land characteristics, are processed to give values of land qualities. Where necessary, for example in estimating moisture deficit, quite complex calculations can be incorporated by means of a subroutine. In the second stage, the relevant land qualities for a land utilisation type are selected and the suitability class is obtained from these. Where the means of combining suitabilities from individual land qualities is that of the method of limitations (p. 176), the overall suitability is obtained by successive IF statements as described for land

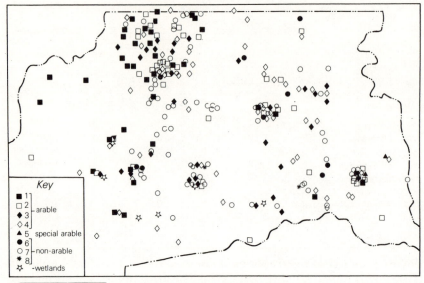

Figure 12.1 Example of automatically printed map of land capability classes, Malawi. From Young and Goldsmith (1977).

capability. Where some other method of combination is employed, appropriate arithmetic or sorting procedures are used. It is essential for the program to be completely specific about the manner of combination and to cover all eventualities. Each different land utilisation type is applied to data from the first site by a program loop; this is set within a further loop which selects the sites in turn. The output can include:

(a) The suitability class of each site for each land utilisation type considered;
(b) the land quality, or combination of qualities, which caused the site to fall into that class, and hence the suitability subclass for each land utilisation type;
(c) computer-printed maps showing suitabilities for each land utilisation type in turn, by means of symbols printed in their correct positions; by further refinements of automated cartography, the whole area can be mapped into suitability classes.

The procedures described so far are no more than can be achieved by manual processing of data, and much extra time is needed in the first instance if the system is to be automated. A suitability classification of quite modest complexity could take something of the order of six man-months to program, test and remove the inevitable crazy results which

Automated Methods in Land Evaluation

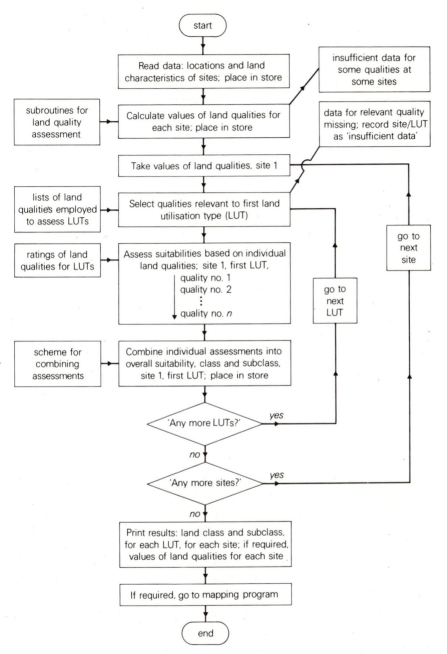

Figure 12.2 Generalised flow chart for land suitability evaluation by computer.

appear at first owing to failure to realise tacit assumptions. The benefits appear when it comes to modifying the system of evaluation. Suppose, for example, that soil depth has been taken as a limitation, and limits of 100, 50 and 25 cm assigned as suitability class boundaries for some crop. Later, evidence may come forward that these were too generous and limits of 80, 40 and 20 cm would be more appropriate. If there are several thousand observation sites and processing has been manual, the new evidence will quite likely be ignored on the grounds of the time needed to reprocess the data. If on the other hand the system has been automated, it is easy and cheap to insert the revised values and reclassify the sites. Progressive improvements of this kind can be made at a more sophisticated level than simple substitution of values or addition of a further land quality; models of predicted crop yields or other production may be developed and incorporated in the system. By such means, an initially rather crude evaluation system can be progressively improved and refined over a number of years. At the present, such developments are only at an early stage.

One of the most advanced and versatile systems for land data storage and retrieval is the Canada Land Data System, operated by the Lands Directorate, Environment Canada, Ottawa. This stores data from more than 3000 digitised maps, including land capability for agriculture, forestry, recreation and wildlife, together with present land use and administrative boundaries. It supplies information in either tabular or map form, combining data of different kinds where required. For example, a table showing areas presently forested and those suitable for forestry within a set of administrative divisions can be produced, or overlay maps combining census boundaries, land capability and present land use. Two aspects of such systems must be set against each other: they are very costly to set up but, once in operation, they enable regional planning to proceed on a geographically well informed basis.

The problem of wasting time by computerisation for its own sake has already been noted. The other danger of using automated methods is epitomised in the well known aphorism 'GIGO – garbage in, garbage out'. Classifications of land capability or suitability produced by a computer can never be any better than the land/land use relationships which were devised and fed into the program. They can easily be very much worse than manually processed results, since the latter are subject to continual monitoring by common sense. The computer is at its most efficient when doing the work of a slave (i.e. research assistant), churning through large numbers of observation sites in an objective and uniform way. In land evaluation as in soil survey, the setting up of systems for classification, evaluation and mapping, tasks requiring skill and judgement, are performed very much better by experienced surveyors.

Further reading

Norris (1970), Rudeforth (1975), Webster (1978a), de Gruijter (1977), Beckett *et al.* (1972), Bie (1975), Moore and Bie (1977), Moore *et al.* (1972), Sadovsky and Bie (1978), Courtney and Nortcliff (1977).

Presentation of Results

13

The quality of a survey is judged by its finished product, and therefore the effort devoted to presentation of the results should be in due proportion to that expended on the survey itself. Presentation is not a postscript to a survey but one of the most critical parts, second only to the initial planning, and sufficient time and resources must be allocated at the planning stage for the production of the maps and report.

A soil survey is intended for use; if the results are not used, the work may just as well not have been done. Hence the aims of the report should be:

(a) to tell the potential user what information is there;
(b) to emphasise the practical importance of that information;
(c) to help each kind of user find the information he needs, and enable him to understand it.

The people who are interested in the findings of a survey come from many walks of life and have different backgrounds and special interests. Those users must be identified and the report directed towards them. If the users are farmers, write the report for farmers. In a land development project, the users range from government ministers, partners of engineering firms, bankers, technical specialists in agronomy, irrigation engineering, etc., to economists. You cannot write a separate report for every one of those, so the interests and technical knowledge of each must be identified and all must be able to locate relevant material in a comprehensible form.

Besides the variety of users, a further problem is that a survey report will include information which is valid for different periods of time. The basic mapped distribution of soil types and properties, including the results of chemical, physical and engineering tests based on the mapping units, has a long-term value over and above the immediate demands which led to the survey. Interpretative material of a physical kind, e.g. crop yield estimates or qualitative land evaluation, has an intermediate life, in due course being rendered obsolete by changes in technology. Economic interpretation has the shortest life of all, often requiring recal-

216

culation in terms of changed prices even before the printing of the report. All these kinds of information must be placed on record, so that if economic, technological or other circumstances change, reference can be made back to the basic data. It is not enough to leave such information on files, as 'backup material'; unless presented in an orderly and adequately annotated manner, such data are unusable by anyone other than the authors. A recently tried practice of putting such information onto microfiche is highly inconvenient for the reader.

Poor presentation has been one reason why so many soil surveys have been put to little use. In a typical report of many national survey organisations, about two-thirds of the text is devoted to detailed descriptions of the soil types present, couched largely in pedological terminology and supported by chemical analytical data of no demonstrated significance. Little space or attention is given to interpretations and guidance on land potential and management. Have such reports been written for the surveyors themselves?

Consultants' reports set a better example. Although they have a captive audience, the clients, attractive presentation and clear exposition are as important as soundness of content for the reputation of a company and the securing of future contracts. Another source which repays study is the recent reports of the US Soil Conservation Service. The section on interpretation, or use and management of the soils, is usually longer than the pedological descriptions and in some cases placed before it. The arrangement of a typical report is as follows:

(1) *How to use this soil survey.* A guide printed inside the front cover, explaining how to locate the soils of an area of interest on the map, and where to find different kinds of information about them in the report.
(2) *General soil map for broad land use planning.* A brief introductory description of soils and the landscapes in which they are found, readable by the non-specialist.
(3) *Use and management of the soils.* Sections on interpretation, land use potential and management, for crops, pasture, woodlands, engineering uses, recreation and wildlife habitat; inclusive of interpretative tables, about half the text.
(4) *Descriptions of the soils.* Series by series, mostly pedological detail but each ending with a paragraph on limitations, land capability and management; rather shorter than the text on interpretation.
(5) *Formation and classification of the soils.* Short and only semi-technical.
(6) *General nature of the County.* Broad physical environment; printed first in some surveys; short.

It comes hard to the soil surveyer, who has spent the last year or more digging pits and rubbing soil between his fingers, that no-one appears to be interested in the results of all this hard work. The desire to justify it by presenting large volumes of pedological detail seems irresistible. But the balance of text space in the survey report should not be in proportion to the effort devoted to different kinds of activity. In particular, much of the systematic mapping effort is subsumed in the map and extended legend. The same situation occurs in engineering, economics and many fields of applied science. The presentation is focused on the potentially useful results, compressing though not omitting the data and reasoning which lead to them.

As a possible means of breaking away from the conventional form of presentation, consider setting out the results in the reverse order to that in which they were obtained. Following the statement of the problem, the actual order of work is likely to have followed the sequence: collection of basic data on soils and their distribution, interpretations based on these data, leading to conclusions and guidelines on use and management; commissioned surveys may then continue to recommendations. In the report, this sequence can be followed backwards, shedding readers at each stage. First, all users wish to know about the recommendations, if any, and the conclusions and management guidelines; non-specialists responsible for policy will close the report at this stage. Technical readers, such as farmers and agronomists, want to know the reasoning behind these results, and thus the basis for the interpretations; they are prepared to take the pedological detail for granted. A very small readership indeed, namely soil scientists charged with implementation of development, extending the results to adjacent areas, or possibly reinterpretation of the basic data, will proceed to the soil profile descriptions and related data.

Two innovations have helped to make reports more readable whilst not losing essential information: the technical appendix and the summary volume. The technical appendix is a means of placing on record basic data on which the conclusions are founded; it is not needed for the immediate purposes of the survey but may be required if reinterpretation is called for. Formal soil profile descriptions and tables of analytical data are sometimes appropriately relegated to the appendix, putting shorter descriptions, technically accurate but in readable prose, into the main text. The summary volume brings together in non-technical language those results that are of interest to policy makers.

Adoption of both these practices leads to four main sections: summary, main text, technical appendices, and maps. In a large survey these will be separate volumes, otherwise sections of a single volume.

The report

Special-purpose soil surveys are directed at a specific object, or problem, such as what will happen if a particular tidal marsh is reclaimed, or where you can safely dispose of toxic wastes. In such circumstances the conventional order of a report can certainly be reversed: start by giving the answers to the problem, follow this with the technical reasons for those answers, and only lastly or as an appendix give the pedological details on which the reasoning is based.

In order to outline a report in terms that will be widely applicable, we shall assume a general-purpose survey, covering an area for which a variety of uses is possible. This could be either a survey by a national soil survey organisation, intended for use over many years, or a commissioned survey intended for a multipurpose land development scheme. Table 13.1 gives an outline for the report on such a survey. In sections 4 to 6 the conventional order of soils–interpretation–recommendations has been followed, but as noted above the sequence of these chapters may be reversed.

Many of these headings are self-explanatory or can be amplified by reference to published reports. For a systematic account of the details, reference may be made to Smyth (1970). Comment here is confined to points of emphasis.

I. The summary

The most important part of a report commissioned as a basis for land development is the 'executive summary'. This is usually the only part read by senior personnel, who need to know how the findings of the survey affect their planning but who do not have the time or specialist interest to study the details of the report. It must be self-explanatory and illustrated wherever required by photographs, diagrams and small-scale maps. Readers should not need to refer to the main text, but individual conclusions and recommendations may be cross-referenced. It should be written in plain language, avoiding technical jargon. Areas mentiond in the text should be clearly marked on the accompanying maps.

A distinction should be kept between conclusions and recommendations. Conclusions are derived from the soils and their estimated behaviour, often under alternative courses of action. Recommendations make a selection from these alternative courses. Thus a conclusion might be that two soil types offer an erosion hazard, one more serious than the other; the recommendation could be that one should be cultivated with appropriate safeguards, the other left under forest. In developed countries it may be better to present the conclusions and leave the users to

Table 13.1 Outline for a soil survey report.

---

vol. I   Summary

vol. II Main report

    0 Introductory sections

    A Systematic general-purpose survey
       how to use the report
       abstract
       acknowledgements
       table of contents

    B Consultant's report
       preface
       terms of reference
       acknowledgements
       table of contents

    1 Background and aims of the survey

    2 The environment
       physical
       agriculture/present land use
       economic and social background

    3 Methods of survey

    4 Soils
       introduction
       legend
       soil mapping units

    5 Land evaluation/soil survey interpretation
       introduction
       land capability/land suitability classification
       land capability/land suitability units
       economic and social analysis

    6 Soil and land management
       principles guiding recommendations
       land allocation to specific uses
       specific recommendations, e.g. erosion control, drainage, irrigation

    7 Closing sections
       references
       glossary of technical terms
       units of measurement

vol. III Technical appendices
       survey methods
       laboratory methods
       soil classification, representative profile descriptions and laboratory data
       specialist field and analytical studies (e.g. borehole data, water analyses,
         climatic/soil moisture calculations)
       interpretative data (e.g. crop yield summaries)

vol. IV Maps
       soil map
       basic interpretative map
       additional interpretative maps

---

make up their own minds. In developing countries, recommendations are always agreed in advance with the clients, as a check that technically desirable measures do not conflict with socio-political constraints. In a multidisciplinary report, the conclusions and recommendations must be in accord with those of other specialists.

II. The main report

The main body of the report explains the methods, findings and interpretations of the survey for a broad readership that does not have specialist knowledge of soil science. It should not be disrupted by lengthy inclusions of technical material that are primarily for reference; these should be consigned to appendices.

As far as possible, factual material should be separated from interpretations. This emphasises the immediate usefulness of the interpretative assessments while at the same time simplifying the task of reinterpretation for other purposes or as external circumstances change.

How to use this report. Explain to farmers, planners and other potential users how to locate a farm, field or other site on the maps, how to find the soils present from the map legends, and where in the text and tables to find information of different kinds. This material is effectively presented inside the front cover.

Abstract. Besides enabling the potential user to judge whether the survey is of interest to him, the abstract is used by bibliographic abstracting services. To be effective it should be short, less than 250 words. Translation into major international languages is desirable. As far as possible, abstracts should give results as opposed to saying what was done. Thus 'In the Eastern Region there are 24 000 ha of good arable land and a further 37 000 ha marginal for arable use, is much more informative than 'The soils of the Eastern Region were classified according to their potential for arable use.'

Table of contents. This outlines the structure of the report and acts as a guide to the reader. The headings should be informative; 'Map unit 21' is not informative, 'Soils of the river flats' is more useful. Separate lists of tables and maps are useful for reference.

Background and aims of the survey. A short account of the circumstances which led to the survey being carried out, and its intended purposes.

The environment or introduction to the area
(a) *Location:* including a small-scale map giving all place names used in the report, with an inset showing location within the country.

(b) *Physical environment:* brief descriptions of climate, geology, geomorphology, hydrology and vegetation, not in comprehensive detail but sufficient to support the description and interpretation of soil data. Much of this information can be effectively presented as small-scale maps.

(c) *Agriculture and/or present land use:* on a similar basis, possibly in more detail than the physical environment if this is relevant to the survey, i.e. the area is already densely settled.

(d) *Economic and social background:* similarly as a context, for example, as a background to the management levels assumed in the recommendations.

Methods of survey. A statement sufficient to enable the user to judge the quality of the data, both to establish confidence in the findings and to enable decisions to be taken on the need for further work. This will include information on base maps and air photographs, density and types of field soil observations, laboratory analyses, and other types of survey carried out or incorporated (e.g. pasture resource surveys). Any techniques specially developed or adapted to overcome problems encountered in this survey should be stated briefly, with details reported in an appendix.

Soils

All of the preceding material has been in a sense introductory, and this is the first major section of results in the report. It should include the following material.

Introduction. To explain the layout of the chapter, to describe in non-technical terms the soil classification employed and how the soil types have been grouped into mapping units, and to state how this chapter is related to the interpretative chapters which follow.

Complete map legend and soil mapping units. This is the section to which the user who has located his farm or other area of interest on the map first turns. It should always form part of the main report, not an appendix, since it is essentially an extension of the map itself. Where there is a large number of units, group according to the landforms with which they are associated, e.g. 'soils of the floodplains', 'soils of the river terraces'. Soil–landform relationships can be effectively illustrated by block diagrams. Include a table of approximate equivalence between the soil types distinguished in the survey, the national soil classification of the country (where not the same) and the FAO classification or US Soil Taxonomy.

For each mapping unit, describe how to recognise the soils and their position in the landscape, e.g. 'usually found on lower slopes below Alpha Series, where the subsoil changes from red to yellowish red, with mottles at depth showing impeded drainage'. These descriptions are intended for farmers, agronomists, engineers and similar technical users. It is not possible to give specific information without using technical terms, but avoid jargon (e.g. sandy loam is acceptable, argillans is not). Technical terms can be defined and explained in a glossary.

Table 13.2 presents a sample main text description of a simple mapping unit, appropriate to a general-purpose survey. In a special-purpose survey more emphasis may be placed on characteristics of particular relevance to a purpose; for example, in a survey for irrigation planning, details should be given of moisture retention characteristics, infiltration rates and saturated hydraulic conductivity.

Detailed descriptions, including for each soil type a representative profile description, range of variation and tables of laboratory data, are intended primarily for other soil scientists and are more appropriately placed in an appendix.

Land evaluation/soil survey interpretations

This and the following are the two sections of principal interest to the largest number of users of the report, those concerned with technical aspects of land use: agricultural planners and extension officers, irrigation design engineers, farmers, foresters, conservationists, etc. In a commissioned survey, the terms of reference will stipulate which type or

Table 13.2   Main text description of a simple mapping unit.

Paparore Series (600 ha) occurs on the low-lying marine terrace along the east side of Rangaunu Harbour. Its profile characteristics are 15–20 cm dark-brown, friable, loamy sand with a very weak fine crumb structure, merging to 30 cm grey, massive, weakly cemented medium sand. This horizon usually has a few fine brown mottles and is underlain at a depth of 50 to 60 cm by very dark-brown, massive, strongly cemented sand (known locally as 'coffee rock'). The soil is acid to strongly acid throughout, with base saturation less than 15%, except where raised by top dressing.

Slightly saline groundwater occurs below the cemented horizon, usually at a depth of between 80 and 100 cm. During prolonged heavy rain, water may be ponded above the cemented horizon, which reduces trafficability and leads to poaching of the surface by stock.

The mapping unit includes irregular patches of poorly drained Te Karae Series which is distinguished by a peaty surface layer: Paparore Series is distinguished from Waiharara Series, which occurs on the adjacent old dune landscape, by the presence of mottling and the extreme cementation of the coffee rock layer.

Present land use is mainly low-intensity cattle rearing and fattening but dairy enterprises maintain better-quality grazing by regular top dressing with phosphate. Plantations of Eucalyptus (esp *E. botryoides*) have shown very rapid early growth. It appears that these trees can utilise the groundwater supply, even where it is slightly saline.

types of land evaluation are to be employed: land capability classification, land classification for irrigation, or a range of land suitability evaluations for different kinds of use.

(a) *Introduction.* Explains the principles of the evaluation system(s) employed and how the results can be applied to planning and management.
(b) *Land classification.* Gives basic definitions of the evaluation classes employed; detailed or formal definitions can be placed in an appendix.
(c) *Land capability/suitability units.* Accounts of each unit employed on the evaluation map or maps; the equivalent of the extended legend to the soil map.
(d) *Economic and social analysis.* Where the evaluations are largely physical, a brief analysis of economic and social aspects is given here; where economic evaluations are employed, results are better given as a separate chapter.

The presentation of a land evaluation survey in its own right, as distinct from an interpretation of a soil survey, is discussed on pp. 180–4.

Soil and land management

In a general-purpose survey, this section will consist of guidelines and broad recommendations, e.g. 'Despite their moderate slopes, the X and Y mapping units have a substantial erosion hazard, and are better left uncultivated or under perennial forage crops which provide complete ground cover.' In a commissioned and special-purpose survey, specific recommendations may be required, such as specified crop rotations and conservation measures for each unit. Such recommendations are derived from the preceding sections on soils and land evaluation, and a reasonable amount of cross-reference should be made to these sections and to the technical appendices.

In a multidisciplinary study, management recommendations on any of the following topics require the participation of the soil surveyor; other specialists mainly involved are noted in parentheses:

(a) choice of crops, crop variety, tree species (agronomist, forester);
(b) soil fertility (agronomist): strategy, recommended application and type of fertiliser, specific nutrient and toxicity problems, design and siting of field trials;
(c) land preparation (agronomist, engineer): primary land levelling with respect to topography, pans and infertile subsoils; crop tillage;

(d) erosion control (agronomist, soil conservation engineer): recommended cropping and cultivation techniques – contour cultivation, strip cropping, shelter belts; mechanical controls;

(e) drainage and irrigation (agronomist, economist, engineer): design and methods of operation taking into account surface topography, land grading, infiltration and deep percolation, surface and ground-water hydrology, water supply and quality, installation and running costs.

Economic analysis. Where the results of the soil survey have been subjected to detailed economic analysis, or where the interpretations include economic land evaluation, this is given as a separate chapter. Specific reference should be made to the assumptions on which it is based as derived from previous material, e.g. crop yield estimates, required conservation works or other land improvements.

Technical appendices

Information that is too technical to be useful to non-specialist readers or data that are primarily for reference are best reported in appendices. The length of the appendices commonly exceeds that of the main text. Nearly all soil survey reports require an appendix for detailed descriptions of individual soil units, including representative profile description, range of variation, impurities, analytical data and classification. Other kinds of information included in technical appendices are:

(a) climatic data, drought hazard calculations, soil moisture regime calculations;

(b) results of soil physical tests, e.g. permeability;

(c) detailed economic calculations;

(d) accounts of standard classification or other reference systems employed, e.g. the definitions in the USBR land classification for irrigation; although accessible elsewhere to the specialist, such material is reproduced for convenience of reference.

III. Maps

Users have two main requirements of maps:

(1) *To locate their area of interest* (farm, field, etc.) and find which soil unit or units occur; they then turn to the text. Farmers, other individual land users and their advisers use a map in this way. To fulfil this purpose the maps must be at a scale which shows areas of interest at

the required level of detail, the base information must be sufficient to locate the map units exactly on the ground, e.g. field boundaries for farmers, and the individual map units must be easily recognisable.

(2) *To see overall distributions;* this is a requirement of land use planners. It is best achieved by good use of colour. A general-purpose soil map is conceived as a quarry of information from which many special interpretations may be made. An interpretative map, on the other hand, is tailored for one specific purpose. For example a map to show land suitability for irrigation development should enable the user to identify precisely those areas that are and are not suitable for development. The fewer the categories used the clearer the map. For this reason and because of the relatively short life of the interpretations, the basic soil map and its derived interpretative maps should be presented separately.

Base maps. The choice of topographic base lies between planimetric topographic maps and air photographs. The advantages of air-photo maps of high definition are obvious – there is a wealth of precise locational detail. Set against this, the production costs of high-quality rectified photo base maps can be substantially higher than conventional topographic maps and identification of mapping units is limited to symbols.

Visual effect. Different mapping units may be distinguished by symbols, monochrome tones and patterns, colour or some combination of those techniques. The use of numerical or mnemonic symbols alone is simplest, cheapest and does not obscure topographic detail. However, where a visual impression of the soil pattern is required, a combination of symbols and colour is needed. The expense of designing and producing effective coloured maps is justified where a large number of copies is required and where the survey will retain its value for many years, and also by the importance of the information presented and the value of maximum visual impact on the users of the survey.

Map legends

The purpose of the legend is to make the map as self-contained as possible. Maps are often used without reference to their accompanying report and for convenient use in the field the legend should be on the map sheet. At the same time the legend must be informative. In addition to identifying each map unit in terms of taxonomic or interpretative group (which will be intelligible only to the surveyor) the legend should relate each unit to its position in the landscape and explain its most significant characteristics (Table 13.3).

Table 13.3 Part of a soil legend.

Landscape unit	Soil reference symbol	Soil name	Pedological classification	US Soil Taxonomy	Soil characteristics
soils of tidal swamps	Ye	Yellitenda Series	practically unripe sulphidic gley	typic sulfaquent	very soft, very saline, heavy clay, high sulphur content
	Sk	Sankwia Series	nearly ripe sulphidic gley	sulfic haplaquent	firm, very saline, heavy clay, high sulphur content below 50 cm
	Ku	Kau-Ur Series	nearly ripe saline gley	typic hydraquent	firm, slightly to moderately saline, heavy clay, non-calcareous, low sulphur content
soils of seasonally flooded low terraces	Sa	Salikene Series	saline gley	salic vertic fluvaquent	poorly drained, neutral to moderately acid, saline, clay; cracks deeply in the dry season
	Ma	Mandori Series	saline acid sulphate soil	sulfaquept	poorly drained, severely acid, saline clay
	Ku	Kudang Series	non-calcareous gley	tropic fluvaquent	poorly drained, weakly acid, non-saline, non-calcareous, clay loam over clay
	Pg	Panang Series	calcareous gley	tropic fluvaquent	imperfectly to poorly drained, calcareous, clay loam over clay

Extended legend. An extended summary of the most important factual and interpreted characteristics of each soil unit may be presented for quick reference as a large table or tables accompanying the map. The extended legend used in systematic general-purpose soil surveys in New Zealand is sufficiently detailed to serve as a surrogate report; information presented for each soil mapping unit includes the map reference symbol, soil name, parent material and subsurface materials, landform, environment, a brief description of a representative profile, a range of physical and chemical properties and interpretations for a variety of uses, e.g. stock-carrying capacity and soil limitations on each potential land use, e.g. flooding, susceptibility to erosion. The extended legend also includes explanatory notes to clarify the headings and the interpretative ratings, acknowledgements and references.

Publicity

A survey commissioned by a client and executed by consultants has its own ready-made customers, usually technical and administrative government departments together with agencies outside the country providing financial support. The print run is laid down in the terms of reference. It is regrettable that many such reports never see the light of day, for they invariably contain information of value beyond the immediate purpose which led to their being commissioned, and sometimes also methodological innovations of wider interest. Governments should be encouraged to give clearance for the wider release of such reports after internal review. The policy of the UK Land Resources Development Centre in publishing its *Land resource studies* has made available over 30 surveys of varied nature and much methodological interest (Young 1978, pp. 468–76).

General-purpose surveys, and in particular the standard mapping programmes of national soil survey organisations, need active publicity if they are to achieve their potential. Standard publicity methods directed towards farmers, land use planners, engineers, bankers, etc., are needed to draw the attention of potential users of the surveys to their existence and value. Methods include short articles in agricultural journals, display stands at shows, local radio, and publicity leaflets explaining what soil surveys can do.

In this respect the US Soil Conservation Service gives a lead. They produce a series of illustrated leaflets, 'Farmers and ranchers: soil surveys can help you', 'Construction engineers: soil surveys can help you', and similarly for land use planners, developers and builders, homebuyers, waste disposal, and recreation area planners, plus an address and telephone guide, 'Where to get information about soil and water conservation'. The style and content is exemplified by extracts from the 'Farmers and ranchers' leaflet:

As a farmer or rancher you don't have time or capital to spend on elaborate agricultural research and experiments or on mapping and studying soils. But you are interested in the results of such studies if they can help you to manage more profitably . . . Farm production depends largely on fitting soil management practices to the soil properties as accurately as possible.

Special crops. You may want to know if new or special crops will work for you. The soil survey of your area describes soil properties that affect crop growth and provides information that could save you costly experiments.

Reclaiming land. Some severely eroded soils respond readily to soil treatments . . . but other soils respond very poorly. A soil survey can help you decide whether added treatment to reclaim soils is likely to succeed.

Range management. A soil survey can help you estimate the likely benefits of management practices. For example, the soil in an area of brush or mesquite may have such low potential productivity that the cost of chaining or chemical removal may not be worth the ultimate yield in forage. On the other hand, there may be rocky areas or hillsides where the soils are capable of producing more forage if properly managed. A soil survey can help you determine such natural differences in productivity.

Publicity is no use unless the soil survey actually does provide information of the kind needed: soil-specific crop yield estimates for farmers, bearing capacities for engineers, subsidence hazard for house-buyers, land suitability comparisons for land use planners. Thinking forward to whether your planned survey will justify its existence in such ways can help in planning the range and balance of survey activities.

Further reading

Smyth (1970).
   Recent County Soil Survey Reports of the US Soil Conservation Service repay study.
   For an example of the 'executive summary', see Hill *et al.* (1978).
   For examples of extended legends, see recent reports of the New Zealand Soil Bureau.
   For presentation in general, examine if possible reports by consultant firms.

Surveys for Irrigation

Surveys for irrigation are amongst the most complex special-purpose soil investigations. The very high engineering and social cost of a large irrigation project and the far-reaching hydrological changes involved justify a comprehensive and detailed appraisal of land suitability. This includes climate, topography, soils, the supply and quality of irrigation water, the environmental impact both within and outside the project area, and the economics of the project.

Three main features distinguish studies for irrigation from soil surveys in general. First, much attention is given to differences of relief, owing to their hydrological significance and consequent economic implications. Secondly, soil studies are directed towards physical properties, namely the ability to absorb water, to retain it for the crop, and to drain away surplus water in a relatively short time. Thirdly, the associated land evaluation is invariably in economic terms, concerning the capacity of the augmented agricultural production which will result from irrigation to repay the capital costs involved.

These features of emphasis are modified by the type of irrigation under consideration, i.e. gravity or overhead application, and the aridity of the environment. Gravity or flood irrigation systems are normally less sophisticated and cheaper per unit area and hence are the most common in developing countries; small differences in topography are critical to the design, operation and costs of such systems. Overhead application methods are less dependent on relief. In arid environments the assessment of salinity and sodicity hazards and the design measures necessary to avoid them become a major feature of surveys for irrigation. For supplementary irrigation in sub-humid regions this aspect is less critical.

Detailed knowledge of site and soil conditions is required for engineering design – for example to determine land levelling needs, the irrigation, drainage and special reclamation requirements of specific soil types, soil conservation measures, and the alignment of canals and drains. Soil information is also necessary to judge the optimum size of farms, choice of crops, application of fertilisers, cultivation, and irrigation scheduling. Surveys for project feasibility and implementation are carried out at a higher intensity than for rainfed crops. A publication scale of between 1: 25 000 and 1: 10 000 is desirable for feasibility studies and even larger scales for design of sophisticated irrigation schemes and for areas where there are soil problems needing precise definition.

In order to anticipate any hydrological problems, special tests of soil water characteristics are carried out, both in the field and in the laboratory.

Soil survey

Design of field survey

Even in intensive surveys, geomorphological units can be a useful basis for mapping, not only because they can be mapped by eye on the ground and on air photographs but because they usually comprise related sequences of soils which respond differently to irrigation. In an alluvial landscape, levées and backswamps, terraces and fans each have distinct depositional sequences with related variations in soil texture, microtopography, and natural drainage. A proportion of soil boundaries may be drawn initially by air photo-interpretation but it will usually be necessary to undertake grid survey within these landscape units to establish soil texture profiles and especially to check against the hidden occurrence of potentially hazardous conditions, such as slowly permeable substrata.

This is one of the few occasions in soil surveying where a grid design may be justified. But it is wrong to consider that irrigation surveys *must* be on a grid; usually, free survey at high intensity, coupled with air photo-interpretation, will still give better value for effort.

Most investigations are carried out to a depth of 1.5 m, with more widely spaced deep borings to 3–5 m to test the permeability of the substrata and the depth and salinity of the groundwater.

Soil mapping units

Mapping units are to be distinguished at the series level by the kind and arrangement of horizons but it is also necessary to map phases of series using criteria of practical importance not distinguished at the series level. The choice of criteria is made according to the special requirements of the crops envisaged; for example, if paddy rice is to be grown, phases may be distinguished according to quite small differences in soil permeability, slope and microtopography. Surface stoniness, sodicity and salinity may be used where these affect the costs of land preparation and reclamation. Significant variations in rooting depth or depth to limiting horizons may also be used where these are not distinguished at the series level.

The higher categories of genetic classification are not generally useful in assessing land suitability or management but it is worthwhile keying the mapping units employed into the US Soil Taxonomy, the FAO soil legend or other recognised systems to facilitate correlation with similar soils elsewhere.

Site characteristics

Special emphasis is placed on site characteristics that influence the application and drainage of water and the costs of land preparation.

Relationships between landform and groundwater hydrology. Freely drained sites in the higher parts of a landscape, e.g. higher river terraces and the upper parts of alluvial fans, will augment the groundwater with surplus irrigation water. This can cause waterlogging and salinity in the lower parts of the landscape, such as floodplains and the toes of alluvial fans.

Slopes and microtopography. The length and steepness of slope is a major factor determining the method of water application. Gravity irrigation for arable crops is not practicable on slopes steeper than 8° (17%), and where there is a risk of erosion due to unstable soil conditions or heavy rains an upper limit of 3° (6%) may be more appropriate. In any event, costs of construction and operation rise rapidly with slope and relief differences.

On sloping land, terracing may be required for erosion control or for basin irrigation (e.g. for rice). Under gravity irrigation, irregular surfaces may suffer local waterlogging in low spots, especially where subsoil drainage is impeded, while high spots receive insufficient water. Irregular surfaces therefore require smoothing to ensure an even distribution of water.

Land shaping is very costly. It may be impracticable where rock, gravel or an indurated layer is close to the surface. It is certainly inadvisable where the result will be great differences in permeability and water retention capacity between the areas of cut and fill. Overhead irrigation is necessary where land shaping for gravity irrigation is impracticable.

Photogrammetric contouring to 1 m intervals may be justifiable for the design and layout of bunds and channels (in earlier times the same result was achieved by meticulous field levelling).

Land clearance costs. A quantitative assessment of surface stones, rock outcrops and vegetation is required to estimate the costs of land preparation.

Flood, erosion and microclimate hazards. The dangers of flooding and soil erosion by surface water, wind erosion and frost due to the drainage of cold air are all influenced by topography. Assessment of hazard under the conditions of the irrigation scheme is required.

Soil characteristics

The soil characteristics of particular relevance to irrigation are listed in Table 14.1. Field assessment of effective rooting depth, texture and structure are common to most soil surveys but particular attention must also be given to:

Table 14.1 Critical soil characteristics for irrigation.

Soil property	Investigations required
effective soil depth and nature of limitation	field measurement at each observation site
particle size distribution	field assessment of soil texture at each observation site and laboratory determination on representative profiles from each mapping unit
structure and stability of structure under irrigation	field assessment at each observation site, and interpretation of ESP and the sodium absorption ratio of the irrigation water
porosity	field assessment and field or laboratory determination of apparent density (dry bulk density) on representative profiles
infiltration rate	a minumum of three replicate measurements for each mapping unit
saturated hydraulic conductivity	replicate field measurements for each horizon of each mapping unit; deep borings for substrata drainage studies
water retention characteristics	field capacity determination on samples collected following infiltration tests; laboratory determination of water retention curves on undisturbed samples from representative profiles
depth to groundwater	systematic measurement in the field, deep borings as necessary
salinity of soil and groundwater	field measurement of electrical conductivity or systematic sampling for laboratory determination
cation exchange capacity (CEC) and exchangeable sodium percentage (ESP)	laboratory determination on representative profiles; where sodicity is identified or anticipated, systematic sampling and analysis may be required
pH	field measurements plus laboratory determinations on representative profiles
carbonates and gypsum	field assessment plus laboratory determinations on representative profiles
toxic substances, e.g. boron, sulphidic materials	laboratory analysis where appropriate; field oxidation and pH measurements for sulphidic materials

Table 14.2 Suitability for gravity irrigation of soils with different infiltration rates. Based on FAO (1979a).

Equilibrium infiltration rate (cm h^{-1})	Suitability for irrigation	
	Rice	Diversified arable
<0.1	suitable	unsuitable because of surface ponding in basins and excessive runoff
0.1–0.3	marginal; excessive water loss by percolation	marginally suitable; excessive ponding or runoff
0.3–6.5	unsuitable; unacceptable loss of water by percolation	suitable; optimum rate between 0.7 and 3.5
6.5–12.5		marginally suitable; small basins or short furrows required to ensure even application of water; lined distributary system needed to reduce seepage losses
>12.5		unsuitable; recommended for overhead irrigation only

(a) the nature and thickness of any limiting horizons, such as calcrete layers, that may be exposed at the surface by land shaping;

(b) accurate, consistent assessment of the finer gradations of soil texture; soil mapping units are very often distinguished primarily on the basis of texture.

Field or laboratory measurements of other critical properties are required for each mapping unit. Sampling and field tests are carried out at representative profile pits where a full description of morphology is also recorded. Measurements of infiltration and hydraulic conductivity are very time-consuming, but they should be performed by the surveyor rather than by an engineering counterpart to ensure accurate identification of the soil on which the measurements are carried out. The general nature of these tests is outlined below; details are given by the US Bureau of Reclamation (1978) and in *Soil survey investigations for irrigation* (FAO 1979a).

Infiltration. Measurements of vertical infiltration into the soil surface serve as a guide to the most appropriate method of irrigation, the size of basins or length of furrow and the optimum rate of water application (Table 14.2). Ideally, measurements should be made under the same conditions as are envisaged for the irrigation development, for example a basin with puddled soil for paddy cultivation, and using water of the same quality. However, a very large volume of water is needed for a basin infiltration test and usually a double ring infiltrometer is used.

Two concentric cylinders are driven into the ground to a depth of 10 cm. Both are filled with water to the same level and measurements of the rate of fall of water are made in the inner ring. The outer ring serves to minimise outward flow of water from the inner cylinder. The values of interest are the initial inflltration rate, over the first hour, and the equilibrium rate when the rate of fall has become constant, which may not be achieved for several hours. At least three replicate tests should be performed at each site, with stations not less than 10 m apart.

Obviously a good seal around the rings is essential. A baked clay soil must be pre-wetted to avoid shattering while the cylinders are driven in. The rings can then be sealed with bentonite. A plastic sheet may be used to protect the soil when adding water to avoid puddling the surface or undermining the cylinders. Infiltration tests are unsatisfactory on cracking clay soils since the water drains rapidly through the fissures and weeks may elapse before those fissures are fully closed.

Saturated hydraulic conductivity. Measurements of saturated hydraulic conductivity or lateral permeability of the different soil horizons are used to assess waterlogging problems and as the basis for designing in-field and regional drainage. For in-field drainage, data are required for depths of 2–3 m. Deeper borings are required for regional drainage studies. Measurements may be made in an 8–10 cm diameter auger hole bored to the required depth. For measurements above the water table the test is best performed following saturation of the site, for example following infiltration measurements. The hole is filled with water and the rate of fall of the water level measured.

Measurements below the water table are made by baling out the auger hole and measuring the rate at which water flows in. Measurements should begin immediately after baling and be completed before 75% of the water removed has been replaced by in-flowing groundwater, otherwise a funnel-shaped water table develops around the hole which reduces the rate of inflow.

Auger holes cannot be made in very stony nor in unstable soils, although a cylindrical perforated metal guard can be inserted to stabilise the sides in sandy materials. The test may be performed stepwise at successive depths to measure variation in layered soils, but to measure the permeability of thin layers at several metres from the surface a cased hole (peizometer) is used.

Large variations in saturated hydraulic conductivity can occur within a few metres, even within the same mapping unit. At least four replicates should be performed and some latitude allowed in interpreting the results. Table 14.3 shows the approximate relationships between texture, structure and permeability. Soils with values of less than 0.1 m per day require excessively close drain spacing, and some artificial improvement of permeability by moling or subsoiling is essential for drainage at

Table 14.3 Approximate relationships between texture, structure and hydraulic conductivity. From FAO (1979a).

Texture	Structure	Saturated hydraulic conductivity	
		$(m\ day^{-1})$	$(cm\ h^{-1})$
coarse sand, gravel	single grain	>12	>50
medium sand	single grain	6–12	25–50
loamy sand, fine sand	medium crumb, single grain	3–6	12.5–25
sandy loam, fine sandy loam	coarse subangular blocky, fine crumb	1.5–3	6–12.5
light clay loam, silt, silt loam, very fine sandy loam, loam	medium prismatic and subangular blocky	0.5–1.5	2–6
clay, silty clay, sandy clay, clay loam, sandy clay loam, silt loam, silt	fine and medium prismatic, blocky and platy	0.12–0.5	0.5–2
clay, clay loam, silty clay, sandy clay loam	very fine or fine prismatic, blocky and platy	0.06–0.12	0.25–0.5
clay, clay loam	massive, very fine or fine columnar	<0.06	<0.25

reasonable cost. Soils with a permeability greater than 10 m per day do not require any field drainage unless the rapid transmission of water is likely to bring about a rise of the groundwater table. Any slowly permeable layer in the profile is likely to disrupt the movement of drainage water.

Water retention characteristics. The capacity of the soil to retain water available to plants has a direct bearing on the feasibility of irrigation and the optimum frequency and amount of applications of water. As water is removed from the soil the tension at which the remaining soil water is held increases. The relationship between water content and water tension is expressed as a soil water retention curve (Fig. 14.1). The shape of the curve depends principally on the pore size distribution, coarse pores draining rapidly at low water tension, very fine pores releasing water only at high tension.

The upper limit of available water is the **field capacity,** the amount of water held in the soil after drainage under gravity. In freely drained sandy soils it is reached within a few hours of saturation. In silts and clays equilibrium is reached only after many days and any water remaining in the soil before equilibrium is attained is available to crops, providing that aeration is adequate. Therefore field capacity does not corres-

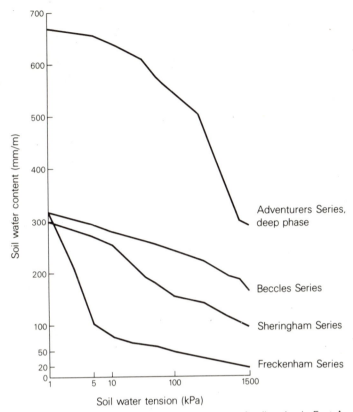

Figure 14.1 Representative soil water retention curves of soil series in East Anglia, UK: Adventurers Series (peat); Beccles Series (sandy clay loam over clay); Sheringham Series (loam to sandy silt loam); Freckenham Series (sand).

pond to a particular soil water tension and must be determined in the field. The soil must be saturated to at least 30 cm below the proposed sampling depth and then covered to prevent loss of water by evaporation. Samples should be collected for percentage moisture determination after 48 h. It is convenient to sample for field capacity following infiltration tests. In the absence of a direct determination of field capacity, an arbitrary value, corresponding to water content at a tension of 10 kPa, may be adopted. For most crops the lower limit of available water, the **permanent wilting point,** corresponds to a soil water tension of about 1500 kPa.

Water is not equally available to plants between field capacity and permanent wilting point. Different crops suffer moisture stress and reduction of potential yield at different soil water tensions, mostly below 100 kPa, and many have moisture-sensitive periods of growth (commonly during fertilisation). For irrigation scheduling and for the design of sophisticated irrigation systems, a full water retention curve is required and allowance must be made for any contributions from the groundwater.

Soil water retention curves are determined in the laboratory on undisturbed soil cores collected in metal cylinders. The samples are saturated with water, then equilibrated at successive increments of tension or air pressure, from 5 to 1500 kPa. Triplicate samples are required from each horizon.

Table 14.4 shows the approximate relationships between available water capacity and soil texture. However, the range of values within any one textural group is considerable; for example total available water capacity in non-swelling clay soils may vary from 120 to 200 mm m^{-1} according to organic matter content, structure and mineralogy, so direct measurements are always preferable.

Salinity. Soluble salts increase the osmotic potential of the soil water thereby opposing uptake of water by the plant. Plant growth may also be impaired by the toxicity of specific ions in solution, most commonly by Na^+, Cl^- and SO_4^{2-}. Although salinity is probably the most widespread soil limitation in arid areas, it is not a stable characteristic of the soil under irrigation. It can be ameliorated by leaching, or induced into the root zone over a few years by rising groundwater due to inadequate drainage. For this reason it is not necessarily an appropriate diagnostic property for soil mapping units and separate soil salinity maps are sometimes prepared.

Table 14.4 Estimated values of available water capacity for soils of different textures (millimetres of water per metre depth of soil). Based on analyses of UK soils (Hall *et al.* 1977, Dent & Scammell 1981b). Values should be reduced proportionally for per cent by volume of stones, and by 10% for tropical conditions.

USDA texture	Total available water capacity		Readily available water capacity (field capacity to 100 kPa)	
	Topsoil	Subsoil	Topsoil	Subsoil
clay (non-swelling)	190	135	55	35
silty clay	210	150	60	35
silty clay loam	240	170	85	45
clay loam	220	150	80	40
sandy clay loam	200	165	105	75
silt loam	235	210	140	125
loam	200	170	120	100
very fine sandy loam	220	190	130	115
fine sandy loam	200	160	120	95
sandy loam	185	140	110	85
loamy sand	120	110	70	65
fine sand	120	100	70	60
medium and coarse sand	105	75	60	45

Table 14.5 Classification of salt-affected soils. After Richards (1954).

	EC saturation extract (mS cm^{-1})	ESP	pH	
saline soils	>4	<15	<8.5	sufficient soluble salts to interfere with the growth of most crops
saline–sodic soils	>4	>15	<8.5	sufficient exchangeable sodium to interfere with the growth of most crops plus an appreciable content of soluble salts
sodic soils	<4	>15	>8.5	sufficient exchangeable sodium to interfere with the growth of most crops but without appreciable quantities of soluble salts

Salinity is usually reported in terms of electrical conductivity (EC) as millisiemens per centimetre (mS cm^{-1}). (The SI unit millisiemen has replaced the equivalent unit in previous use – millimho, mmho.) In the field, measurements of the EC of a saturated soil paste can be made using a portable conductivity meter but interpretations of crop response are usually based on the electrical conductivity of a saturation extract – a solution obtained under vacuum from a saturated soil paste.

Reclamation costs associated with drainage improvement and leaching must be estimated in any land evaluation for irrigation. Leaching tests may be performed in the field using the proposed irrigation water.

Cation exchange capacity (CEC) and exchangeable sodium percentage (ESP). The cation exchange capacity is a measure of the soil's ability to retain and supply plant nutrients. Minimum values for satisfactory irrigated cropping are considered to be 3 milliequivalents per 100 g (meq 100 g^{-1}) soil in the upper 30 cm for rice and 4 meq 100 g^{-1} for other arable crops.

An exchange complex dominated by calcium is desirable and this is usually the case where the pH value is greater than 5.5. A high exchangeable sodium percentage is often associated with an excess of soluble salts and pH values greater than 8.5. An ESP greater than 15 causes unstable structure which inhibits drainage and leaching.

Table 14.5 presents a simple classification of saline and sodic soils, but the limiting values given are only indicative, not fixed critical values. The effects of increasing ESP worsen gradually and are apparent at lower values in smectite clays than in kandite clays.

For non-calcareous soils, cation exchange capacity and exchangeable cations are usually determined by leaching with 1M ammonium acetate solution at pH 7. For calcareous soils, a mixture of barium chloride and triethanolamine buffered at pH 8.1 should be used (Hesse 1971). Where soluble salts are present they may be determined separately and subtracted from the total soluble plus exchangeable cations to arrive at the cation exchange capacity, or they may be removed by leaching with a deionised glycol–ethanol solvent (Loveday 1974). Sodium can be determined individually on the leachate by flame photometry and the exchangeable sodium percentage calculated as

$$ESP = \frac{\text{exchangeable Na} \times 100}{\text{CEC}}$$

Water quality. The quality of irrigation water and groundwater may be more significant to land suitability than soil quality. Details of analyses and interpretations of water quality are given by Ayers and Westcot (1976). The principal factors of interest are the total salinity (EC_w) and the sodium absorption ratios (SAR):

$$SAR = \frac{\text{Na}}{\sqrt{[(Ca + Mg)/2]}}$$

where concentrations of ions are in milligrams per litre. Water with a high SAR gradually replaces other cations on the exchange complex with sodium, increasing the exchangeable sodium percentage and bringing about permeability and workability problems and sodium toxicity.

Land evaluation

In planning an irrigation scheme there are four main questions: where is it to be, how much water is available, how much irrigable land, and will it pay? The first is answered through soil and hydrological surveys of a range of possible sites, linked by qualitative land evaluation. The second question requires quantitative hydrological studies, the third special-purpose soil survey; the maximum size of a scheme is constrained by whichever proves to be in shorter supply, irrigation water or irrigable land. The last question calls for economic land evaluation.

Surveys to locate potential sites are conducted at reconnaissance or semi-detailed scales. Land evaluation at this stage must be a suitability evaluation directed at the major kind of land use, irrigated agriculture. Land capability classification is not appropriate. The evaluation can be in qualitative terms, backed by sample economic feasibility studies at a generalised level. No special techniques over and above those described for land suitability evaluation are called for.

Once a single site or a small number of alternatives have been selected there may be two further stages, a feasibility survey followed by studies for detailed design. The layout of irrigation works, roads, farms and fields is a matter of engineering and agricultural land use planning, drawing upon detailed soil survey. The principal role of land evaluation is at the feasibility stage, to answer questions of whether the scheme is technically and economically viable. The final decision to invest is taken following this feasibility survey.

There is no question that land evaluation for the feasibility survey must be in economic terms. One evaluation system is by far the most widely used, that of the US Bureau of Reclamation (1953), called *Land classification for irrigation*. This fulfils its intended purpose so well that there is no need to look to alternatives. The USBR system is a form of economic land evaluation of potential suitability for irrigation. Although not employing the same terminology, the procedures are largely compatible with those of the FAO system. A requirement for irrigation developments to be based on surveys in accordance with USBR specifications is incorporated into US law.

There are six land classes, abbreviated definitions of which are as follows (note that 'arable' is used with the meaning 'irrigable'):

- Class 1: *Arable*. Lands that are highly suitable for irrigation, being capable of producing sustained and relatively high yields of a wide range of crops at reasonable cost. They are smooth lying with deep soils, open soil structure allowing easy penetration of roots yet good available moisture capacity, and free from harmful quantities of salts. These lands potentially have a relatively high payment capacity.
- Class 2: *Arable*. Lands of moderate suitability for irrigation, being lower than class 1 in productive capacity, adapted to a somewhat narrower range of crops, more expensive to prepare for irrigation or more costly to farm. These lands have an intermediate payment capacity.
- Class 3: *Arable*. Lands that are suitable but approaching marginality for irrigation. They have substantial soil, topographic or drainage limitations. A greater risk is involved in farming these lands than classes 1 and 2, but under proper management they are expected to have adequate payment capacity.
- Class 4: *Limited arable or special use*. These lands may either have excessive deficiencies that can be corrected at high cost, but are suitable for irrigation of high-value crops such as vegetables or fruits; or they may have excessive non-correctible deficiencies precluding arable use but permitting use as irrigated pasture or orchard. They are capable of supporting a farm family if operated in farms of sufficient size or in association with better lands. Class 4 lands may have a range of payment capacity, under intensive use, greater than that of arable classes.
- Class 5: *Non-arable*. These lands are non-arable under existing conditions, but have a potential value sufficient to warrant segregation for

special study; or their arability (sic) is dependent upon additional project construction. The designation of class 5 is tentative and must be changed to the proper arable class or to class 6 prior to completion of the land classification.

- Class 6: *Non-arable*. These lands do not have sufficient payment capacity to warrant consideration for irrigation.

These definitions incorporate three aspects: physical properties of topography and soil, ability to grow a range of crops, and payment capacity. The last refers to the potential of the irrigated land, under sound management, both to provide an acceptable income to the farmer and to pay off costs of the capital works. There is a fairly close correspondence with the suitability classes in the FAO system: classes 1 to 3 are equivalent to S1 to S3, class 4 to the phase of conditionally suitable (Cs), class 5 covers land for which prior to economic analysis it is not known whether it will be N1 or S3, and class 6 covers the order not suitable (N). By requiring that class 5 should not appear on the final map, the USBR system groups together land which in FAO terms would be separated into currently not suitable (N1), on economic grounds, and permanently not suitable (N2).

There are three kinds of subclasses. The reason for placing land into other than class 1 is indicated by letters s, t or d to indicate deficiencies in soils, topography and drainage respectively. The special-use land, class 4, may be indicated as suitable for pasture (P), fruit (F), rice (R), vegetables (V), housing development (H), sprinkler irrigation (S) or subirrigation (U). Position subclasses indicate whether land otherwise suited to irrigation has a problem because its position is isolated (i), high (h) or low (l).

Survey procedures follow those of a special-purpose soil survey followed by economic land evaluation. It is specified in the manual (USBR 1953) that field survey should employ a standard mapping symbol, e.g.

$$\frac{3std}{C22BX}u_2f_2$$

in which 3 is the land class, s, t and d are soils, topographic and drainage deficiencies, C is a type of land use (cultivated), the remaining lower symbols refer to productivity, land development costs, water requirements and drainability, and u and f refer to need for levelling and flooding hazard. This is a satisfactory field procedure but by no means essential to the approach, and some surveyors may prefer conventional soil mapping units. The USBR manual gives general specifications for soil, topographic and drainage properties applicable as limits to each land class. Thus class 1 land should have sandy loam to clay loam, an effective depth of 150 cm to rock or 90 cm to gravel, pH <9.0, total soluble salts <0.2%, slopes <4%, an even surface requiring no grading, low clearance costs (boulders or vegetation) and free drainage. These are intended as guidelines, requiring modification to meet local circumstances.

The initial surveys of soils and topography are converted into quantitative specifications of the operations needed for land preparation and development, e.g. land clearance, grading, farm water distribution, drainage, and soil improvements such as leaching (to remove excess salts) or subsoiling. These land development specifications are next translated into costs. The anticipated crop yields and farm gross margins are estimated, leading to estimates of the repayment capacity. The sequence of procedure is virtually the same as that described in Chapter 11. Thus although the survey is initially in terms of soils, topography and drainage, the resulting mapping units are ultimately put into irrigation suitability classes on the basis of payment capacity.

The USBR system can be recommended for general application to irrigated land evaluation with one reservation. The intensity of observations and the stated 'minimum requirements' are intended for US conditions, namely those of high costs and high returns. Thus for detailed surveys of new lands, the requirements include base maps at 1:4800, borings or pits to 1.5 m depth at a minimum density of 6 per square kilometre, segregation of areas of 0.1 ha (class 6) or 1 ha (other classes) and a '97% accuracy' (!). The levels of intensity given are not always necessary or desirable for surveys of developing countries where the anticipated returns per unit area may be much lower. Survey contracts should therefore state that methods will be 'based on' those of the USBR manual unless it is intended to follow these specifications rigorously with consequent high survey costs.

Further reading

FAO (1979a), Loveday (1974), Mitchell (1976), Makin *et al.* (1976), US Bureau of Reclamation (1953), Doorenbos and Pruitt (1977).
A manual *Guidelines on land evaluation for irrigated agriculture* is in preparation by FAO.

Applications

If you think that soil survey or land evaluation could be of help in some question of land use planning or management, the first thing to find out is whether a survey has already been carried out for the area. This is a matter of library search or enquiry, starting points for which could be the local offices of the Ministry of Agriculture, the Soil Survey, the national (topographic) survey organisation, an agricultural research station or a university (Appendix A). If so, is the survey at a scale suitable for your needs? A check for this is to take the published map and see if it could be used as a working document for the kinds of planning or management you have in mind; look also for the number of mapping units shown and the approximate size of the units mapped. There may not be enough detail for the purpose in mind, or occasionally there may be too much. What kind of a survey is it? Many early soil maps were purely 'pedo-logical' in the narrow sense of the term, that is, the soils were classified and mapped without providing any interpretations concerning the potential land use or management of the different units distinguished. Other surveys explicitly restrict their interpretations to agricultural uses. Being a more recent development, it is less likely that a land evaluation survey will exist for the area.

The next thing to check is whether the survey is reliable. The status of the organisation which carried it out is some guide, although not a guarantee. The survey does not necessarily have to be recent. As far as accuracy of mapping is concerned, there is no evidence that standards have ever differed very much from those of today. Where age can be a bar is if an obsolete method of describing and naming the soils was used, and insufficient data are given to interpret the descriptions in present-day terms. If in doubt, it may be worth commissioning a soil surveyor to check the reliability in the field by random sampling points or traverses.

Supposing that a survey exists, at an appropriate scale and apparently reliable, the next question is whether it provides the information needed. In this respect there are three possibilities.

First, the information may be directly obtainable from the map, the extended legend or the interpretative tables and descriptions in the accompanying report. In this case you have located the information required.

Secondly, the mapping units and boundaries may appear to be suitable, but the type of information required is not given for these units. It might be, for example, that information is needed on swelling and shrinkage properties of soils, but the existing survey only provides interpretations of an agricultural nature. Where this happens it is quite likely that the questions can be answered by undertaking further tests based on the mapping units already surveyed. In the example above, it has repeatedly been shown that soil engineering properties correlate well with land facets and with soil series. The further investigations can be concentrated on collecting information directly bearing upon the purpose in hand, without need to repeat the time-consuming process of mapping boundaries.

In countries where a substantial proportion of the area has been covered by systematic detailed survey, e.g. the United States, New Zealand and the Netherlands, applied studies can be directed towards land suitability evaluation for given purposes or other special interpretations. Quite often it will be possible to commission a land evaluation survey using an existing soil map as one source of data.

There remains the third possibility, that the existing survey does not appear to have the potential to provide information, even with supplementary investigations, in which case we are back to the position in which no previous survey exists.

In many countries this last situation will be most common. There are then four alternatives: to commission a general-purpose soil survey, to commission a special-purpose soil survey, to commission a land evaluation survey, or to decide to manage without.

A general-purpose soil survey (p. 2) will produce a map which can give information for a variety of different purposes, agricultural and non-agricultural, but it may not have the potential to answer individual questions very precisely. One of the strongest arguments for a general-purpose soil survey is that it will last for quite a long time. From past experience, there is every reason to expect a good general-purpose survey to remain usable for at least 20–30 years. Furthermore, special-purpose interpretative studies, including land suitability evaluation, can be superimposed onto an existing general-purpose soil map.

But if there is an immediate and very specific object in mind, a general-purpose survey will not do. The clearest illustration is the case outlined in Chapter 14: that when planning an irrigation scheme a lot of information on soil water characteristics is needed, calling for deep borings and specialised field and laboratory tests. Even if a good general-purpose soil survey exists, no-one would dream of risking investment in an irrigation scheme without further investigations. If what is needed is information on a few soil characteristics, which must fall within specified limits of accuracy, then commission a special-purpose soil survey.

One further point to consider is whether a soil survey as such is best suited to the purpose, or whether to take the approach of land evaluation. As discussed earlier, this distinction is not clearcut; soil survey interpretation is a form of land evaluation, while few land evaluation surveys have been carried out that do not incorporate a soil survey. The difference is rather one of emphasis. Soil survey is likely to be the best starting point if the information needed is a matter of technical interpretation of morphological, physical or chemical soil properties, and if the variations in these properties lie at the centre of the problem in hand. In a soil survey, the basis for interpretation of the results is a soil map. In land evaluation, greater emphasis is placed at the outset on the potential use of the land. If it is a team investigation, the staff may include agronomists, livestock specialists, foresters or other professionally concerned with land use. Economic assessment can form a major component. The sequence of enquiry is set out in Figure 15.1.

Applications

To date, most applications of soil surveys have been to arable farming in one form or another, whether for farm management and advisory services, or to land development projects. There is nevertheless a wide range of applications, listed in Table 15.1; some of these have been discussed earlier, in particular the use of soil surveys in regional planning (Ch. 1) and in irrigation (Ch. 14).

Land development projects

By far the most widespread use of soil surveys in developing countries is in land development projects, financed in part from outside the country. The donors wish to see that their money is put to sound use; the recipient governments wish to make the most of the scarce funds available. As noted above (pp. 9–10) there are four stages at which soil and land evaluation surveys play a part: project location, project feasibility, project planning, and management. The most critical stage is the feasibility survey, which precedes the final decision to go ahead with investment.

In feasibility surveys in the past, the use made of information derived from soil survey and land evaluation has been less than its potential. This was partly because the planners were not provided with the information they required. Too much time was spent on soil mapping and not enough on activities directed towards interpretation and land evaluation. Soil survey was employed principally for the purposes of elimina-

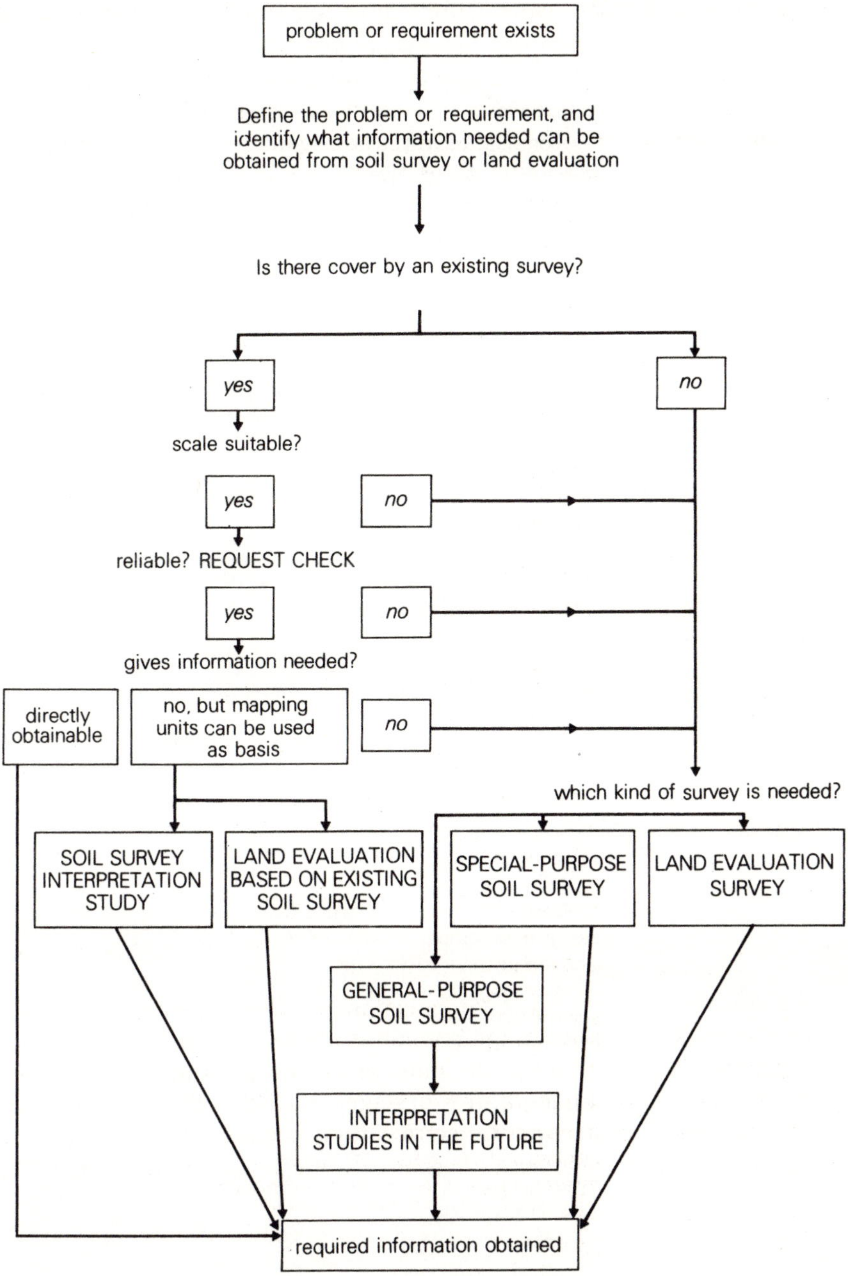

Applications

problem or requirement exists

Define the problem or requirement, and
identify what information needed can be
obtained from soil survey or land evaluation

Is there cover by an existing survey?

yes   no

scale suitable?

yes   no

reliable? REQUEST CHECK

yes   no

gives information needed?

directly   no, but mapping   no
obtainable   units can be used
              as basis

which kind of survey is needed?

| SOIL SURVEY INTERPRETATION STUDY | LAND EVALUATION BASED ON EXISTING SOIL SURVEY | SPECIAL-PURPOSE SOIL SURVEY | LAND EVALUATION SURVEY |

GENERAL-PURPOSE
SOIL SURVEY

INTERPRETATION
STUDIES IN THE FUTURE

required information obtained

Figure 15.1 Schematic sequence of enquiry for information from soil survey or land
evaluation.

247

Table 15.1 Applications of soil and land evaluation surveys.

Evaluation for multiple or competing kinds of land use

    planning   national, regional and local land use conflicts, particularly in the urban fringe zone

    development   location and extent of projects
                          allocation of land for different uses
                          avoidance of hazards
                          land management
                          economic appraisal

Arable farming

                          land requirements of crops
                          nutrient and fertiliser requirements
                          soil requirements of specialised crops, e.g. horticulture, viticulture, fruit, and of new crops and varieties
                          response to new techniques, e.g. direct drilling
                          supplementary irrigation
                          agricultural advisory work
                          productivity estimates
                          erosion and degradation
                          drought limitation
                          land reclamation
                          economic appraisal

Livestock farming

                          carrying capacity
                          degradation and erosion hazard
                          nutrient requirements
                              minor nutrients e.g. copper, cobalt deficiencies
                          drought limitation
                          wetness/drainage limitation

Irrigation

                          selection of sites
                          extent of irrigable land
                          avoidance of hazards, e.g. salinisation
                          design of schemes
                          land reclamation
                          water management, including scheduling
                          soil and crop management
                          economic appraisal

Forestry

                          selection of sites
                          tree species selection
                          planting and management practices
                          forest road siting, design and maintenance
                          avoidance of hazards, e.g. windthrow

Table 15.1   (contd)

Engineering	
roads	routing
	foundations
	sources of aggregate
	hazards, e.g. landslides
building	earth structures
	foundations
	hazards, e.g. site stability, corrosion of steel and concrete
	vulcanism, flooding
	water supplies
	drainage
waste disposal	domestic and industrial wastes
	toxic wastes
Water	
	catchment and reservoir location
	hazards to water quality e.g. salinity, acidity, toxic substances
	drainage
	land reclamation
Environmental impact	
	total environmental impact assessment
	soil erosion and degradation
	river flow and sediment load
	salinisation, acidification
Wildlife habitat	
	location of nature and game reserves
	management, design for conservation
	vegetation and fauna, including wetland and associated aquatic habitats
Recreation	
	national and regional parks, urban recreational parks and playing fields
	coastal, lake and other specialised sites
	camp sites
	carrying capacity
	design for access and conservation
Financial and legal	
	rating, taxation
	insurance
	collateral on loans
Military	
	terrain evaluation
	training areas

ting clearly unsuitable land, i.e. the mountains and swamps; for guarding against serious environmental hazards like soil erosion and salinisation; and for apportioning land between arable, grazing, forestry and other major kinds of use. It was through the occurrence of environmental disasters in the 1940s and 1950s that the need for soil surveys in development projects first became recognised. The financial losses that can result from neglect of hazards are so great that this function alone would justify soil surveys.

Given the much wider range of information which soil survey and land evaluation are now in a position to supply, there is a further range of applications. The first is in land management recommendations, produced through cooperation between the soil surveyor and the agronomist, forester or other specialist. Details such as kinds of crop rotations, lengths of fallow or grass–legume ley, levels of fertiliser and other material inputs should be soil-specific, that is, made specifically for the different soil types present. By no means all the soil mapping units will differ substantially enough to warrant separation for this purpose and a grouping of the basic mapping units into **soil management units** can usefully be made. Secondly, estimates of inputs should also be soil-specific; the farming operations and material inputs are needed as the basis for economic analysis, and these are likely to vary as between heavy-textured and light-textured soils, well and imperfectly drained areas, level and sloping land, and other environmental differences. Thirdly, it is basic both to physical planning and to economic analysis that crop yield estimates and other estimates of production should be made. Finally, an attempt should be made to predict soil response to changes in land use. This is an extension of the hazard avoidance function. Changes in kind of land use or an increase in its intensity will have consequences for soil organic matter, nutrients, structure and physical properties. Techniques for predicting soil response are as yet little developed, but it is incorrect to plan for changed land use conditions in the future solely on the basis of soil properties as they are at present.

In summary, soil and land evaluation surveys for development projects can provide soil-specific information of the following kinds:

(a) environmental hazards which may arise;
(b) land suitability for different kinds of land use;
(c) recommendations for land management;
(d) estimates of inputs required, both for initial land improvements and for subsequent farming or other production;
(e) crop yield or other production estimates, under specified input levels;
(f) predictions of soil response to changes in land use.

At a later stage, if the project goes into operation, it is valuable if the local soil survey unit can monitor soil and other environmental changes; as yet this has not often been done. The major soils-related activity following implementation of the scheme will be agricultural extension. It is sometimes held that advisory staff in developing countries cannot make use of soil maps, either because the staff are of a lower educational standard or because the farming practices being advocated are so elementary that soil type is irrelevant. This is not wholly true. Within the area covered by each local adviser there will only be a limited range of soil types. Simple keys for recognition of these can be devised, and explained in the field by a visit from a soil surveyor. Recommendations for basic farming practices, e.g. crop rotations, can then be linked to soil type. To achieve such a state of affairs takes time and effort, involving the soil surveyor in a lot of work after the map is completed. If it can be achieved, however, it is a means of avoiding the disappointments that can arise where a single overall recommendation is applied to an area with diverse management requirements.

Land development in the urban fringe zone

The sharpest conflicts of land development occur in the urban fringe zone where there are competing demands on land for food production, industrial crops (including fibres and possibly in the near future 'energy farming'), urban expansion and industrial development with associated roads, airports and port facilities. Worldwide, land of high value for food production is severely limited and conflicts with urban and industrial use frequently arise. Once the decision has been made to develop land for urban growth, this is in effect irrevocable. Sound quantitative physical data on land suitability for alternative uses are required, on which economic and political assessments for urban growth alternatives can be based. Ideally, these data should be based on detailed soil survey, from which estimates of productivity under specified management can be derived. Failing this, it is necessary to fall back on qualitative ratings of the soil and land characteristics that control productivity (e.g. Wilson *et al*. 1975).

Soil engineering characteristics assume particular importance where urban and industrial development is envisaged. The hazard avoidance role of soil survey and allied geomorphological investigations include assessment of risk from flooding, slope instability, erosion, earthquakes, volcanic activity and permafrost.

Because of high land values in the urban fringe zone, the large capital investment in urban and industrial development, and also the high returns per unit area of specialist horticulture and agriculture supplying urban populations, the economic value of soil and land evaluation surveys is correspondingly great. This justifies detailed and thorough soil and land evaluation surveys.

Forestry

For forestry plantations, soil survey and land evaluation serve three functions: in the selection of sites for plantations, in competition with other potential uses; in the selection of tree species; and in establishment and management practices. Forest site evaluation pays particular attention to the growth potential for timber, site and climatic hazards including windthrow and slope stability, crop establishment and management costs, and landform and soil properties that affect access roads and crop extraction.

Climatic factors include the length of growing season and accumulated temperature, the balance between rainfall and potential water demand, effects of frost and snow, and windthrow hazard in relation to topographic exposure. Topographic factors also include slope steepness, form and stability. Soil factors include natural drainage and the possibilities of drainage improvement; effective rooting depth and anchorage and the possibilities of breaking up pans and indurated horizons that restrict rooting; available water capacity; nutrients and the response to fertiliser; and the soil pattern in relation to the economic benefits of uniform treatment of large blocks of land.

These factors affect choice of sites, choice of species, management practices and the costs of establishment, management and extraction. For example, extensive areas of acid, poorly drained or peaty soils have a restricted choice of tree species, may require deep ploughing and other drainage improvement, initial and perhaps periodic fertilisation and relatively expensive road construction for access and extraction. Very often forestry is allotted sloping land or sandy, infertile soils since it makes effective use of such land where agriculture is marginal or environmentally unacceptable. Forestry may also be advocated where watershed protection is the prime consideration.

Surveys for logging of natural forests are based initially on forest inventory. Once the amounts and kinds of timber resources have been determined, further considerations include location and topography and soil engineering properties for extraction roads. Where regeneration or replanting is demanded, the land characteristics already discussed for forestry plantations must be considered.

Engineering

The principal characteristics of soil and substratum which affect earth structures and foundations are the compressive strength, shear strength and sensitivity, i.e. reduction of strength from the undisturbed to the remoulded state which follows earth moving or 'pumping' by traffic, consolidation, permeability and drainage. Where steel or concrete structures are involved, corrosivity is sometimes significant.

Most of these properties are related to the particle size distribution, in particular the content of silt and clay, and to the nature of the clay minerals. In the case of cohesive strength and its relation to water content, the proportion of swelling smectite clays and in volcanic regions the content of allophane is critical. In the case of coarse materials of high frictional strength, the roundness of the particles exerts a significant influence. Soil strength is also influenced by the previous stress history of the material; underconsolidated materials such as flow till and unripe soils are very sensitive to disturbance.

Major civil engineering works are invariably designed on the basis of specialised site investigations, normally extending to greater depths than in the case of conventional soil survey. These site investigations are expensive and time-consuming and one value of soil survey is to serve as a base for sampling, eliminating obviously unsuitable areas, and extending test results beyond the sampling sites. Since a number of engineering properties of soils are dependent on particle size distribution, drainage, topography and parent material there is a useful correlation between engineering properties and soil series or land facets; such links have been demonstrated in polar, temperate and tropical environments.

For minor works, e.g. those involving shallow foundations or road subgrades, engineering interpretations of general-purpose soil maps may be employed directly; in some countries a data bank of engineering properties has been built up based on parent materials and land facets. A special-purpose **geotechnical map** may be produced, based initially on land systems and facets mapped by air photo-interpretation and compiling engineering test data for each mapping unit, paying particular attention to properties of the deeper parts of the regolith, and also hazards such as flooding, landslides and earthquakes.

Some applications of soil engineering surveys are as follows:

(a) roads and airport runways: alignment, foundations, sensitivity to pumping;
(b) sources of aggregate: for roads, buildings, dams, etc.;
(c) damage to structures by frost action;
(d) corrosion damage: iron and steel, cement;
(e) salt weathering of structures;
(f) runoff potential, hydrologic forecasting;
(g) landslide hazard;
(h) septic tank absorption fields;
(i) waste acceptance and treatment.

Financial and legal purposes

When buying farmland, soil productivity estimates provide an independent check on potential profitability, additional to that estimated from the existing farming systems. When buying a building site there can be many unsuspected hazards: flooding, high water table, landslides, subsidence leading to foundations settling and walls cracking. Soil survey interpretation indicates where such hazards are likely, so that measures can be taken to protect against them or else the land avoided.

For land rating and taxation purposes, land evaluation provides an objective means of assessing potential productivity, independent of current management practices. Taxation systems obtained in this way have been devised in Germany and the USA. For the development of previously unsettled land by private capital, loan capital is required and land evaluation is a means of checking the soundness of the proposed development.

Military purposes

A specialised form of survey, known as **terrain evaluation,** has been developed in the USA and the UK for military purposes. The unique problem in a military situation is to be able to assess the terrain of land to which you have no field access. The characteristics required are particularly those which concern movement of tanks and other vehicles, and hence compaction, trafficability, swell–shrink properties of soils and waterlogged ground are of importance.

The technique commences with mapping of land systems and land facets by air photo-interpretation. Assessment of the relevant engineering properties is made by attempting to identify the parent material and approximate soil type from photo-interpretation, and conducting tests on apparently analogous ground to which there is access. These techniques are currently being refined by the application of satellite imagery.

Recent trends

This book is written at a time when techniques and approaches to soil survey and land evaluation have emerged from a period of relative stagnation and are moving forward rapidly; more than half the references listed date from 1975 onwards. It is hazardous to predict which way an applied science is moving, since some of the avenues along which advances are currently being made may prove to be dead ends. He who jumps on two bandwagons moving in different directions risks losing his footing. With this note of caution, an attempt will be made to identify some current trends in methods of soil and land evaluation surveys and in their applications. Two such trends have been noted above: the greater use made of engineering interpretations of soils data, and the increasing applications of soil surveys in the urban fringe zone.

Physical properties of soils

In soil survey, greater attention is being given to soil physical properties. It is an anachronism that the 'standard' set of laboratory determinations, given in nearly all survey memoirs, does not include water retention characteristics. It has long been recognised that mere contents of N, P and K, which are almost invariably presented, are ephemeral soil properties, appropriate for decisions on what fertilisers to apply to a crop in the following year but of very limited value in predicting long-term productivity. Both in temperate and tropical regions, attention is being given to questions of soil degradation, and to the soil properties which can affect this. Of particular interest are surveys to estimate the capacities of different soil types to tolerate high intensities of arable use.

Land resources

There is a growing recognition that land resources do not consist of soils alone. For crop production, landforms, climate and soils all contribute to potential productivity; in forestry and pasture resources, an ecosystem approach is applicable. As a consequence, soil survey organisations need to give greater attention to agro-climatology, including the recruitment of specialist staff. This is illustrated by recent studies of potential land productivity by the FAO, in which it has been found that climate plays an equal or greater part than soils in differentiating between areas with varying potential for crop growth. More generally, organisations involved in planning and management are finding that their needs are served by a range of natural resource studies, including surveys of landforms, climate and vegetation, rather than by soil surveys alone.

Information systems

Broadening the data base of soil survey, by increasing the scope of observations and measurements and increasing the area of detailed survey, brings with it the problem of handling the data. An increasing interest is being shown in the potentialities of soil information systems and land resource data banks. This is a natural consequence of the potential offered by sophisticated computing facilities. Soil surveys have always had the problem of how to handle many hundreds or thousands of observations, and it is in tasks involving the relatively routine processing of large numbers of items that computers are especially efficient. The application of sophisticated methods of statistical analysis is also being thoroughly tested, although the potential benefits to practical soil survey are uncertain.

In land evaluation, soils information can be combined with climatic data to produce predictive models. An example is the prediction of drought risk and optimum economic levels of irrigation provision (Dent & Scammell 1981). It seems probable that models for predicting crop yields will soon be developed, although as yet there has been more success in relating yields (retrospectively) to year-to-year climatic fluctuations than to soils.

If survey data are gathered with computer storage, retrieval and mapping in mind, a range of single-factor maps and special-purpose interpretations can be rapidly generated by computer-graphic techniques (e.g. Nichols & Bartelli 1979, Rudeforth 1975, Ragg 1977). The possibility of generating special-purpose interpretative maps by interpolation between closely spaced reference points avoids one limitation of conventional soil survey, namely that the critical limits of soil parameters for some purposes do not coincide with the surveyor's field boundaries; such interpolation, however, is only justified where there are no clear visible landscape boundaries.

Interpretation, credibility and communication

To date, the use made of soil surveys has been far below their potential. This situation has been caused partly by problems of credibility and communication. For a number of reasons, few countries have devoted more than a barely significant fraction of their national effort in scientific research to soil survey. A national general-purpose survey only begins to serve its function of providing interpretations for a variety of problems as they arise when a substantial degree of uniform, semi-detailed or detailed coverage has been achieved. This goal is likely to be achieved in a number of countries, including the USA, within the next 20 years. With its achievement, there is likely to be less effort devoted to pure soil mapping, and more on interpretations, effective presentation and putting the results of surveys to use.

The trend towards directing survey activities towards specific purposes, rather than mapping for its own sake, is already apparent. It has come about through the discovery that narrowly 'pedological' soil maps are frequently put on the library shelf but never to practical purposes. In developing countries, resource inventories at reconnaissance scales are currently out of favour, again for the reason that little or no development seems to result from them at first; it is possible that this pendulum may swing back, since some countries are finding lack of a complete coverage a handicap to coherent planning. Present emphasis in surveys for developing countries is in identifying realistic development alternatives, and directing survey activities towards these.

A pedological map is incomprehensible, and therefore of no value, to the average land user or planner. Each kind of user requires either a special-purpose survey directed towards his needs, or else an interpretation or evaluation specifically in terms of the kinds of use, techniques or aspects of management with which he is concerned. Detailed soil maps are required as a basis for most such intepretations, but the range of interpretations needed to serve different requirements extends far beyond the agricultural bias of most existing survey data. The techniques of land evaluation have provided a means of integrating soils with other land resource data, and of showing how physical surveys can be translated into economic terms.

There is also some progress being made in the direction of communication. The USA is well advanced in this respect, with an active publicity programme and information service, and several national survey organisations have recently carried out studies to find out what users require. Survey reports, particularly those of consultant firms, often include a summary aimed at the non-specialist reader, giving the main results in easily understood language.

Moves towards better communication should lead in turn to improvements in the methods of soil survey and land evaluation. The user will acquire a better understanding of what survey information is available and how it can be applied. The surveyor will be in a position to set the requirements of the user against his own knowledge of the vagaries of soil distribution and to plan the survey accordingly.

Further reading

Davidson (1980), Jarvis and Mackney (1979), Mitchell (1973), Robertson (1970), Mackney (1974), Young (1973a).

For engineering applications: Bartelli (1978), FAO (1973), National Institute for Transport and Road Research (1976), Dowling (1968) and British Standards Institution (1967).

Other non-agricultural applications: Simonson (1974) and Bartelli (1978).

Recent trends: Arnold *et al.* (1977) Swindale (1978), Young (1978), Hills (1979), Beatty *et al.* (1979) and FAO (1980).

Soil survey organisations, universities, consultant companies and other institutions concerned with soil and land evaluation surveys could usefully build up a collection of examples of surveys for study and reference. Keeping to English-language reports, a basis would be a selection from the County Soil Survey Reports of the US Soil Conservation Service, reports of the national Soil Surveys of England and Wales, Scotland (not identical in methods with England and Wales), Australia, New Zealand, Kenya (including land suitability evaluation) and Canada. For applications in a densely settled environment, see reports of the Netherlands Soil Survey. For developing countries, see the Land Resource Studies (nos 1–31) of the UK Land Resources Development Centre, which contain a wide range of different scales and purposes (reviewed in Young 1978); reports of FAO surveys; and, if they can be obtained, reports of surveys by consultant companies.

Appendix A
How to Obtain Soil Maps

It is not always a straightforward matter to find out if a soil map exists for a given area. Some maps are published in rather obscure sources, some remain unpublished. There are two methods, written enquiry or bibliographic search.

In the general case, an enquiry addressed 'The Director, Soil Survey of (country), Ministry of Agriculture, (capital city), (country)' will probably find its way to whatever organisation exists; ask for either a full list of published soil maps for the country or whether coverage exists for your area of interest. For the USA, obtain the leaflet 'Where to get information about soil and water conservation' from the Information Division, Soil Conservation Service, Department of Agriculture, Washington DC. For the UK, write to the Soil Survey of England and Wales, Rothamsted Experimental Station, Harpenden, Herts, or to the Soil Survey of Scotland, Macaulay Institute for Soils Research, Craigiebuckler, Aberdeen. For the larger British Commonwealth countries write to the Soil Survey concerned, e.g. New Zealand Soil Bureau, Private Bag, Lower Hutt. Both Canada and Australia have separate provincial or state surveys based in the relevant state Department of Agriculture and, at a national level, for Canada, the Soil Research Institute, Agriculture Canada, Central Experimental Farm, Ottawa, Ontario, and, for Australia, CSIRO, Division of Soils, Melbourne. For smaller Commonwealth countries, information may be held by the Land Resources Development Centre, Tolworth Tower, Surbiton, Surrey, England. For French-speaking overseas countries, a general source is the Service Central de Documentation de l'ORSTOM, 70–74 route d'Aulnay, 93-Bondy, France. The United Nations organisation concerned with soil survey and land evaluation is the Soil Resources Management and Conservation Service, Land and Water Development Division, FAO, Via delle Terme di Caracalla, 00100-Rome, Italy.

For bibliographic search, some useful starting points are as follows:

(a) FAO 1965/1973. *Catalogue of maps, Soil Map of the World Project*, 3rd edn, 1965 (published), 4th edn, 1972 (produced internally), Rome: FAO. Contains 500 pages, covering, in addition to soils, topographic and other thematic maps. The FAO library of soil maps may be inspected by appointment.

(b) Orvedal, A. C. 1975–81. *Bibliography of the soils of the tropics*. Vol. I (1975): *Tropics in general and Africa*; Vol. II (1977): *South America*; Vol. III (1978): *Middle America and West Indies*; Vol. IV (1981): *Islands of the Pacific and Indian Oceans*. Washington DC: Office of Agriculture, Development Support Bureau, Agency for International Development.

(c) Annotated bibliographies with titles *Soils of Xxxxx* produced by the Commonwealth Bureau of Soils, Rothamsted Experimental Station, Harpenden, Herts, England. A price list of countries for which these are available is obtainable on request. In addition, the Commonwealth Bureaux provide a broad documentation service, including computerised search facilities, details of which are supplied on request.

(d) *Land resource bibliographies* produced by the Land Resources Development Centre, address as above. Twelve countries have been covered to 1980.

If what you require is a very generalised indication of what kinds of soil are likely to occur in some distant part of the world, refer to the 18 map sheets and 10 volumes of FAO–Unesco (1970–80). *Soil map of the world 1: 5000 000*. Paris: Unesco. This map should be used with much caution owing to the small scale, paucity of surveys over large areas, and the fact that parts are by now superseded by more recent surveys. An updated version is maintained by FAO, Rome.

The principal abstract periodicals for soils and related information are *Soils and fertilizers* (Commonwealth Agricultural Bureaux, Farnham Royal, Slough, Berkshire, England); *Bibliography of Agriculture* (National Agricultural Library, Oryx Press, Phoenix, Arizona, USA); and *Geo Abstracts* (Geo Abstracts Ltd, University of East Anglia, Norwich, England).

Appendix B
Discounted Present Value

In projects which require land improvements, it is necessary to incur capital expenditure in the first year or early years in return for benefits, in the form of increased production and profits, received in future years. In irrigation schemes and many other agricultural projects, initial capital expenditure leads to a build-up towards a steady state of increased production after a number of years. In forestry, the benefits are received at intervals (thinning and felling) over periods of between 15 and 60 or more years. Cash-flow discounting is a way of setting initial capital expenditure against future benefits, or more generally of balancing costs incurred and benefits received at different periods in the future.

Money invested at the present earns interest, and acquires a higher value in future years. If the interest rate is 10%, £100 invested this year becomes £110 in one year's time, £121 in two years, or in the general case,

$$100 \times (1+r)^n \qquad \text{in } n \text{ years time}$$

where r is the interest rate expressed as a fraction, i.e. 10% as 0.1. Thus the money value of expenditure incurred now increases in the future since the capital spent on a land improvement could alternatively have been placed in some interest-earning investment.

It would be possible to compare expenditure and benefits at different periods by adding compound interest and bringing all the values to some common date in the future. Since, however, the decision to invest is made now, it is better to carry out the process in reverse and bring all costs and benefits to their equivalents at the present time, called their **present value.** Discounting can be regarded as the reverse of addition of interest. Taking a discount rate r of 0.1 (10%), expenditure or cost of £100 in one year's time has a present value of $100/(1+0.1)=£90.90$. The present value of £100 spent or received two years hence is $100/(1+0.1)^2=£82.6$; another way of looking at this is to say that a foreseen expenditure of £100 in two year's time could be met by setting aside £82.6 now in an investment earning 10% compound interest. The discounting procedure is exactly the same whether dealing with a cost or a benefit. In the general case, a cost incurred or benefit received of £P in n year's time has a present value V of

$$V = P \frac{1}{(1+r)^n}$$

The value $1/(1+r)^n$ is called the **discount factor,** used to multiply any actual cost or benefit to give its present value (Table B.1).

After an initial period, maintenance costs and benefits often even out to a steady amount each year. A short cut to the calculations is then possible using tables of cumulative discount factors. For example, at a discount rate of 10%, £100 received in years 1 to 5 inclusive has a present value of $90.90+82.60+75.10$

+68.30+62.10=£379. The cumulative discount factor is thus 3.79. To calculate the present value of a cost or benefit in years 5 to 20 inclusive, take the multiplier for 20 years and subtract that for 5 years (Table B.2).

The procedures are the same whether one assumes a commercial rate of interest (and thus discounting), currently of the order of 15% in many countries, or whether the calculation is done in terms of an assumed lower 'social' rate of interest. A simplified example of the calculation is given in Table 11.2 (p. 197). For a discussion of the basis of the 'social' rate of interest, together with opportunity costs, shadow pricing and other assumptions often employed in accounting for governmental development projects, see textbooks on cost–benefit analysis (e.g. Dasgupta *et al.* 1972, Hansen 1978, Overseas Development Administration 1972).

Table B.1 Discount factors: calculation of the present value of a future cost or benefit in year n.

Year	5%	6%	7%	8%	9%	10%	12%	15%	20%
1	0.952	0.943	0.935	0.926	0.917	0.909	0.893	0.870	0.833
2	0.907	0.890	0.873	0.857	0.842	0.826	0.797	0.756	0.694
3	0.864	0.840	0.816	0.794	0.772	0.751	0.712	0.658	0.579
4	0.823	0.792	0.763	0.735	0.708	0.683	0.636	0.572	0.482
5	0.784	0.747	0.713	0.681	0.650	0.621	0.567	0.497	0.402
6	0.746	0.705	0.666	0.630	0.596	0.564	0.507	0.432	0.335
7	0.711	0.665	0.623	0.583	0.547	0.513	0.452	0.376	0.279
8	0.677	0.627	0.582	0.540	0.502	0.467	0.404	0.327	0.233
9	0.645	0.592	0.544	0.500	0.460	0.424	0.361	0.284	0.194
10	0.614	0.558	0.508	0.463	0.422	0.386	0.322	0.247	0.162
11	0.585	0.527	0.475	0.429	0.388	0.350	0.287	0.215	0.135
12	0.557	0.497	0.444	0.397	0.356	0.319	0.257	0.187	0.112
13	0.530	0.469	0.415	0.368	0.326	0.290	0.229	0.163	0.093
14	0.505	0.442	0.388	0.340	0.299	0.263	0.205	0.141	0.078
15	0.481	0.417	0.362	0.315	0.275	0.239	0.183	0.123	0.065

Table B.2 Discount factors: calculation of the present value of a future constant annual cost or benefit in years to 1 to n inclusive.

Year	5%	6%	7%	8%	9%	10%	12%	15%	20%
1	0.95	0.94	0.93	0.93	0.92	0.91	0.89	0.87	0.83
2	1.85	1.83	1.80	1.78	1.76	1.74	1.69	1.63	1.53
3	2.72	2.67	2.62	2.58	2.53	2.49	2.40	2.28	2.11
4	3.54	3.46	3.38	3.31	3.24	3.17	3.04	2.85	2.59
5	4.32	4.21	4.10	3.99	3.89	3.79	3.61	3.35	2.99
6	5.07	4.91	4.76	4.62	4.49	4.36	4.11	3.78	3.33
7	5.78	5.58	5.38	5.21	5.03	4.87	4.56	4.16	3.60
8	6.46	6.20	5.97	5.75	5.53	5.33	4.97	4.49	3.84
9	7.10	6.80	6.51	6.25	6.00	5.76	5.33	4.77	4.03
10	7.72	7.36	7.02	6.71	6.42	6.14	5.65	5.02	4.19
12	8.86	8.38	7.94	7.54	7.16	6.81	6.19	5.42	4.43
15	10.38	9.71	9.11	8.56	8.06	7.61	6.81	5.85	4.68
20	12.46	11.47	10.59	9.82	9.13	8.51	7.47	6.26	4.87

References

Agricultural Development and Advisory Service 1977. *Suitability mapping.* ADAS Tech. Rep. 31, UK Min. Agric.

Agricultural Land Service 1966. *Agricultural land classification.* UK Min. Agric. Tech. Rep. 11.

American Society of Photogrammetry 1968. *Manual of color aerial photography.* Falls Church, VA: American Society of Photogrammetry.

American Society of Photogrammetry 1975. *Manual of remote sensing,* 2 vols. Falls Church, VA: American Society of Photogrammetry.

Arens, P. L. 1977. Edaphic criteria in land evaluation. In *Land evaluation standards for rainfed agriculture.* World Soil Resour. Rep. 49, 24–31. Rome: FAO.

Arnold, R. W. (ed.) 1977. *Soil resource inventories.* Agron. Mimeo 77–23, New York State Coll. Agric. Ithaca, NY: Cornell University.

Arnon, D. I. 1972. *Crop production in dry regions,* 2 vols. Aylesbury: Hill.

Avery, B. W. 1962. Soil type and crop performance. *Soils Fertil.* **25,** 341–4.

Avery, B. W. 1980. *Soil classification for England and Wales (higher categories).* Soil Survey Tech. Monogr. 14. Rothamsted, Harpenden: Soil Survey.

Ayers, A. S., and D. W. Westcot 1976. *Water quality for agriculture.* Irrig. Drainage Paper 29. Rome: FAO.

Ball, D. F., and W. M. Williams 1968. Variability of soil chemical properties in two uncultivated brown earths. *J. Soil Sci.* **19,** 379–91.

Bartelli, L. J. 1978. Technical classification system for soil survey interpretation. *Adv. Agron.* **30,** 247–89.

Beatty, M. T., G. W. Petersen and L. D. Swindale (eds) 1979. *Planning the uses and management of land.* Madison, Wisconsin: American Society of Agronomy.

Beckett, P. H. T. 1971. The cost-effectiveness of soil survey. *Outlook Agric.* **6,** 191–8.

Beckett, P. H. T., and R. Webster 1971. Soil variability – a review. *Soils Fertil.* **34,** 1–15.

Beckett, P. H. T., R. Webster, G. M. McNeil and C. W. Mitchell 1972. Terrain evaluation by means of a data bank. *Geog. J.* **138,** 430–56.

Beek, K. J. 1978. *Land evaluation for agricultural development.* ILRI Pubn. 23. Wageningen: International Institute for Land Reclamation and Improvement.

Beek, K. J. 1981. From soil survey interpretation to land evaluation. Parts 1 and 2. *Soil Survey Land Evaluation* **1,** 6–12 and 23–30.

Bibby, J. S., and D. Mackney 1969. *Land use capability classification.* Soil Survey Tech. Monogr. 1. Rothamsted, Harpenden: Soil Survey.

Bie, S. W. (ed.) 1975. *Soil information systems.* Wageningen: Pudoc.

Bie, S. W., and P. H. T. Beckett 1970. The costs of soil survey. *Soils Fertil.* **33,** 203–17.

Bie, S. W., and P. H. T. Beckett 1971. Quality control in soil survey. *J. Soil Sci.* **22,** 32–49 and 453–65.

Bie, S. W., A. Ulph and P. H. T. Beckett 1973. Calculating the economic benefits of soil survey. *J. Soil Sci.* **24,** 429–35.

Bleeker, P., and J. G. Speight 1978. Soil–landform relationships at two localities in Papua New Guinea. *Geoderma* **21,** 183–98.

Blyth, J. F., and D. A. Macleod 1978. The significance of soil variability for forest soil studies in north-east Scotland. *J. Soil Sci.* **29,** 419–30.

Boulton, G. S., and M. A. Paul 1976. The influence of genetic processes on some geotechnical properties of glacial tills. *Q. J. Engng Geol.* **9,** 159–94.

Brink, A. B., J. A. Mabbutt, R. Webster and P. H. T. Beckett 1966. *Report of the working group on land classification and data storage.* MEXE Rep. 940. Christchurch, Hants: Military Engineering Experimental Establishment.

References

British Standards Institution 1967. *Methods of testing soils for civil engineering purposes.* British Standard 1377: 1967.

Brunsden, D., J. C. Doornkamp and D. K. C. Jones 1979. The Bahrain surface materials resources survey and its application to regional planning. *Geog. J.* **145,** 1–35.

Buol, S. W. and W. Couto 1981. Soil fertility-capability assessment for use in the humid tropics. In *Characterization of soils in relation to their classification and management for crop production,* D. J. Greenland (ed.), 254–61. Oxford: Oxford University Press.

Burgess, T. M. and R. Webster 1980. Optimal interpolation and isarithmic mapping of soil properties. *J. Soil Sci.* **31,** 315–42 and 505–24.

Burrough, P. A., P. H. T. Beckett and M. G. Jarvis 1971. The relation between cost and utility in soil survey. *J. Soil Sci.* **22,** 359–94.

Carroll, D. M. 1973. Remote sensing techniques and their application to soil science. *Soils Fertil.* **36,** 259–66 and 313–20.

Carroll, D. M., R. Evans and V. C. Bendelow 1977. *Air photo-interpretation for soil mapping.* Soil Survey Tech. Monogr. 8. Rothamsted, Harpenden: Soil Survey.

Charter, C. F. 1957. The aims and objects of tropical soil surveys. *Soils Fertil.* **20,** 127–8.

Chorley, R. J., D. R. Stoddart, P. Haggett and H. O. Slaymaker 1966. Regional and local components in the areal distribution of surface sand facies in the Breckland, Eastern England. *J. Sed. Petrol.* **36,** 209–20.

Christian, C. S., and G. A. Stewart 1968. Methodology of integrated surveys. *Unesco Nat. Resour. Res.* **6,** 233–80.

Collins, W. G., and J. L. van Genderen 1978. *Remote sensing applications in developing countries.* Birmingham: University of Aston, Remote Sensing Society.

Cooke, R. U., and J. C. Doornkamp 1974. *Geomorphology in environmental management.* Oxford: Oxford University Press.

Courtney, F. M. 1973. A taxonometric study of the Sherborne soil mapping unit. *Trans Inst. Br. Geogs* **58,** 113–24.

Courtney, F. M., and S. Nortcliff 1977. Analysis techniques in the study of soil distribution. *Prog. Phys. Geog.* **1,** 40–64.

Cracknell, B. E. 1978. *The evaluation activities of the Ministry of Overseas Development.* London: Manpower Planning Unit, Ministry of Overseas Development.

CSIRO Australia 1953–80. *Land research series,* nos 1–30. Melbourne: Commonwealth Scientific and Industrial Research Organisation.

CSIRO 1960–8. *Atlas of Australian soils.* 10 sheets, each with handbook. Melbourne: Melbourne University Press.

Cuanallo, H. E. de la C. and R. Webster 1970. A comparative study of numerical classification and ordination of soil profiles in a locality near Oxford. *J. Soil Sci.* **21,** 340–52.

Curtis, L. F., J. C. Doornkamp and K. J. Gregory 1965. The description of relief in field studies of soils. *J. Soil Sci.* **16,** 16–30.

Dasgupta, P., A. Sen and S. Marglin 1972. *Guidelines for project evaluation.* New York: United Nations.

Davidson, D. A. 1980. *Soils and land use planning.* London: Longman.

Dent, D. 1980. Acid sulphate soils: morphology and prediction. *J. Soil Sci.* **31,** 87–100.

Dent, D. L., and P. Scammell 1981a. Evaluation of long-term irrigation need using soil and crop characteristics and meteorological data. *Soil Survey Land Evaluation* **1** (3).

Dent, D. L., and P. Scammell 1981b. Irrigation need. In *Soils of Norfolk,* W. M. Corbett (ed.). Rothamsted, Harpenden: Soil Survey.

Department of Agriculture, Zambia 1977. *Land use planning guide.* Lusaka: Ministry of Lands and Agriculture.

Doorenbos, J., and A. H. Kassam 1979. *Yield response to water.* Irrig. Drainage Paper 33. Rome: FAO.

References

Doorenbos, J., and W. O. Pruitt 1977. *Crop water requirements*. Irrig. Drainage Paper 24. Rome: FAO.

Dowling, J. W. F. 1968. Land evaluation for engineering purposes in Northern Nigeria. In *Land evaluation*, G. A. Stewart (ed.), 147–59. Melbourne: Macmillan.

Dowling, J. W. F., and P. J. Beaven 1969. Terrain evaluation for road engineers in developing countries. *J. Inst. Highway Engr.* **14**, 5–22.

Dumanski, J. (ed.) 1978. *Manual for describing soils in the field*. Ottawa: Agriculture Canada.

FAO 1973. *Soil survey interpretation for engineering purposes*. Soils Bull. 19. Rome: FAO.

FAO 1974a. *Approaches to land classification*. Soils Bull. 22. Rome: FAO.

FAO 1974b. *Shifting cultivation and soil conservation in Africa*. Soils Bull. 24. Rome: FAO.

FAO 1976. *A framework for land evaluation*. Soils Bull. 32. Rome: FAO.

FAO 1977. *Guidelines for soil profile description*, 2nd edn. Rome: FAO.

FAO 1978. *Report on the agro-ecological zones project*. Vol. 1: *Methodology and results for Africa*. World Soil Resour. Rep. 48. Rome: FAO.

FAO 1979a. *Soil survey investigations for irrigation*. Soils Bull. 42. Rome: FAO.

FAO 1979b. *A provisional methodology for soil degradation assessment*. Rome: FAO.

FAO 1980. *Report on the second FAO/UNFPA expert consultation on land resources for populations of the future*. Rome: FAO.

FAO–Unesco 1974. *Soil map of the world*. Vol. 1: *Legend*. Paris: Unesco.

FAO–Unesco 1970–80. *Soil map of the world 1: 5000 000*. Vols 1–10. Paris: Unesco. (Each volume consists of a text volume and one or more map sheets.)

Forster, B. A. 1977. *Report on the land units of the Wagait Aboriginal Reserve*. Tech. Bull. 20, Animal Ind. Agric. Branch. Canberra: Department of Northern Territories.

Gibbons, F. R. 1961. Some misconceptions about what soil surveys can do. *J. Soil Sci.* **12**, 96–100.

Goosen, D. 1967. *Aerial photo interpretation in soil survey*. Soils Bull. 6. Rome: FAO.

de Gruijter, J. J. 1977. *Numerical classification of soils and its application in survey*. Wageningen: Pudoc.

Haantjens, H. A. 1965a. Practical aspects of land system surveys in New Guinea. *J. Trop. Geog.* **21**, 12–20.

Haantjens, H. A. 1965b. *Agricultural land classification for New Guinea land resources surveys*. CSIRO Div. Land Res. Reg. Surv. Tech. Memor. 65/8. Canberra: Commonwealth Scientific and Industrial Research Organisation.

Hall, D. G. M., M. J. Reeve, A. J. Thomasson and V. F. Wright 1977. *Water retention, porosity and density of field soils*. Soil Survey Tech. Monogr. 9. Rothamsted, Harpenden: Soil Survey.

Hansen, J. R. 1978. *Guide to practical project appraisal. Social benefit–cost analysis in developing countries*. Project Formul. Eval. Ser. 3. New York: United Nations.

Hesse, P. R. 1971. *A textbook of soil chemical analysis*. London: John Murray.

Hill, I. D. (ed.) 1978. *Land resources of central Nigeria. Agricultural development possibilities*, 7 vols. Surbiton, Surrey: Land Resources Development Centre.

Hills, R. C. 1979. *Surveys of free resources: is there a role in planning and project implementation?* Devel. Stud. Centre Occas. Pap. 16. Canberra: Australian National University.

Hodgson, J. M. (ed.) 1974. *Soil survey field handbook*. Soil Survey Tech. Monogr. 5. Rothamsted, Harpenden: Soil Survey.

Hodgson, J. M. 1978. *Soil sampling and soil description*. Oxford: Oxford University Press.

Jarvis, M. G., and D. Mackney 1979. *Soil survey applications*. Soil Survey Tech. Monogr. 13. Rothamsted, Harpenden: Soil Survey.

References

Kassam, A. H. 1980. Agro-climatic suitability for rainfed crops of winter barley, upland rice, groundnut, sugarcane, banana/plantain and oil palm in Africa. In *Report on the second FAO/UNFPA expert consultation on land resources for populations of the future*. Rome: FAO.

Kellogg, C. E. 1937. *Soil survey manual*. Dept Agric. Misc. Publ. 274. Washington DC: Department of Agriculture. (For a revised edition, see Soil Survey Staff 1951.)

Klingebiel, A. A., and P. H. Montgomery 1961. *Land capability classification*. Agric. Handb. 210. Washington DC: Department of Agriculture.

Kuchler, A. W. 1967. *Vegetation mapping*. New York: Ronald.

Land Resources Development Centre 1966–80. *Land resource studies*, nos 1–31. Surbiton, Surrey: Land Resources Development Centre.

'Longman' 1961–80. *Tropical agriculture* series. London: Longman. (The series includes 12 books on individual crops, with climatic and soil requirements.)

Loveday, J. (ed.) 1974. *Methods of analysis for irrigated soils*. Farnham Royal, Slough: Commonwealth Agricultural Bureaux.

Mackney, D. (ed.) 1974. *Soil type and land capability*. Soil Survey Tech. Monogr. 4. Rothamsted, Harpenden: Soil Survey.

Mahler, P. J. (ed.) 1970. *Manual of multipurpose land classification*. Min. Agric. Publ. 212. Teheran: Ministry of Agriculture.

Makin, M. J., T. J. Kingham, A. E. Waddams, C. J. Birchall and B. W. Eavis 1976. *Prospects for irrigation development around Lake Zwai, Ethiopia*. Land Res. Study 26. Surbiton, Surrey: Land Resources Development Centre.

Mansfield, J. E., J. G. Bennett, R. B. King, D. M. Lang and R. M. Lawton 1975–7. *Land resources of the northern and Luapula Provinces, Zambia: a reconnaissance assessment*, 6 vols. Land Res. Study 19. Surbiton, Surrey: Land Resources Development Centre.

Milne, G. 1935–36. *A provisional soil map of East Africa, with explanatory memoir*. London: Crown Agents.

Mitchell, A. J. B. 1976. *The irrigation potential of soils along the main rivers of Eastern Botswana: a reconnaissance assessment*. Land Res. Study 7. Surbiton, Surrey: Land Resources Development Centre.

Mitchell, C. W. 1973. *Terrain evaluation*. London: Longman.

Mitchell, C. W., and J. A. Howard 1978a. *The application of Landsat imagery to soil degradation mapping at 1:5000000*. AGLT Bull. 1/78. Rome: FAO.

Mitchell, C. W., and J. A. Howard 1978b. *Land system classification. A case history: Jordan*. AGLT Bull. 2/78. Rome: FAO.

Mitchell, C. W. *et al.* 1979. An analysis of terrain classification for long-range prediction in deserts. *Geog. J.* **145,** 72–85.

Moore, A. W., and S. W. Bie (eds) 1977. *Uses of soil information systems*. Wageningen: Pudoc.

More, A. W., J. S. Russell and W. T. Ward 1972. Numerical analysis of soils: a comparison of three soil profile models with field classification. *J. Soil Sci.* **23,** 193–209.

Moss, R. P. 1968. Land use, vegetation and soil factors in south-west Nigeria, a new approach. *Pacific Viewpoint* **9,** 107–26.

Moss, R. P. 1969. The appraisal of land resources in tropical Africa: a critique of some concepts. *Pacific Viewpoint* **10,** 18–27.

Mulcahy, M. J., and A. W. Humphries 1967. Soil classification, soil surveys and land use. *Soils Fertil.* **30,** 1–8.

Munn, R. E. (ed.) 1979. *Environmental impact assessment. Principles and procedures*. SCOPE Rep. 5, 2nd edn. Chichester: Wiley.

Murdoch, G., R. Webster and C. J. Lawrance 1971. *A land system atlas of Swaziland*. Christchurch, Hants: MVEE.

References

National Institute for Transport and Road Research 1976. *Geotechnical and soil engineering mapping for roads and the storage of materials data.* Draft TRH 2. Pretoria: Council for Scientific and Industrial Research.

Nichols, J. D., and L. J. Bartelli 1979. Computer generated interpretive soil maps. *J. Soil Water Conserv.* **29**, 232–5.

Norris, J. M. 1970. Multivariate methods in the study of soils. *Soils Fertil.* **33**, 313–18.

Nortcliff, S. 1978. Soil variability and reconnaissance soil mapping: a statistical study in Norfolk. *J. Soil Sci.* **29**, 403–18.

Northcote, K. H. 1971. *A factual key for the recognition of Australian soils,* 3rd edn. Glenside, South Australia: Rellim.

Olson, G. W. 1974. Land classifications. *Search, Agric.* **4**, 1–34.

Overseas Development Administration 1972. *A guide to project appraisal in developing countries.* London: HMSO.

Pimental, D. and M. Pimental 1979. *Food, energy and society.* London: Arnold.

Purseglove, J. W. 1968. *Tropical crops. Dicotyledons,* 2 vols. London: Longman.

Purseglove, J. W. 1972. *Tropical crops. Monocotyledons,* 2 vols. London: Longman.

Pyatt, D. G., D. Harrison and A. S. Ford 1969. *Guide to site types in forests of north and mid-Wales.* Forestry Commission, Forest Record 9. London: HMSO.

Ragg, J. M. 1977. The recording and organisation of soil field data for computer aerial mapping. *Geoderma* **19**, 81–9.

Ragg, J. M., and R. Henderson 1980. A reappraisal of soil mapping in an area of southern Scotland. *J. Soil Sci.* **31**, 559–80.

Richards, L. A. 1954. *Diagnosis and improvement of saline and alkali soils.* Agric. Handb. 60. Washington DC: Department of Agriculture.

Robertson, V. C. 1970. Land and water resource planning in developing countries. *Outlook Agric.* **6**, 148–57.

Rowan, A. A. 1977. *Terrain classification.* Forestry Commission, Forest Record 114. London: HMSO.

Rudeforth, C. C. 1975. Storing and processing data for soil and land use capability surveys. *J. Soil Sci.* **26**, 155–68.

Ruthenburg, H. 1980. *Farming systems in the tropics,* 3rd edn. Oxford: Oxford University Press.

Sadovsky, A. D., and S. W. Bie (eds) 1978. *Developments in soil information systems.* Wageningen: Pudoc.

Scott, R. M., R. Webster and C. J. Lawrance 1971. *A land system atlas of western Kenya.* Christchurch: Her Majesty's Government.

Shaxson, T. F., N. D. Hunter, T. R. Jackson and J. R. Alder 1977. *A land husbandry manual.* Lilongwe, Malaŵi: Ministry of Agriculture.

Simonson, R. W. (ed.) 1974. *Non-agricultural applications of soil surveys.* Amsterdam: Elsevier.

Smyth, A. J. 1970. *The preparation of soil survey reports.* Soils Bull. 9. Rome: FAO.

Soil Survey Staff 1951. *Soil survey manual.* Agric. Handb. 18. Washington DC: Department of Agriculture.

Soil Survey Staff 1966. *Aerial-photo interpretation in classifying and mapping soils.* Agric. Handb. 294. Washington DC: Department of Agriculture.

Soil Survey Staff 1975. *Soil taxonomy. A basic system of soil classification for making and interpreting soil surveys.* Agric. Handb. 436. Washington DC: Department of Agriculture.

Speight, J. G. 1974. A parametric approach to landform regions. *Inst. Br. Geogs. Sp. Pubn* **7**, 213–30.

References

Speight, J. G. 1977. Landform pattern description from aerial photographs. *Photogrammetria* **32**, 161–82.

Stewart, G. A. 1968. *Land evaluation*. Melbourne: Macmillan.

Stobbs, A. R. 1970. Soil survey procedures for development purposes. In *New possibilities and techniques for land use and related surveys*, I. H. Cox (ed.), 41–64. Berkhamsted: Geographical Publications.

Swindale, L. D. (ed.) 1978. *Soil-resource data for agricultural development*. Honolulu: University of Hawaii.

Sys, C. 1978. Evaluation of land limitations in the humid tropics. *Pédologie, Ghent* **28**, 307–35.

Sys, C., and J. Riquier 1980. Ratings of FAO/Unesco soil units for specific crop production. In *Report on the second FAO/UNFPA expert consultation on land resources for populations of the future*, 55–96. Rome: FAO.

Taylor, N. H., and I. J. Pohlen 1970. *Soil survey method*. NZ Soil Bureau Bull. 25. Wellington: New Zealand Soil Bureau.

Thomas, D. 1973. Urban land evaluation. In *Evaluating the human environment*, J. A. Dawson and J. C. Doornkamp (eds), 88–108. London: Arnold.

Thomas, P., F. K. C. Lo and A. J. Hepburn 1976. *The land capability classification of Sabah*, 4 vols. Land Res. Study 25. Surbiton, Surrey: Land Resources Development Centre.

Thompson, M. C., and F. G. Sturrock 1976. *Report on farming 1975–76. Changes in the production and profitability of farming with standards for farm business analysis. Eastern counties of England*. Agric. Econ. Unit, Rep. 66. Cambridge: Department of Land Economy.

Townshend, J. R. G. (ed.) 1981. *Terrain analysis and remote sensing*. London: George Allen & Unwin.

Trapnell, C. G., J. D. Martin and W. Allan 1948–50. *Vegetation–soil map of Northern Rhodesia*, 1st edn, 1948; 2nd edn, 1950. Lusaka: Ministry of Agriculture.

US Bureau of Reclamation 1953. *Bureau of reclamation manual*. Vol. V: *Irrigated land use*. Pt 2: *Land classification*. Denver, Colorado: USBR.

US Bureau of Reclamation, 1978. *Drainage manual*. Washington DC: US Government Printing Office.

Vincent, V., R. G. Thomas and R. Anderson 1961. *An agricultural survey of Southern Rhodesia*. Pt I: *The agro-ecological survey*. Pt II: *The agro-economic survey*. Salisbury: Ministry of Agriculture.

Vink, A. P. A. 1975. *Land use in advancing agriculture*. Berlin: Springer.

Webster, R. 1971. Wilk's criterion: a measure for comparing the value of general purpose soil classifications. *J. Soil Sci.* **22**, 254–60.

Webster, R. 1978a. *Quantitative and numerical methods in soil classification and survey*. Oxford: Oxford University Press.

Webster, R. 1978b. Optimally partitioning soil transects. *J. Soil Sci.* **29**, 388–402.

Webster, R., C. M. Lessells and J. M. Hodgson 1976. Decode – a computer program for translating coded soil profile description into text. *J. Soil Sci.* **27**, 218–26.

Western, S. 1978. *Soil survey contracts and quality control*. Oxford: Oxford University Press.

White, L. P. 1978. *Aerial photography and remote sensing for soil survey*. Oxford: Oxford University Press.

Wilson, A. D., J. E. Cox and J. C. Heine 1975. *Agricultural and horticultural implications of the ARA urban growth alternatives study*. Pt 2: *Soil resources of the Auckland region*. Auckland: Ministry of Agriculture.

268

References

Wilson, R. T. 1979. Recent resource surveys for rural development in southern Darfur, Sudan. *Geog. J.* **145,** 452–60.

Wischmeier, W. H., and D. D. Smith 1965. *Predicting rainfall-erosion losses from cropland.* Agric. Handb. 282. Washington DC: Department of Agriculture.

Woode, P. R. 1981, 'We don't want soil maps. Just give us land capability'. The role of land capability surveys in Zambia. *Soil Survey Land Evaluation* **1,** 2–5.

Young, A. 1973a. Soil survey procedures in land development planning. *Geogr. J.* **139,** 53–64.

Young, A. 1973b. Rural land evaluation. In *Evaluating the human environment,* J. A. Dawson and J. C. Doornkamp (eds), 5–33. London: Edward Arnold.

Young, A. 1974. The appraisal of land resources. In *Spatial aspects of development,* B. S. Hoyle (ed.), 29–50. Chichester: John Wiley.

Young, A. 1976. *Tropical soils and soil survey.* Cambridge: Cambridge University Press.

Young, A. 1978. Recent advances in the survey and evaluation of land resources. *Prog. Phys. Geog.* **2,** 462–79.

Young, A., and P. F. Goldsmith 1977. Soil survey and land evaluation in developing countries: a case study in Malawi. *Geog. J.* **153,** 407–38.

Index

Index